HOW JEWISH IS JEWISH HISTORY?

THE LITTMAN LIBRARY OF
JEWISH CIVILIZATION

Dedicated to the memory of
LOUIS THOMAS SIDNEY LITTMAN
*who founded the Littman Library for the love of God
and as an act of charity in memory of his father*
JOSEPH AARON LITTMAN
יהא זכרם ברוך

*'Get wisdom, get understanding:
Forsake her not and she shall preserve thee'*

PROV. 4: 5

The Littman Library of Jewish Civilization is a registered UK charity
Registered charity no. 1000784

How Jewish Is Jewish History?

MOSHE ROSMAN

Oxford · Portland, Oregon

The Littman Library of Jewish Civilization

The Littman Library of Jewish Civilization
Chief Executive Officer: Ludo Craddock
Managing Editor: Connie Webber
PO Box 645, Oxford OX2 OUJ, UK
www.littman.co.uk

————

Published in the United States and Canada by
The Littman Library of Jewish Civilization
c/o ISBS, 920 NE 58th Avenue, Suite 300
Portland, Oregon 97213–3786

First published 2007
First published in paperback 2009

A catalogue record for this book is available from the British Library

The Library of Congress catalogued the hardback edition as follows:
Rosman, Murray Jay.
How Jewish is Jewish History? / Moshe Rosman.
p. cm.
Includes bibliographical references and index.
ISBN-13: 978–1–904113–34–8
1. Jews—Historiography. 2. Judaism—Historiography. 3. Historiography. I. Title.
DS115.5.R67 2007   909´.4924—dc22 2007020760

ISBN 978–1–904113–85–0

Publishing Co-ordinator: Janet Moth
Copy-editing: Kate Clements
Proof-reading: Philippa Claiden
Index: Bonnie Blackburn
Production: John Saunders
Designed by Pete Russell, Faringdon, Oxon.
Typeset by Hope Services, Abingdon, www.hopeservices.co.uk
Printed in Great Britain on acid-free paper by
Biddles Ltd., King's Lynn. www.biddles.co.uk

*To my children and my children-in-law,
and their children*

May you forever regard the history spoken of here as your own

Preface

ॐ

THIS BOOK was sparked by three experiences, two academic and one intensely personal. In the winter of 1989, while on sabbatical from my home institution, Bar-Ilan University in Israel, I had the privilege of serving the first of two stints as a visiting professor at the University of Michigan. Peter Novick's book *That Noble Dream* had just appeared and it eloquently articulated the crisis of identity and confidence that postmodern mores had caused in the historical profession. Spending that semester in Ann Arbor listening to lectures, participating in discussions, and reading material that reflected this crisis set me on a path to attempt to understand the ramifications of postmodernism for my own subspecialty of history, Jewish history. One result of this was a new graduate course I began teaching at Bar-Ilan entitled 'Methods and Topics in Historiography', which became the vehicle by which I could explore the relationship between historiography and postmodernism, and allowed me to hone my own ideas against the lively arguments of my students.

The second academic experience was a conference held at the Graduate Theological Union in Berkeley in the early summer of 1997. This was a gathering of all of the scheduled authors of the collective work *Cultures of the Jews: A New History*, under the virtuoso leadership of its editor, David Biale. The discussions with colleagues at this, my first conference in Berkeley, led to a revelation: on every parameter (intellectual, cultural, religious, and so on) I was at the right end of the spectrum. Having fancied myself a liberal for all of my sentient life, the discovery that, at least in relative terms, I was a conservative was disconcerting. This discovery did, however, help me understand my reaction to postmodernism and showed me how I might go about formulating a position. At the Berkeley conference, I appreciated the fact that at least some of those who disagreed with me were willing to engage with my views, and I think it is fair to say that the rational discourse held there, and subsequently by email, influenced thinking and even changed positions on both sides of the divide.

The third experience officially began on 24 June 1998 when I was diagnosed with a blood cancer called multiple myeloma and told that median survival, with treatment, was thirty months—and what a treatment it has been. This is not the place to tell that story; however, the disease is relevant in two ways. First, it entailed long stays in Hadassah University Medical Center in Jerusalem, as well as limited mobility and strength for considerable periods when I was not hospitalized. This meant that I could not conduct the archival research that had become my stock-in-trade and I sought out projects based on books rather than archival documents. Second, faced with mortality, I wanted to make a more personal statement about my profession than the standard monograph genre permits. Although under no illusions as to my intellectual power or originality, I felt that after more than a decade of studying and reflecting on these problems, I could at least state the issues and the stakes for Jewish history that postmodernism set. Also, as some of my friends have remarked, since being visited by the Angel of Death, I have been more willing to speak my mind and less reticent about criticizing colleagues.

With all of this in the background, but with no explicit plan, as academic occasions arose and my health permitted I began writing articles relating to aspects of the postmodern challenge. By 2004 I realized that although each piece had been conceived separately, they were all connected to the same larger theme. Together they might define what I regard as a vital problem for Jewish historiography and which no one, save the postzionist camp (and they only secondarily), had confronted.[1]

At the 2004 Association for Jewish Studies Annual Conference in Chicago I broached the idea to Connie Webber of the Littman Library, and with her encouragement I set about transforming my collection of articles into a book. Chapters 2 to 7 are based on those articles; each has been revised and updated (Chapters 6 and 7 were first translated from Hebrew) so as to fill a particular niche in the book and in its argument. The Introduction, Chapter 1, and the Conclusion were newly written to create a context for the articles, to link them, and to consummate the argument.

The names and publication venues of the original articles (material from which is used here by permission) are as follows: 'Defining the Post-Modern Period in Jewish History', in E. Lederhendler and J. Wertheimer (eds), *Text and Context: Essays in Modern Jewish History and Historiography in Honor of Ismar Schorsch* (New York: Jewish Theological Seminary, 2005); 'Hybrid with What? The Variable Contexts of Polish Jewish Culture', in

---

[1] Note that the collection, Kepnes, *Interpreting Judaism in a Postmodern Age*, has chapters on most fields of Jewish studies and even on the Holocaust and Zionism, but nothing on the discipline of Jewish history per se.

A. Norich and Y. Eliav (eds), *Jewish Cultures and Literatures* (Providence: Brown Judaica Series, 2007); 'From Counterculture to Subculture to Multiculture: The "Jewish Contribution" Then and Now', in J. Cohen and R. I. Cohen (eds), *The Jewish Contribution to Civilization* (Oxford: The Littman Library of Jewish Civilization, 2007); 'A Prolegomenon to Jewish Cultural History', *Jewish Studies: An Internet Journal (JSIJ)*, 1 (2001), 109–27; 'The Art of Historiography and the Methods of Folklore' [Omanut hahistoriyografiya veshitot hafolklor], *Zion*, 64 (2000), 209–18; 'Jacob Katz and the Feminist Revolution' [Ya'akov katz lenokhaḥ hamahapeikha hafeministit], in I. Bartal and S. Feiner (eds), *Jacob Katz Reconsidered* [Iyun meḥadash bemishnato hahistorit shel ya'akov katz] (Jerusalem: Zalman Shazar Center, 2007).

Reviewing what I have written, I am struck by how clearly I am an example of Jerome Bruner's cultural psychological Self which I discuss in Chapter 5: that is a Self that is a product of history, 'Self from the past to the present'. Discerning readers will not be surprised to learn that I am the grandson of early twentieth-century Jewish immigrants from Russia to the USA, who grew up to be both thoroughly American and thoroughly Jewish, with a significant religious commitment and an American university education, married to the daughter of Holocaust survivors, and living in Israel.

In different phases of my life I have been intimately familiar with four key Jewish metahistories, which I explain in Chapter 1. As a child and a teenager I studied in schools where the Orthodox religious metahistory held sway. As a young man I spent many years at the Jewish Theological Seminary of America, where the acculturationist metahistory was a veritable credo. Since 1979 I have lived and worked in Israel, where a modified Zionist metahistory still sets the intellectual agenda of the institutions with which I have been affiliated. I have also been an active participant in the international Jewish academic community, and have witnessed the development of the multicultural metahistory, including its postzionist tributary.

That said, however, I dare to expect that readers who disagree with me will not use my biography, and particularly my religious, Israeli and American commitments, as an excuse to dismiss my analysis out of hand, but will judge it on its merits. Indeed, the precedent of my Berkeley experience gives me hope that a composition such as mine can be seen, not as the platform of some imaginary party, but as the genesis of a serious conversation that potentially should include everyone who cares about Jewish history.

This book is an attempt by a Jewish historian to come to terms with postmodernism. I know that I will appear too postmodern for some, and insufficiently so for others, but I am postmodern enough to understand that this can only be the first word. I look forward to hearing what others will have to say.

Acknowledgements

༜

DURING the long gestation of this book many colleagues and friends have given me ideas, shared insights, taught me whole subjects, provided references, criticized the substance and style of chapters, reproached me, lent advice and offered support. Their input has ranged from barely more than a word, to hours of conversation in an ongoing relationship, to written critiques. I have not accepted all of what they have offered, and some of them have endured criticism from me, but I am grateful to all and feel privileged to belong to a real—conference and email enabled—'republic of letters'. I list the names of those I remember in alphabetical order, asking forgiveness from those I have forgotten over the long years, and regretting that I cannot publicly detail each individual's kindness to me: David Assaf, Gershon Bacon, Israel Bartal, Elisheva Baumgarten, David Biale, Miriam Bodian, Daniel Boyarin, Kimmy Caplan, Haim Cedar, Jeremy Cohen, Richard Cohen, Yaacob Dweck, Todd Endelman, Shmuel Feiner, Baruch Feldstern, Adam Ferziger, Edward Fram, Marla Frankel, Zvi Gitelman, Jacob Goldberg, François Guesnet, Ira Harris (whom I thank belatedly), Kathryn Hellerstein, Elliott Horowitz, Gershon Hundert, Andrzej Kaminski, Arthur Kiron, James Kugel-Kaduri, Jack Kugelmass, Eli Lederhendler, Joshua Levinson, Olga Litvak, Ivan G. Marcus, Michael Meyer, Dan Michman, Eyal Mizrahi, Ken Moss, David Myers, Ben Nathans, Anita Norich, Adi Parush, Iris Parush, Elchanan Reiner, David Resnick, Yaacov Ro'i, Dena Roth, Robert P. Roth, David Ruderman, Michael Satlow, Scott Spector, David Stern, Adam Teller, Magda Teter, Jack Wertheimer, Marcin Wodziński, Shira Wolosky, Bracha Yaniv, Larry Zalcman and Steven Zipperstein.

The crucial last phase of work was done while I enjoyed the hospitality and superb research facilities of the University of Pennsylvania's Center for Advanced Judaic Studies. My sincere thanks to the Center's Director, David Ruderman, and to the administrative and library staff for their indispensable help in bringing my idea to realization. I also want to thank the staff of the Bar-Ilan University Department of Jewish History, ably led by Kokhava Akrabi, for all of their help.

Connie Webber of the Littman Library has been a talented coach, dispensing the right mix of wisdom, patience, criticism, encouragement and urging, to get this manuscript to the finish line. Janet Moth has conscientiously shepherded the book into print. I also would like to thank Kate Clements, John Saunders, and Pete Russell for their work. Ludo Craddock has co-ordinated the entire effort with efficient competence and good humour.

My brother, David L. Rosman, lovingly and unselfishly gave the doctors, nurses and staff of Hadassah the raw material they needed to do God's work in keeping me alive. My other brother, Leonard B. Rosman, has stood at the ready, supporting me however he could in my rage against the night. Throughout the experience—frequently, the ordeal—of the past nine years, my parents, Norman and Elayne Rosman, have continued, long after they deserved to go off duty, to nurture and care for me. My children have found the way to enable me to continue being their father; sharing their lives and their choices has been the greatest motivation and the greatest reward for staying alive.

My wife Lynne has known exactly how to confront the stranger who threatened to destroy our life. Her determination, resourcefulness, and love have pulled me from the depths and led me to this moment. I am deeply grateful for her understanding of what this project has signified for me and for her willingness to undergo ever more hardships to ensure its completion.

Jerusalem,
Hanukah 5767/December 2006

Contents

Note on Transliteration

THE TRANSLITERATION of Hebrew in this book reflects consideration of the type of book it is in terms of its content, purpose, and readership. The system adopted therefore reflects a broad approach to transcription, rather than the narrower approaches found in the *Encyclopaedia Judaica* or other systems developed for text-based or linguistic studies. The aim has been to reflect the pronunciation prescribed for modern Hebrew, rather than the spelling or Hebrew word structure, and to do so using conventions that are generally familiar to the English-speaking reader.

In accordance with this approach, no attempt is made to indicate the distinctions between *alef* and *ayin*, *tet* and *taf*, *kaf* and *kuf*, *sin* and *samekh*, since these are not relevant to pronunciation; likewise, the *dagesh* is not indicated except where it affects pronunciation. Following the principle of using conventions familiar to the majority of readers, however, transcriptions that are well established have been retained even when they are not fully consistent with the transliteration system adopted. On similar grounds, the *tsadi* is rendered by 'tz' in such familiar words as bar mitzvah, mitzvot, and so on. Likewise, the distinction between *ḥet* and *khaf* has been retained, using *ḥ* for the former and *kh* for the latter; the associated forms are generally familiar to readers, even if the distinction is not actually borne out in pronunciation, and for the same reason the final *heh* is indicated too. As in Hebrew, no capital letters are used, except that an initial capital has been retained in transliterating titles of published works (for example, *Shulḥan arukh*).

Since no distinction is made between *alef* and *ayin*, they are indicated by an apostrophe only in intervocalic positions where a failure to do so could lead an English-speaking reader to pronounce the vowel-cluster as a diphthong—as, for example, in *ha'ir*—or otherwise mispronounce the word.

The *sheva na* is indicated by an *e*—*perikat ol*, *reshut*—except, again, when established convention dictates otherwise.

The *yod* is represented by *i* when it occurs as a vowel (*bereshit*), by *y* when it occurs as a consonant (*yesodot*), and by *yi* when it occurs as both (*yisra'el*).

Names have generally been left in their familiar forms, even when this is inconsistent with the overall system.

INTRODUCTION

Writing Jewish History in the Postmodern Climate

੭

O VER THE PAST GENERATION or so, intellectual life in the Western world has undergone a revolution. Postmodern sensibility has spawned a range of theoretical innovations—deconstructionist, post-structuralist, feminist, postcolonial, cultural studies, and others—that have had far-reaching implications for research and writing in all text-related disciplines in the humanities and social sciences. A central tenet of postmodern discourse—that there can never be objective description, only subjective interpretation—has been a serious obstacle to most academic disciplines trying to maintain their integrity and their self-confidence. If we cannot say something objective, if we cannot determine some truth, why say anything?

Jewish studies are no exception. In fact, given Jews' inextricable involvement with many of the key events, turning points, processes, and trends in the politics, culture, society, and intellectual life of the *modern* world, Jews and things connected to them have been particularly susceptible to the *postmodern* critique. Such modern phenomena as nationalism, capitalism, liberalism, social science, and academic discourse have had significant Jewish dimensions, and also have been subject to withering postmodern criticism.

Beyond such problems, however, the study of Jewish history—indeed, all of Jewish studies—has come into question as a result of the postmodern approach. If nothing can be defined objectively, how can we identify a unitary, continuous, coherent Jewish People with a distinct culture and history? Is there a recognizable object for the subject of Jewish studies to study? And if we do assume there is a Jewish People with its own collective history, how can this history be researched and written in the shadow of postmodern postulates that seem to assert that facts are 'constructed', not 'found'; that narratives are always ideological tracts, never simply descriptive disquisitions?

Has Jewish history also entered a—or *the*—postmodern phase? If so, what is the relationship between the Jewish past and the Jewish present? Is there some findable key to Jewish history across periods, or is there an infinite number of *meta*-historical interpretations of its meaning? In a world that is coming to be organized according to a multicultural paradigm, can the Jews and their history fit in? What is the relationship between Jewish culture and history and the culture and history of the non-Jews among whom the Jews lived and live? How do a feminist perspective and analysis through the prism of gender transform the Jewish historical master-narrative? Can Jewish history call on the methodologies of other disciplines to help it accomplish its task in the new postmodern context?

These are the questions that this book seeks to address. However, before tackling these specific issues it is necessary to clarify what general challenges postmodern thought and practice pose for Jewish history, and on what basis Jewish historiography can meet them. Why have certainties such as the very existence of our subject and the accepted method by which we practise it become problematic, and how can we contend with such problems?

Clarification requires engaging with the subject of postmodernism, notoriously associated with opaque jargon and tangled expression. Perhaps here, in a Jewish context, it can be made to speak, as the Torah is said to do, 'in the language of humans'.[1] 'Postmodern' is a term that has been used in myriad ways since the 1960s. For historians it refers, typically, to theories of language, texts, and literature that have served as the foundation for a critique of traditional historical practice, sometimes called 'new historicism'. This critique utilizes as its primary tool of analysis a self-conscious examination of the rhetoric used in writing historical narratives.[2] On the basis of this, critics have posited, first of all, that language does not describe anything neutrally, or objectively. Language is a cultural code. Like any code it encrypts meaning. Every language encodes the values, ideologies,

---

[1] Babylonian Talmud, *Berakhot* 31*a*.

[2] For introduction to postmodern theory, see Derrida, *Positions*; id., *Of Grammatology*; Foucault, *Discipline and Punish*; id., *Foucault Reader*; Huyssen, *After the Great Divide*; Kuhn, *Structure of Scientific Revolutions*; Best and Kellner, *Postmodern Theory*; Lyotard, *The Post-Modern Condition*; Habermas, *Lectures on the Philosophical Discourse of Modernity*; and Ophir, 'Postmodernism: A Philosophical Position' (Heb.). On the new historicism, see Appleby, Hunt, and Jacob, *Telling the Truth About History*; Ankersmit, *History and Tropology*; Ankersmit and Kellner (eds), *New Philosophy of History;* Berkhofer, *Beyond the Great Story*; Munslow, *Deconstructing History*; Novick, *That Noble Dream*, 522–629; Jenkins, *Postmodern History Reader*; and the many books in the series *The New Historicism: Studies in Cultural Poetics*, edited by Stephen Greenblatt. My personal guide over the shoals of postmodernism has been Shira Wolosky.

and power relations inherent in the culture it serves. It automatically applies these to the phenomenon it happens to be describing. Therefore, any description through language 'always already' offers an interpretation of that which it purports to represent.

For example, whether at the outset of a historical composition one calls the geographical area between the Mediterranean Sea and the Jordan river Canaan, Coele-Syria, Palestine, Erets Yisra'el, Erets Yisro'el, Israel, Palestine/Israel, the Holy Land, or the Promised Land already implies a political, ideological, religious, and cultural stance. Each term signals the broad outlines of the description that will follow, and these descriptions will be different from each other—they are, perforce, interpretations. Unintentionally, all descriptions are 'thick descriptions';[3] that is, they interpret the meaning of the object of their description as they are in the act of representing it. The interpretation is part and parcel of the description. From this it follows that there is no separation between fact and interpretation. As soon as I have decided to call that territory Israel, I have defined to a great degree what will qualify as 'fact' and what will not. In this sense interpretation precedes description and determines the 'facts'. Therefore one might say that all is interpretation. There is no way of proving which interpretation is true, or even preferable, because there is no way to get outside the language in which the interpretation is couched. This means that representation is not a function of the thing being represented but of how the representer uses the language. This, in turn, depends upon that representer's perspective. Thus, cognitive determinations are always relative to one's perspective and anything can legitimately be described from multiple perspectives. Meaning is fluid and unstable.

Consider, for example, events in Ukraine in 1648–9 when Ukrainian peasants and Cossacks rose up against Polish rule, and killed many Jews in the process. This is referred to by Poles as 'the civil war', by Ukrainians as 'the war for independence', and by Jews as 'the persecutions of 1648–9' (*Gezerot Taḥ-Tat*). These titles represent the different meaning of these events to each of these groups; they are not attempts to falsify, but a result of the differing perspectives from which they 'view' what happened. However, as new information becomes available and, even more so, as holders of these interpretations become more conscious of how their interpretation is contingent upon other attitudes they hold (nationalist

---

[3] This a term that originated with Ryle, *Collected Studies*, and was popularized by Geertz in *The Interpretation of Cultures*. See Chapter 5 at n. 4.

ideology, self-image as victim, sense of being cheated by history, desire to glorify the collective past, current opinions about the nations descended from the parties to the conflict), their interpretation is subject to modification. In Jewish historiography, the Shabatean movement has been regarded by various scholars at different times as a perverse aberration of Jewish religion, as an overdue assertion of the mystical side of Judaism, as a Jewish version of the Reformation, as the engine of Jewish modernization, as a chain of loosely related local events, and more.

Since meaning is contingent and unstable, one of the basic principles of postmodern scholarship is that phenomena cannot be said to have an 'essential' nature. 'Judaism is . . .', 'Judaism teaches . . .' are the kinds of statements that must always be qualified by placing them in a spatial, temporal, and social context. In a certain place, at a certain time, under certain conditions, 'this Judaism was . . .' and 'that Judaism taught . . .'. That is, Judaism has been variably construed depending on the context. Thought of in this spirit, commonly used terms imply such contextual contingency: 'Biblical Religion', 'Rabbinic Judaism', 'Ashkenazi Judaism', 'Sephardi Judaism', 'Liberal Judaism', and so on. The 'essence' of key concepts such as Judaism and Jewish is always constructed by some and then contested by others.

The problem of constructivism versus essentialism is central to this book because it entails a core conundrum for Jewish history (and probably for any subject of study, even postmodernism itself). If the word 'Jewish' signifies no essential features continuous over time and place, if it can be—or if it has been—constructed in an infinite number of ways, if it is always and everywhere contingent, then, as a practical matter, how do we go about defining the subject which we seek to research and write about? How do we initially recognize something as Jewish and mark it as a proper component of our study? If Jewish can be everything, is it anything? Is there a 'Jewish history' to write about? Chapters 1 to 4 confront different facets of this challenge.

Another aspect of the relationship between language and reality that postmodern theory expounds is the fact that the only way humans can relate to reality is through the mediation of language—language that is always already laden with encoded significance. One might say, then, that language doesn't merely mediate or interpret reality, it constructs it. Why does the Talmud class the deaf, the imbecile, and the child together as not being responsible for their actions and not legally culpable in most situations? The answer is presumably because in ancient times all three were not readily or perfectly socialized. What hindered the deaf-mute person's socialization was the lack of language. The deaf-mute's parent could not, as she would do for a hearing child, use language to label articles, people, situations, and processes, and thus construct for the child conventional reality that he might eventually share with everyone else in society.

In postmodern practice, a language-constructed reality, once formed, is treated as a text to be read and interpreted by being deconstructed; that is, by exposing its metaphysical assumptions and internal contradictions.[4] For example, many traditional expositors of halakhah (Jewish law: a classic example of a set of texts—in this case prescriptive, legal ones—intended to forge a certain reality) contend that, historically, these laws made life more felicitous for women, protected their honour and implied that they had a high status, perhaps even superior to that of men. They did this by exempting them from performing about a third of the 613 commandments, requiring from them modest dress and behaviour, limiting their role in public life, and teaching them a curriculum different from that of men, by methods designed specifically for them. However, a deconstructive reading of these laws and the society they organized suggests that they can be interpreted as based on the desire to perpetuate gender hierarchy, and to keep women in the role of social facilitators of male cultural fulfilment, depriving women of the cultural capital that men's education and ritual performance provided, and subordinating them to male authority at almost every turn.

Furthermore, if language constructs reality, if, as Jacques Derrida famously wrote, 'There is nothing outside of the text'[5] (and, conversely, everything—archaeological finds, film, performance, ritual, games, crimes, sport, and so on—is textual, that is, can be 'read' and analysed as a text might be), then is there a context—a reality—that the text reflects or to which it relates? And if there is, how can we be sure, how can we test, that our language is allowing us to perceive it? No 'event', 'process', or 'personality' can be accessed in a non-linguistically mediated way to check the accuracy of the description; there are only other texts (even if not in conventional 'textual form'), 'primary sources', or 'secondary sources', to which this latest description (also a text) can refer and against which it can be compared.

Our description seems to have no referent we can point to that stands independent of language, because the language we use to do the pointing can only point to what is contained within it. This means that there is indeterminacy of both subject and object. Are the discussions in the Talmud records of actual

---

[4] Based on the definition in the *Oxford English Dictionary*.

[5] Derrida, *Of Grammatology*, 158.

conversations between living people reflecting the contestations of their lives, or are they redacted texts created to exert power over us, the readers? Does the story of Yohanan ben Zakai, establishing the academy at Yavneh at the time of the destruction of the Temple in Jerusalem, report something that happened, or does it instruct us as to how to understand other texts?

This raises one of the directing principles of postmodern analysis. Modernist critics looked to evaluate texts in terms of objectivity; postmodern critics try to detect power and interests. One of the central assertions of one of the most important postmodern theorists, Michel Foucault, was that knowledge—like much social and cultural activity—is always a tool for gaining power. The text is designed to assert its author's authority. Actually, in Foucault's estimation, the author-function is not the writing of the text but the imposition of authority through it.[6] One of the most important steps in deconstructing a text is to identify this authority and who stands behind it.

Postmodern theory also maintains that all narrative follows certain conventions and uses a limited number of figures of speech or literary devices (usually called *tropes* in postmodern discourse). Historical narrative is no exception. As Hayden White pointed out, historical narrative always construes its subject as a plotted story with a beginning and middle, building to a climax, and replete with tropes to procure the reader's understanding: 'The events are *made* into a story by the suppression or subordination of certain of them and the highlighting of others, by characterization, motific repetition, variation of tone and point of view, alternative descriptive strategies, and the like.' Moreover, every culture offers only a limited number of plot structures in which a story can be cast. In the West there are four: tragedy, comedy, romance, and satire. The key step for the historian author is to consider which plot structure fits the story to be told. Once the choice is made, based on the writer's prior hypothesis regarding the phenomenon he or she is describing, the signal is given and the reader 'gradually comes to realize that the story he is reading is of one kind rather than another . . . And when he has perceived the class or type to which the story that he is reading belongs, he experiences the effect of having the events in the story explained to him'. The plot structure is what primarily imparts the meaning and, in line with its conventions, determines the details to be included in the story.[7]

---

[6] Foucault, 'What Is an Author?'; cf. id., *Archaeology of Knowledge*.

[7] White, 'Historical Text as Literary Artifact'; quotations from pp. 85, 86. See other relevant essays in his collections *Metahistory* and *Content of the Form*.

Thus, for example, if one regards the founding of the State of Israel as basically a heroic event, the story of Israel's establishment will be told as a romance with a happy ending and the tropes employed will be ones calculated to portray those who worked to establish the state as heroes, and their actions as courageous and salutary. Behaviour contrary to this image will be treated as unimportant or exceptional, or will be ignored altogether. If, rather, one believes Israel's founding to be a tragic mistake, then the story will indeed be a tragedy full of suffering and injustice, while just motivations and acts of courage, fairness, and sacrifice will be discounted or overlooked. The overriding importance of plot structure and literary devices in conveying and receiving the message of the historical account means that historical narrative approaches a type of literature.

Cognitive relativism, indeterminacy of subject and object, power assertions, and the literary nature of historical narrative, as I have outlined them above, have been apprehended as threatening by many traditional historians. Witnessing the application of these principles by some extremists, they have recoiled in horror.[8]

A good example of such extreme application is the Israeli postmodern academic Ilan Pappé, who spoke of the new type of narrative to be produced in postmodern academe: 'Every story like this will be told according to the ideological or moral sense of the teller, even before full source material will be found that describes in unimportant accuracy what occurred . . . it is not new historical sources that open for us interesting and urgent questions about our past, but a new moral consciousness . . . Opinionatedness and moral concern constitute the ideological foundation for the new view.'[9] For Pappé and his confrères, the historian's task is to tell a story that serves a moral purpose; that would, for example, 'try to understand, and perhaps also to repudiate, the human misfire of both [Arab and Jewish] societies that could have built class solidarity, but surrendered to the emasculating power of nationalism on both sides'.[10] In telling such stories '[factual] accuracy is

---

[8] For responses to postmodern critiques of historiography (some combative, some conciliatory), see e.g. Iggers, *Historiography in the Twentieth Century*; Bentley, *Modern Historiography*; Evans, *In Defense of History*; Ermarth, *Sequel to History*; Spiegel, 'History, Historicism and the Social Logic of the Text'; Haskell, 'Objectivity Is Not Neutrality'; id., 'Curious Persistence of Rights Talk'; Hollinger, *In the American Province*; Toews, 'Intellectual History'; Katz, *A Time for Inquiry, a Time for Reflection*; Topolski, 'Double Image of Postmodernism'; Zagorin, 'History, the Referent and Narrative'.   [9] Pappé, 'New Agenda' (Heb.), 130, 136.   [10] Ibid. 130.

barren, ideology fecundates'.[11] That is, source material, being always manipulated, is hardly relevant. Once the writer, guided by moral ideology, has hit upon the edifying tale to be told, it is virtually guaranteed that he or she will be able to find and construe the sources to support it.

This appears to be cognitive relativism in the service of a moral absolutism grounded in political correctness. The morally edifying story is the one mandated by what is politically correct; other stories, while possible, are not worthy of being told. To traditional historians, who search for sources and try to read them, and who admit to bias but are prepared to change their preconceived notions if convinced that such is warranted, Pappé's style of writing is simply political or ideological propaganda. As Georg Iggers exclaimed in response to this type of exposition and to extreme postmodern epistemology in general: 'Were one to accept the premises of this critique, meaningful historical writing would be impossible.'[12]

Most postmodern scholars have not gone down the route chosen by Pappé. Typically, they garnish their critiques with disclaimers that their epistemology does not mean that history cannot be written (for example, 'We could accept the death of normal history without declaring the death of history doing itself'[13]). In their own work they not only deconstruct historiographical texts in order to write about how history is represented, but they also aim to represent history.[14]

Many postmodern critics of conventional historiography utilize the tools of traditional, so-called 'positivist', historiographical methods, based

---

[11] Pappé, 'New Agenda' (Heb.), 135–6.

[12] Iggers, *Historiography in the Twentieth Century*, 11. See also Bentley, *Modern Historiography*, 141–5; cf. Nietzsche, 'On the Uses and Disadvantages of History'; Megill, *Prophets of Extremity*. Historians' anxiety was reflected, for example, in the overwhelming response to Peter Novick's *That Noble Dream*, which traced the history of the idea of objectivity in American historical writing, concluding with a section on 'objectivity in crisis'. Novick declared that, as of the 1980s, 'as a community of scholars united by common aims, common standards, and common purposes, the discipline of history had ceased to exist' (ibid. 628). The book went through five printings in four years, which is unusual for an academic monograph, was reviewed in many publications, and was the subject of a panel session at the American Historical Association annual meeting in December 1990, which attracted 'a crowd that filled the aisles, the floor space in back of the room, and spilled into the corridor outside': American Historical Society, 'Peter Novick's *That Noble Dream*', 675.

[13] Berkhofer, 'Challenge of Poetics to (Normal) Historical Practice', 450; cf. White, 'Historical Text as Literary Artifact', 97, 99.

[14] Cf. Conforti, *Past Tense* (Heb.), introduction.

on the assumptions that first, knowledge is verifiable by logical argument or empirical proof, and second, their portrayal had a real referent. They go through the process of research, evidence gathering, close reading, rational enquiry, and logical deduction to arrive at new knowledge (proving, among other things, that positivist-style objectivity is impossible!). They also sometimes speak of trends and they isolate themes.[15]

In addition, as much as postmodern historians insist on cognitive relativism and the absence of referent, many, like Pappé, also insist on a lack of moral relativism. In this connection, Thomas Haskell noted 'the curious persistence of rights talk in "The Age of Interpretation" . . . Such talk implies something highly controversial: the existence of an objective moral order accessible to reason.'[16] Indeed, many postmodernists see it as their duty to serve the needs of such a moral order.

The assertion of moral objectivity while denying cognitive objectivity is difficult to maintain. The limiting case, the Shoah, demonstrates that such a stance is untenable. From a moral perspective, 'Auschwitz has changed the basis for the continuity of the conditions of life within history'.[17] Therefore, 'it would seem self-evident that such a monstrous manifestation of human "potentialities" would not be forgotten or repressed . . . [However], postmodern thought's rejection of the possibility of identifying some stable reality or truth beyond the constant polysemy and self-referentiality of linguistic constructs challenges the need to establish the realities and truths of the Holocaust.'[18] A situation where it is morally unacceptable to deny the occurrence of the Shoah, but it is impossible to establish and represent the existence of such occurrence, is patently absurd.[19]

Faced with this paradox, some of the leading postmodern theorists (Jean-François Lyotard, Hayden White, and Dominique LaCapra) did not re-embrace positivism, but did declare the need to find a manner in which to represent faithfully the events of the Shoah. In his own way, each sought

---

[15] e.g. Foucault, *Archaeology of Knowledge*; id., *History of Sexuality*; cf. Iggers, *Historiography in the Twentieth Century*, 121. Although presenting the case for 'objectivity in crisis', Novick's book also used an impeccably positivist method; see Haskell, 'Objectivity Is Not Neutrality', 130, 151–7.

[16] Haskell, 'Curious Persistence of Rights Talk'; cf. Wolosky, 'Moral Finitude and the Ethics of Language'.

[17] Habermas, *Eine Art Schadensabwicklung*, 163, trans. and cited in Friedlander (ed.), *Probing the Limits of Representation*, 3.

[18] Friedlander (ed.), *Probing the Limits of Representation*, 3, 4–5.

[19] Iggers, *Historiography in the Twentieth Century*, 13.

a new voice, a new rhetorical mode, or new categories of historical analysis to do this. Their intricate and rather abstract attempts have not been conclusive. Undertaking this task, however, implied their understanding that the events of the Shoah—and by analogy other historical events—existed and, in theory at least, can be represented.[20]

Postmodern theory, therefore, requires nuanced responses from historians. Rather than view it as a bête noir or angrily dismiss it as mere jargonized cant, many historians have come to understand that, beyond its historiographically problematic epistemology (which even leading postmodern historical critics cannot sustain in practice), what, at base, postmodernism demands from the historian is a more profound version of what modernist objectivism advertised: a self-consciously critical stance. Nothing—not sources, not interpretative procedures (hermeneutics), not rhetorical conventions, not one's own motivations, not one's own interpretations—can be taken for granted and left unexamined. The attempt must be made to multiply sources and perspectives as much as possible, while admitting that the resultant descriptions will always imply interpretations, will always be contingent, and will never be complete.

Gender, class, race, ethnicity, geographical location, cultural heritage, sociology, anthropology, demography, psychology, economics, and so on[21]— all offer a unique perspective from which to produce a different, and valid, portrayal-cum-interpretation of past events. There is no 'God's-eye view' of history that humans can produce. There are histories, not one unitary history.[22]

Consequently, historians have broadened the historical field of enquiry both methodologically and with respect to content. The history of every-

[20] Lyotard, *The Differend*, 56–7 (cf. id., *Peregrinations*, 45–6, where, in his tributary historical account of his friend Pierre Souryi, Lyotard presented a traditional positivist-style representation); LaCapra, 'Representing the Holocaust'; White, 'Historical Emplotment'. White did suggest appropriating the idea of 'intransitive writing' from Roland Barthes and Berel Lang. Cf. Friedlander's introduction to *Probing the Limits of Representation*, 5–6, 9–12.

[21] In fact, the trend towards 'social science history' preceded the postmodern revolution and was criticized by postmodernists as trying to overgeneralize and be scientistic while losing sight of the individual. I include social science disciplines in this list because they do each offer a characteristic perspective that could serve as one point of departure for a historiographic account; see Iggers, *Historiography in the Twentieth Century*, 51–94, and Novick, *That Noble Dream*, 382–7.

[22] Cf. Novick, *That Noble Dream*, 540.

day life has taken on as much importance as the history of politics and wars, if not more. Similarly, the history of women, slaves, minorities, Africans, and Asians now often overshadows the attention given to 'dead white European males'. Methodologically, history has attempted to incorporate a plethora of other disciplines into its deliberations. There is psychohistory, economic history, cultural history, demographic history, etc., etc.

The field and methodology of Jewish history have also been broadened, albeit with some tardiness. Since the Second World War, and especially since the 1970s, a distinctive cohort of Jewish historians (by which I mean historians who write about Jewish history, whether they are personally Jewish or not) has sought to move away from previously dominant intellectual and religious history, focused on the 'dead white European males' of the Jewish experience, rabbis and spiritual giants, and from the history of persecution centred on Jewish suffering. They have tried to adapt methodologies from other branches of the humanities as well as the social sciences, and have examined Jewish society from new perspectives such as gender, economics, and cultural studies. Chapters 5, 6, and 7 offer three examples of this shift and its attendant problems.

Against extreme postmodern practice, a position that has evolved among historians, including those writing Jewish historiography, is that language, non-transparent and a priori interpretative as it is, is our only means to access reality; but there *is* a reality to be accessed and it *can be* accessed. On the one hand, as David Biale has put it, 'the realm of the "facts-in-themselves" lies beyond our unmediated reach'. As a Platonic ideal these surmised facts may act as 'a limiting case on the interpretive imagination, but they remain inaccessible, in and of themselves, divorced from interpretation'.[23] On the other hand, however, many historians would agree with Joan Scott that 'social and political structures aren't denied, rather they must be studied through their linguistic articulation'.[24]

Language does enable us to perceive an existing reality, even if language itself necessarily colours that perception.[25] For example, the events of 1933–45 with respect to the Jews did not constitute a subject until, among

[23] Biale, 'Between Polemics and Apologetics', 178.

[24] Scott, personal communication, as cited in Iggers, *Historiography in the Twentieth Century*, 132.

[25] Iggers, *Historiography in the Twentieth Century*, 129–33 and works cited there; also Ginzburg, *History, Rhetoric and Proof*; Haskell, 'Objectivity Is Not Neutrality', 156–7; Spiegel, 'History, Historicism and the Social Logic of the Text'; Stone, 'History and Postmodernism', 217–18.

other things, language gave them a name: Shoah, Holocaust, or *Ḥurban* (Yiddish: *Khurbn*). It was the name that lent them coherence and constructed them into a unity, a wholeness that could be reflected and acted upon.[26] In this sense language created the 'reality' of the Shoah. (Note that each name has different nuances as to what precisely it denotes and hence constructs this reality somewhat differently.) Notwithstanding the role of language, the reality of these events (however they might be labelled)—and the horrendous suffering they engendered—surely existed before language constructed them in such a way as to make them accessible to deliberation. Conversely, there are still debates as to which events properly belong under the Shoah rubric. The absence of appropriate identifying language can cause some aspects of reality to disappear.

The effect of postmodern theory on historiography has been summed up by Elizabeth Ermarth: 'The challenge to the hegemony of historical thinking may seem to some like a challenge to be resisted. It seems to me like an invitation to take responsibility for the conventions that we have naturalized . . . The challenge points up their fragility, their contingency . . . The play of postmodern writing seeks to guarantee vitality, to affirm what remains open to surprise and capable of new formation'.[27] Contingent, yes; conjured up out of nothing, no.

Many historians are convinced that, in contrast to cognitive relativism and radical multiperspectivism, postmodern theory can point to, and be regulated by, a notion of intersubjectivity. People form a community and develop conventions for realizing its objectives and its truths, conventions that are contingent, and subject to continual modification by means of rational debate in response to changing social, cultural, and technological circumstances.[28]

---

[26] Ofer, 'Linguistic Conceptualization of the Holocaust', 588, noted that the term 'Shoah' was established in general use about two years after the war had ended, and that 'linguistic conceptualization of the fate of European Jewry under the Nazis reveals the process of the internalization of the Holocaust among the Jews of Palestine—the Yishuv—and Israel' (p. 567). Among ultra-Orthodox (*ḥaredi*) Jews 'Khurbn' is the common term of choice. Outside Israel, 'Holocaust' came into vogue in the late 1950s, preceding the great awakening of Holocaust consciousness in the USA and elsewhere. In Russia people usually use the word 'Katastrofa'. I am indebted to my colleague Dan Michman for initiating me into this subject.

[27] Ermarth, *Sequel to History*, 213–14.

[28] Iggers, *Historiography in the Twentieth Century*, 12; Haskell, 'Curious Persistence of Rights Talk' and 'Objectivity Is Not Neutrality'; Hollinger, *In the American Province*; cf. Novick's presentation and critique of this stance in *That Noble Dream*, 570–2.

One can also imagine a community of communities where some of the conventions of some of the communities are transvalued and become the norm for all. There are, then, standards for evaluation even if they are neither sacrosanct nor eternal. Such practice has been variably termed soft perspectivism, moderate historicism, moderate objectivism, and reformed positivism.[29]

Functioning within the communities of historians, academia, and modern societies, historical interpreters must play by the rules of those communities—or, being critically conscious of the rules themselves and how they intrude into procedures, convince their communities (as postmodernists have succeeded in doing to some extent) that the rules need to be modified. A constructed narrative is contingent, but it cannot be arbitrary; it must adhere to the intersubjective criteria of the community it seeks to inform, or bring about change in those criteria. The meaning it offers must resonate with those it addresses. Resonance can, of course, be negative; but if the interpretation is in consonance with the rules, it has the right to be heard and the potential for overturning communal orthodoxy.

As to the postmodern postulate that history is but another form of literary narrative, traditional historians have defiantly clung to their belief that there still is a distinction to be made between historical and fictional narratives.[30] The philosopher and literary scholar Menahem Brinker has thrown the historians a lifesaver by contending that, while linguistics, literary studies, and philosophy have combined to negate any distinction between the two genres of narrative based on language, style, technique, themes, or motivation of the reader, one 'ancient and very clear distinction' remains: namely, 'a different contract of the writer with the readers'.

A work of fiction, as opposed to a work of history, is not committed to reporting on actual events and persons . . . In a historical composition the author is committed not only to writing about existent people and events but also to an effort to distinguish between what actually happened and what merely seemed to happen

---

[29] Harvey, *The Historian and the Believer*, 230–4, 252–3, anticipated the postmodern epistemological challenge when, in the 1960s, he distinguished between hard and soft perspectivism. On moderate historicism, see Haskell, 'Curious Persistence of Rights Talk'. For the other terms see Rosman, *Founder of Hasidism*, 7, and 'Critical Scholarship', 540.

[30] For responses of cultural anthropologists to an analogous problem in their 'literary' discipline, see Clifford and Marcus (eds), *Writing Culture*, esp. introduction by Clifford (pp. 1–26).

or could have happened but didn't. This differing commitment of the [two types of] author is not, of course, a private matter concerning only them. This is an institutionalized intention that defines the expectations of the reader from the institution of history or the institution of belles-lettres.[31]

To this commitment of intention we might add historians' commitment to allowing their descriptions and interpretations to be circumscribed by the limits of the historical evidence, unlike fiction, which may use evidence as a point of departure, but not as a bridle on imagination. It is evidence which, as Biale hinted, places limits on interpretative imagination. Roger Chartier has expressed it succinctly: 'Even if a historian writes in a "literary manner", he does not produce literature'; '[a historian's] narrative constructions aim at reconstructing a past that really was'.[32] One might add, even if it can never be exactly as it really was.

Historians, then, have found a basis—however epistemologically messy (as life itself tends to be)—on which they can continue to work by identifying sources, analysing them critically, and constructing descriptions and meaningful interpretations of the past within agreed-upon, if tentative, conventions. However, there is now a more diverse range of approaches and methods, a broader pluralism of subjects and sources, much more self-consciousness about what we are doing and how we do it, and greater sophistication in criticizing sources.

The historical perspective dubbed 'Jewish' is, of course, subject to all of the problems and considerations discussed up to this point. What applies to writing historiography applies to writing Jewish historiography. In particular, the problem of definition that postmodern anti-essentialism poses for Jewish history is one of much concern for Jewish historiographers, and I will return to it at various points.

There is more to it, however. The postmodern climate also offers a measure of succour to the writing of Jewish history. The postmodern project aims, in part, to destabilize conventional academic subjects of enquiry; to bring in plural readings and interpretations; to concentrate on the text itself; to amplify unheard voices of unprivileged groups; and to examine the power relations inherent in intellectual, social, and cultural phenomena no less than political ones.[33] On these grounds, the Jews certainly appear to be the type of group that, under the new historiographical regime, might

[31] Brinker, 'Literature and History' (Heb.), 39.
[32] As quoted in Iggers, *Historiography in the Twentieth Century*, 140, 12.
[33] Bentley, *Modern Historiography*, 140–1.

be granted a greater voice as a legitimate, but neglected, component in the historical record.[34]

The expansion of the definition of what is 'historical' that results from the utilization of new types of sources (for example, statistics, local records, art, folklore, and religious ritual) encompasses subjects such as local and organizational history, the history of minorities and marginal groups, the history of social institutions, culture, 'way of life', material culture, *mentalité*, and much more. By using such rubrics, study of the Jews can move from the margins of historiographical treatments to their centre. As an attempt to solve perennial social problems, Jewish social institutions are no less interesting a priori than those of the majority or any other group. Much can be gained by comparing the institutions of the majority with those of the minority and in understanding the symbiosis between them. Culturally speaking, it is clear that Jews have played a significant role as cultural intermediaries and cultural agents in many places and periods. Economically, scholarly focus on the micro, in addition to the macro, reveals the key roles of Jews at the lower economic levels of the places where they lived. The new conception of the methodologies and subjects of history has helped turn Jewish history into a legitimate, even mainstream, subject for historical research.

Beyond this fundamental legitimacy, Jewish history in the Diaspora is the history of a semi-enfranchised, subordinate minority group, who typically made text and its interpretation a central focus of life, and whose political life was atypical and usually overshadowed by intellectual, social, and cultural developments. It is therefore tailor-made to serve as a fresh vantage point from which to view and interpret important, if somewhat unconventional, questions of history.[35] For example, in the area of power relations, how have unequal power relations been managed? How did a largely powerless group secure its existence? Has violence been the only or primary means of gaining rights for such a minority? With regard to text, what has been the relationship between text and society? Or between text and culture? Or text and power? On communal conflict: when, historically, has conflict within a community tended to be creative, and when dysfunctional? What were the consequences of preventing conflicts and what of letting them take their course? How did cultural institutions interact with social hierarchies based on class, gender, and possession of cultural capital?

---

[34] Cf. Fischer, *Historians' Fallacies*, 144; in 1970, Fischer denied the existence of 'Jewish history' because the Jews were merely an 'ethnic-religious group'.

[35] On the uses or contribution of the study of Jewish history, see Chapters 1 and 4.

This list of issues could easily be lengthened. Jewish history can open up new conversations with and about the past.

In fact, over the last two generations Jewish history has been given a voice. In university departments, on library shelves and publication lists, and at academic conferences, the subject of Jewish history has flourished. True, review of this new prominence reveals a social motive alongside an intellectual one. It is meant to confirm Jews' position in the larger society, with the salient reality that most of this academic activity has been financed by money coming from Jewish donors. Still, there is no question that the academic establishment and academic history have become hospitable to the Jewish perspective and the story it has to tell. The number of Jewish historians is legion and the number of publications they produce is prodigious. Yet the position of Jewish history and Jewish studies is not completely secure. Another problem that I will consider in this book is how academic Judaism is adjusting to the 'new academy' which has created conditions different from those of the 1960s and 1970s when Jewish studies took root (see especially Chapter 4).

Among the effects of postmodern sensibility on Jewish historiography, one practical effect stands out. Lyotard, one of the prophets of postmodernism, said, 'I define *postmodern* as incredulity towards metanarratives.'[36] There is now an assumption that there is no immanent meaning in history as a whole, and hence no grand metanarrative or metahistory that unifies all of history. Master-narratives of historical experience—metanarratives or metahistories—have been demolished by postmodernist indeterminacy and multiperspectivism. As Iggers declared: 'There is no longer the possibility of a grand narrative that gives history coherence and meaning. The idea that has been central to Judaeo–Christian faith since biblical antiquity has been questioned, namely, that history has a transmundane purpose and direction.'[37] In the Jewish case, as Eli Lederhendler has observed,

History on a grand scale is a model we no longer *choose*. To write a comprehensive history requires the selection of a red thread of continuity, an organizing principle or theme. It means going back to the notion of an 'essence' of the Jewish experience that can be distilled from the whole. It means imposing a superstructure based on that essence, choosing a defining characteristic of each successive 'stage' of development. It is, in fact, a teleological model that departs only slightly from traditional, Judaic theological models.[38]

---

[36] Lyotard, *The Post-Modern Condition*, p. xxiv.

[37] Iggers, *Historiography in the Twentieth Century*, 141.

[38] Lederhendler, *Jewish Responses to Modernity*, 193–4. See also Frankel, 'Assimilation and the Jews', 15–16.

Consequently, the classic Jewish metahistories—religious, nationalist, acculturationalist—have largely been disowned, together with the sweeping historical surveys that were driven by them. What David Myers has called the 'retrodictive impulse, the attempt to scour the past for themes or subjects that form a coherent, linear chain of historical development'[39] has been subdued (see Chapter 1). Instead, Jewish historians have tended to write narrowly focused monographs, like their colleagues in other subdisciplines, hoping that by chopping history up into smaller chunks they can interpret 'individual' phenomena ('history') without presuming to impose a pattern on the whole ('HISTORY').

There is a problem with this expedient, however. No matter how small the piece, it implies a general theory into which it fits. It seems that there is no evading commitment to some metahistory, even if it is only latent.[40] A good example of this can be found in the microhistory writing that has become so prevalent. Whether it be one town, one neighbourhood, or one peasant, each micro-description can be extrapolated to the macro-level of society and culture—even civilization—as a whole. In every case, only a conception of the macro as the context for the micro enables the latter to be understood, while, in turn, the micro elucidates more details of the macro. The description of a small part always turns out to be the nucleus of a description of the whole. As the eminent historian Anthony Grafton said about the most famous microhistory, Carlo Ginzburg's *The Cheese and the Worms*, 'Ginzburg . . . turned to the records of two inquisition trials, both with the same defendant: a Friulian miller . . . nicknamed Menocchio . . . In these protocols . . . Ginzburg heard the rough, materialist voice of a peasant civilization'. Analogously, one might say that Ivan Marcus's history of the ritual for initiating medieval Jewish boys into the formal education process used one kind of ritual as a mirror reflecting the larger medieval Jewish culture.[41]

In Jewish historiography, all the individual monographs on Jews in various countries written since the 1970s, ostensibly disconnected from some

---

[39] Myers, 'Between Diaspora and Zion', 96. As he noted, Myers borrowed this term from Isaiah Berlin, but in my opinion gave it his own, new, and original, interpretation; cf. Berlin, 'History and Theory', 7. Myers was apparently referring to attempts at grand metanarratives; however, it seems to me that all historical accounts, even the most restricted in scope, are based on the perception of some coherence in the past and must 'retrodict' to be so. See below.

[40] Berkhofer, 'Challenge of Poetics to (Normal) Historical Practice'.

[41] Grafton, *History's Postmodern Fates*, 63 (on pp. 62–9 Grafton discusses the phenomenon of microhistory and its significance); Marcus, *Rituals of Childhood*.

grand thesis about all Jews, have contributed to the development of a new master-narrative: the 'multicultural' narrative which posits that the local context was always determinative of Jewish culture and identity, and each Jewish community was hybrid with the hegemonic culture and society in which it was embedded (see Chapters 1 and 3). Such a view is postmodern enough in its multiperspectivism, but its 'meta-ness' contradicts the spirit of postmodernism.

In light of this, the challenge is to produce a coherent picture that is not a teleological view, holding that history always has a *telos*, a goal, to which it is inexorably heading. In teleological history developments take on inevitability; they are self-generated or even fated. Is it possible, rather, that themes in history can be deduced in a de facto manner, without prejudicing the analysis of yet to be discovered sources? (See Chapter 2.) Can there be historical coherence without that coherence taking on a teleological aspect? In fact, not only the grand schemes, but any description—whatever its scale—cannot escape being, as Myers defined it, at least partially *retrodictive* (that is, if not attempting to trace a *linear* development, then still searching for a basis for coherence). Can it, however, avoid being *predictive*? This is, I believe, a fundamental tension that all historians must live with.

Postmodernism has shaken the confidence of many historians—Jewish ones perhaps more than most. This book is an attempt to delineate aspects of the problem of postmodernism for Jewish history and to offer suggestions as to how Jewish historiography might evolve in the postmodern climate. It places essays focused on different topics into a larger historiographical framework, addressing theoretical challenges that postmodernity raises for Jewish history (Chapters 1 to 4), and the possibility of adaptation of new methods and perspectives (Chapters 5 to 7) to postmodern Jewish historiography.

ONE

Some a priori Issues in Jewish Historiography

۞

ANYONE WHO SETS out to write about Jewish history—no matter
what period or place—confronts basic questions about the enterprise
before actually undertaking the task. One's position on these fundamental
problems creates a framework within which the research will be presented
and by which the narrative will be significantly affected. Before the development of the postmodern consciousness discussed in the Introduction, the
engagement of Jewish historians with these issues was usually oblique and
tacit, their positions typically presented as part of the conclusions of their
research. However, it is now apparent that these positions represented prior
assumptions that, in part, guided that research, and influenced its interpretation and presentation. The new postmodern sensibility has made us aware
of this, and we now self-consciously assess our approach to these a priori
issues before writing our narratives, even before reading the sources. In this
way we can understand the beliefs about the nature of the history we are
studying, which we bring to the research and writing we are doing. This
knowledge can result in healthy self-criticism. Understanding the mechanisms of a syndrome does not mean, however, that a person who understands
does not display its symptoms. One of the 'certainties' of postmodern discourse is that we can never escape the effects of our deeply held convictions.
The more extreme version of this is that we cannot escape them *at all*; the
more moderate one, that we can never *completely* escape them.[1] In this chapter we will consider a key five of these a priori issues.

---

[1] Compare Berkhofer, 'Challenge of Poetics to (Normal) Historical Practice',
447–50, and White, *Tropics of Discourse*, 57–60, with Funkenstein, *Perceptions of Jewish
History*, 21, and Iggers, *Historiography in the Twentieth Century*, 100, 144–5. This debate
is a continuation of a discussion first conducted in the 1930s in the wake of the publication of Karl Mannheim, *Ideology and Utopia* in English. See Novick, *That Noble Dream*,
159–60.

What Are the Jews?

The first key issue concerns the definition of the subject we are writing about. Jewish history pertains to the Jews, but *what* are 'the Jews'? Here is a sampling of the manifold answers that have been offered to this question.[2] Some say that the Jews are practitioners of the religion called Judaism. This formulation is problematic on several counts. First, not all those commonly regarded as Jews, and written about by historians of the Jews, were associated with Jewish religion. Certainly in the modern period, especially after 1800 or so, one could adopt a secular Jewish identity, devoid of any religious content, yet still be recognized by both other Jews and by non-Jews as Jewish. From so-called 'salon Jewesses' at the start of the nineteenth century,[3] to early twentieth-century Bundists and labour Zionists, and early twenty-first-century former Soviet Jews of a certain type,[4] there were many different sorts of people who had nothing to do with Jewish religion, yet are considered to be part of 'Jewish history'. There were even some formal adherents of other religions—such as some nineteenth-century bourgeois Jewish converts to Christianity for the sake of social and economic advantage, or Christians of Jewish ancestry who were sent to Nazi death camps—who might be included in our subject.

Second, even those who were observant of Jewish religion (particularly in the pre-modern period) would hardly regard their religious affiliation as coterminous with their Jewishness. What a modern consciousness would define as religious commitment and religious behaviour—belief in God, performance of religious rituals, commitment to observance of religious commandments—was to them a function of their Jewishness, not its genesis or essence. Their Jewish identity—based on facts of genealogy,

---

[2] The subject treated here has been raised in many different ways and seems to be taking on ever greater urgency: see e.g. Baron, 'Problems of Jewish Identity'; Meyer, *Jewish Identity in the Modern World*; Cohen and Horenczyk (eds), *National Variations in Jewish Identity*; Silberstein (ed.), *Mapping Jewish Identities*; Ben-Rafael, *Jewish Identities*; Walzer, Lorberbaum et al., *Jewish Political Tradition*.

[3] In her doctoral dissertation Natalie Goldberg-Naimark has argued forcefully that the term 'salon Jewess' is a misnomer because the cultural style championed by these women had very little to do with conducting salons. It was much more typified by correspondence, meeting at spas, and other venues and modes of communication.

[4] For typology of Soviet and post-Soviet Jews and their Jewish identity, see Zvi Gitelman's many studies, e.g. 'Jews and Judaism in the USSR', and 'Jewishness in Post-Soviet Russia and Ukraine'.

parentage, upbringing, status, culture, sociology, and even psychology—
preceded, warranted, and was expressed and reinforced by their religious
commitment; it was not contingent upon it. This partially explains why
religiously committed Jews still related to their secular counterparts as
Jews, even if they considered them to be 'imperfect' ones. Historically, to
the religious the problem with the secular was their failure to assume the
religious commitment that Jewish identity entails, but the identity itself
was not in doubt because it was seen to stem from other sources.[5]

Third, Judaism itself is difficult to define and has a history containing
many varieties. It has become fashionable in the scholarly literature, and in
some contexts, to talk about 'Judaisms'.[6] Do all of these qualify their devo-
tees for membership in a religiously determined Jewish category? Or are
some religious iterations of what began as Judaism so unrecognizable as to
be a different religion? By a definition based on *religious criteria* (beliefs, ritual practices, customs, mores, commitments) are Karaites, Conversos, and
Donmeh, Jews by virtue of patrilineal descent (whether Reform or Soviet),
those Isaac Deutscher famously called 'non-Jewish Jews',[7] ancient Hebrew-
Christians, or modern 'Jews-for-Jesus' part of 'the Jews'? The arguments
over this question are often furious. In everyday life, as in historiography,
all but the last two groups are commonly, although not unexceptionally,
regarded as part of Jewish history despite their religious non-normativity.
The ancient Hebrew-Christians and modern Jews-for-Jesus are usually
excluded because by embracing a competing belief system with different
social and cultural associations, their relationship with Jewishness has
become adversarial rather than constituent. In defining Jewishness, then,
more is involved than religion.

A few lines above I made reference to biological determinants—genealogy, birth, parentage—of Jewishness. Endogamous marriage was a hallmark throughout most of Jewish history. So can Jews be defined as a group
that shares the same genes? This is a highly charged matter.[8] On the one

---

[5] For discussion of this problem in the context of 19th-century central Europe, see
Ferziger, *Exclusion and Hierarchy*.

[6] For a description and analysis of Judaism, see Satlow, *Creating Judaism*; cf. Shaye
Cohen, *Beginnings of Jewishness*.

[7] That is, Jewish heretics who rejected Judaism and cut ties to the Jewish community, yet were typical of Jews because of such characteristics as their liminality, their marginality, and their roles as cultural mortar and social pestle—people such as Spinoza,
Heine, Marx, Luxemburg, Trotsky, and Freud. See Deutscher, *The Non-Jewish Jew*, 25–7.

[8] Kahn, *Are Genes Jewish?*

hand, Jews have often regarded themselves as belonging to the same extended family. Postmodern Jews sometimes jocularly refer to themselves as 'MOT'—members of the tribe. Throughout history the ties between them have been commonly understood as quasi-familial, engendering family-type obligations of mutual responsibility. There have been, however, significant incidences of exogamous marriage sprinkled through Jewish history. Conversion to Judaism—a religious ritual that leads to subsequent acceptance as belonging to the Jews in lieu of biologically determined criteria—has been possible for thousands of years. Most important of all, for long periods the Jews have existed as 'a highly fragmented population living under a considerable range of cultural and geographical conditions and reacting to [differential] possible selective factors'.[9] The result of all of these circumstances is that the Jewish gene pool has tended towards containing more variety rather than less. Although certain genetic markers may persist among Jews,[10] a walk down the street of any large Israeli city observing the phenotypes of passing people confirms that genetic variety is persistent.[11] If the Jews are an extended family, it is one with many adopted children; the Jewish gene pool is of wide radius and varying depth.

More problematic, discussion of common ancestry and shared genes readily slides into racial discourse. If the majority of Jews are biologically related, does this mean that they share character and behavioural traits in addition to physiological ones? Are Jews biologically conditioned to be prone both to carry Tay-Sachs disease and to be entrepreneurs? When, in the nineteenth and early twentieth centuries, racial theory was in vogue, ascribing behaviour to hereditary determinants shared by all people of common ancestry, and nations were commonly perceived as being ethnically based, many Jews seriously or casually spoke of the Jews as a race (see Chapter 4). Such terms as 'the Jewish soul', 'the Jewish heart', or 'the Jewish head', denoting certain sensibilities and proclivities that virtually all Jews supposedly share (or should share), are today shorthand terms for a Jewish

---

[9] Shapiro, *The Jewish People*, 62.

[10] See e.g. Hammer, Skorecki, et al., 'Y Chromosomes of Jewish Priests'.

[11] In this connection we might note that the Diaspora Museum (Beit Hatefutsot) in Tel Aviv contains a prominent exhibit consisting of projected colour photographs of Jews apparently intended to emphasize the tremendous variety of phenotypes they encompass, and thereby countering any racial notion of Jewishness. For one attempt to explain the genetic basis for the variety in Jewish phenotypes, see Thomas, Weale, Jones, et al., 'Founding Mothers of Jewish Communities'. See also Mourant, Kopec and Sobczak, *Genetics of the Jews*; Patai, *Myth of the Jewish Race*.

cultural ethos. At some points in history, however, they may have been a reflexive expression of an unspoken commonplace belief in race as determinative of 'quintessential' personality and behaviour.[12]

In the wake of the terrible fate suffered by the Jews in the twentieth century, partially as a consequence of racial theory, and the general discrediting of such theory since the Second World War, Jewish intellectuals today would not contemplate classifying the Jews as a race, and would certainly not write their history as a racial one. Moreover, as already noted, the more than two millennia-long existence of the conversion and intermarriage options (granted, that in some eras this has been only theoretical) means that even if racial theory had any credibility, the Jews could not conform to it.

Modern commentators (and some Jews), however, perplexed by the phenomenon of Jewishness and its resistance to ready definition, still sometimes take refuge in what, upon reflection, is a biological—even racial—characterization. Consider, for example, statements on the nature of Jewish identity by two celebrated novelists. Nadine Gordimer: 'It's something inside you, in your blood and in your bones.'[13] Philip Roth: 'Their being Jews issued from their being themselves . . . It was as it was, in the nature of things, as fundamental as having arteries and veins.'[14] Or the startling formulation of Yuri Slezkine: ' "Jews", for the purposes of this story, are the members of traditional Jewish communities (Jews by birth, faith, name, language, occupation, self-description, and formal ascription) and their children and grandchildren (whatever their faith, name, language, occupation, self-description, or formal ascription).'[15] According to this notion, the

[12] Endelman, 'Anglo-Jewish Scientists and the Science of Race'; Satlow, *Creating Judaism*, ch. 10.   [13] *Ha'arets*, English edn, 14 Nov. 2005, p. 9.

[14] *The Plot Against America*, 220.

[15] Slezkine, *The Jewish Century*, 3. The apparent reason for Slezkine's limiting Jewishness to three generations is because in his book he is describing the century spanned by approximately three generations of Russian Jews. Does his biologically based definition of Jewishness hold for the fourth and subsequent generations as well? Compare this quasi-racial casting of Jewish identity with Sartre's observation on the use of race as the default category for Jewish collective identity: 'That Jewish community which is based neither on nation, land, religion—at least in contemporary France—nor material interest, but only on an identity of situation . . . if the Jews want to draw a legitimate pride from this community, they must indeed end up by exalting racial qualities' (*Anti-Semite and Jew*, 85). Notably, he wrote this in 1944 while the Nazi racially based persecution of the Jews was still going full throttle.

second and third generation's connection to Jewishness needs be no more than a biological connection to 'traditional' Jews. Similarly, some fundamentalist rabbis insist that Jewish identity is literally borne in the genetic material of the ovum of the mother.[16] By contrast, some observers, although willing to count genealogy as a factor in Jewish identity, have jettisoned biology as insufficient for defining Jewishness.[17] Contemporary demographers have dispensed with it altogether.[18]

In the modern era, one of the most common and most important categories of group designation is 'nation'. There is a multiplicity of definitions of this term, and it is evident that there are different types of nations. However, in the sense of modern European nationalism, which is the context within which modern historiographical discourse about the Jewish nation developed, a nation may be regarded as an aggregation of people of common ethnic origin, history, and cultural heritage (including language, myths, and other cultural markers), who believe they share a collective identity, collective responsibility, and a collective fate, and live mostly within a common contiguous territory, with mutual economic ties, and who are organized, or aspire to organize, politically.

In the nineteenth century, as the nations of Europe crystallized politically and the nation more and more came to displace other categories of group identity (such as religion, local political organization, region, culture, feudal or clan ties), historians saw their task as the writing of the history of the nation (usually their own), and the grounding of national identity in that history. Since then the subject matter of the discipline of history has, in large measure, been organized along national lines, with historians traditionally specializing in French history, American history, Chinese history, and so on. When in the nineteenth century Jewish historians began to research and explicate the story of the Jews, they tried to adjust their subject to this model, defining the Jews as a nation analogous to other nations with a history that could provide the foundation for a national collective identity.[19]

At a time when Jews, who understood that the traditional basis for Jewish existence had badly eroded, were searching for the modus vivendi that would

[16] Kahn, *Reproducing Jews*, 129–33, and *Are Genes Jewish?*, 10.

[17] e.g. Baron, 'Problems of Jewish Identity', 36; Halbertal, 'Last Judgment', 28–9.

[18] See below and Chapter 2, the section entitled 'Who Is a Jew?'.

[19] For differing analyses and interpretations of Jewish nationalist historiography, see Barnai, *Historiography and Nationalism* (Heb.); Conforti, *Past Tense* (Heb.); Myers, *Re-Inventing the Jewish Past*; Raz-Krakotzkin, 'The National Narration of Exile' (Heb.); Rein, 'The Historian as a Nation Builder' (Heb.).

assure a secure Jewish life in the modernizing world, the national option offered a conceptual framework within which Jews could claim treatment on a par with other people. In principle, according to enlightened thinking, all nations are, at least prima facie, equal. A nation is entitled to its national rights regardless of its size, power, or the peculiarities of its culture. If the Jews are a nation, they are just as eligible as any other nation for the perquisites of nationhood, and should be able to relate to the other nations as a peer, no longer as a subordinated, marginal, oft-persecuted minority group. Individually, Jews, as members of a nation, are on the same level as the members of other nations, and are not unclassified aliens, merely tolerated or worse by the natives of the 'real' nations they reside among.

In addition, as secular trends became ascendant, and traditional modes of Jewish group identification (for example, religious law and practice, autonomous communal organization, kinship) and traditional conceptualization of the Jews' situation in the world (Exile[20]) progressively lost meaning for large groups of Jews, the nation concept offered a secular definition of Jewishness that modern, secular Jews could adopt. For people who self-identified as Jewish, but no longer adhered to religious and other traditional categories, the nation offered a rubric that made sense in the modern context and which, once accepted as applicable to the Jews, required no further defence.

Its applicability to the Jews was not, however, obvious. Many claimed that the Jews, lacking—for many centuries at least—a common territory and polity, a common vernacular language and other cultural accoutrements, and even a common history—by being dispersed in many lands and sharing in the life of other nations—were emphatically not a nation.[21]

---

[20] Raz-Krakotzkin, 'The National Narration of Exile' (Heb.), ch. 1 (quoting from English summary, p. viii): 'The concept of exile should be regarded as the core of Jewish historical consciousness and self-definition.' In the modern context this concept can appear to be an ethnocentric—and therefore problematic or even irrelevant—interpretation of history.

[21] See e.g. Sartre, *Anti-Semite and Jew*, 66–7, 91, and *passim*, who based his assertion in this regard on Hegel. Lenin, Stalin (see Lumer, *Lenin on the Jewish Question*; Vaksburg, *Stalin Against the Jews*), and many others also did not consider the Jews to be a nation. Similarly, contemporary critiques of Jewish claims to nationhood, notably by some Israelis, are rife: see e.g. Silberstein, *Postzionism Debates*, 71–84; Ram, 'Zionist Historiography and the Invention of Modern Jewish Nationhood'. One famous attack on the idea of Jewish nationhood was Neusner, 'Ideas of Jewish History', and it is discussed below.

Not only non-Jews thought this way. Those many Jews whose strategy for solving the 'Jewish problem' (for finding an appropriate modus vivendi for Jewish existence under the conditions of modernity) hinged primarily upon Jews becoming emancipated, fully fledged citizens of their countries of residence wanted to prove themselves as part of the nation whose state it was in which they lived. They were interested in eliminating any national elements from Jewish identity.[22]

One response to this critique of Jewish nationhood was to admit that, by conventional criteria, the Jews, perhaps, did not qualify; however, as Simon Dubnow maintained, the Jewish nation was actually at a more advanced stage of nationhood than the others. According to Dubnow, 'historical nations'—those that had a contribution to make to the history of humanity—passed through three stages. The first and lowest was the tribal stage, when the nation fended only for itself, followed by the political stage, with the establishment of governing institutions and the state, which could be used for the benefit of people outside the nation as well. The third stage was cultural, when the nation could make available to all humanity its cultural resources without the limitations of governmental institutions. In the history of the world only one nation, the Jews, had successfully weathered the loss of its political and territorial base and reached the highest stage where it could contribute the riches of its spirit, unfettered, to humanity. So the Jews, having attained the apogee of nationhood, were the historical nation par excellence.[23] In a similar vein, Salo Wittmayer Baron noted that 'gradually the [Jewish] nation emancipated itself from state and territory . . . If a Frenchman, whose nation has been rooted in its soil for millennia, can regard history and not the soil as essential to his own national feeling, how much more deeply ingrained is this conviction in the mental make-up of the Jews.'[24]

In contrast to the approach of Dubnow and Baron, which presumed to redefine nationhood, Zionists insisted that Jews could even qualify for conventional nationhood—if Jewish history were understood properly. They periodized Jewish history to the effect that for most of it, from the Israelite conquest of the twelfth century BCE to the Arab conquest of the seventh

---

[22] See e.g. Montefiore, *Dangers of Zionism*, esp. pp. 9–14; cf. Baron, 'Problems of Jewish Identity', 37.

[23] See Conforti, *Past Tense* (Heb.), ch. 2.

[24] Baron, *Social and Religious History of the Jews*, i. 17; Conforti, *Past Tense* (Heb.), ch. 3.

century CE, the Jews were in at least de facto possession of their national territory, Erets Yisrael (even if they did not rule it politically), which also served as the focal point for the national life of those who did not live there. Moreover, their religious and other behaviour—as well as the Shabatean messianic episode (intensively studied by Zionist and Israeli scholars)—demonstrated how virtually all Jews (at least until the late eighteenth century) considered the territory of Erets Yisrael to be the rightful home of the Jews, whether most Jews were there or not, or whether most of its population was Jewish or not.

Hebrew served the functions of a national language unifying Jews throughout the world for most of Jewish history. Furthermore, although there were many Jewish vernaculars, all of them contained significant Hebrew fundamentals and other elements, so that even though they were mostly non-Hebrew, they served to bolster Jewish national consciousness. Politically, even when Jews did not rule their own territory they still manifested Jewish collective political will and took collective political actions. They also maintained autonomous political institutions, such as the Patriarch in Palestine, the Exilarch in Babylonia, the Nagid in Egypt, and the Council of Four Lands in Poland, all of which contributed to a national self-consciousness. Socially, Jews maintained networks linking their various communities through trade, intellectual exchange, and endogamous marriage. Culturally, the high degree of observance of Jewish law (halakhah) by Jews the world over, for most of Jewish history, ensured shared values, shared behaviours, shared myths, and shared identity. Calendar, holidays, dietary restrictions, sabbath, circumcision, public recital of the Torah, a library of canonical books—all concretized a common *mentalité* and the belief that all Jews had a common national biography.[25]

In light of all this, the Zionist position was 'that the Jews, historically, were a "nation" in every important sense of that infinitely tricky and provocative term can hardly be gainsaid. Some historians have gone so far as to argue that it was the Jews (with the Greeks)[26] who were the original inventors of the concept, at least in the Western world, apart from constituting the prototypical case of the actual phenomenon.'[27]

---

[25] See e.g. Dinur, *Historical Writings* (Heb.), iv. 1–172; Baer, *Studies in the History of the Jewish People* (Heb.), i. 11–46, ii. 9–143.

[26] Cf. Anthony Smith, *The Antiquity of Nations*, 127–53, and *The Nation in History*.

[27] Vital, *Future of the Jews*, 146; cf. Raz-Krakotzkin, 'The National Narration of Exile' (Heb.), ch. 3.

But then came the modernist, social-constructivist critique of all nationalism, to the effect that the very idea of 'nation' was not a 'natural' or even 'primordial' phenomenon. Three influential books — Gellner's *Nations and Nationalism*, Anderson's *Imagined Communities*, and Hobsbawm and Ranger's *Invented Traditions* (especially Hobsbawm's essay with that title which opened the book, and a later chapter, 'Mass-Producing Traditions: Europe 1870–1914') — articulated the argument that the concept of 'nation' was both constructed and recent. The Anderson–Gellner–Hobsbawm trinity contended that the construct of nation was conceived as a way of providing the modern industrial state with an indispensable standard culture that it could promote as a means of uniting all of its citizens and directing their efforts towards the good of the collective. It rested on its members believing that they held various characteristics in common. Through these they shared the same 'national' identity. The point is that the members themselves defined the links between them, other than physical proximity, that enabled them to *imagine* themselves as being a community. These connections had no prior or independent existence.

Those who see themselves as a Palestinian nation, for example, could, by attending to one set of links instead of another, just as easily imagine themselves as part of an Arab nation. Those who think that only people of European heritage whose mother tongue is French constitute the French nation might instead imagine their nation to include all people born in France. Israelis might decide that their nation is 'Israeli', and no longer connected to the 'Jewish' nation,[28] whereas Orthodox Jews could conceivably define themselves as the only true Jews and sever ties with all others who call themselves by that name. All it takes to create a national identity is to enunciate one set or another of variables as essential to defining the collective. Once the nation is 'imagined' it creates a narrative that presents the group's beliefs about itself and its history[29] and invents common traditions — holidays, rituals, historical narrative, and so on — that concretize the putative primordial ties binding the past and present generations of the nation together, and uniting all of the current members wherever they may be.[30]

---

[28] This position is already implied in some of the writing by the prominent Israeli author A. B. Yehoshua. See for example the issue of the periodical *Alpayim* (Heb.) (2005) devoted to a colloquium on his interpretation of antisemitism (p. 28), as well as his book *For Normalcy*.

[29] Bhabha (ed.), *Nation and Narration*. On the Jewish-Zionist case, see Raz-Krakotzkin, 'The National Narration of Exile' (Heb.).

[30] Conforti, *Past Tense* (Heb.), ch. 5.

This portrayal has had a de-legitimizing effect on nationalism. True, an imagined nation need not be a 'false' one (Is the love between adoptive parent and child false? Is the love between birth parent and child based only on ties of biology?), and the constructed nature of the concept nation together with its nearly universal acceptance, however recent, might argue for its utility rather than its illegitimacy. However, critics have argued that a constructivist perspective implies that since the nation is merely a possible, but not a necessary, way to organize human collective life, and nationalism has had such violent and unjust collateral effects, perhaps the time has come to consider a new way to accomplish the task. Certainly, newly concocted nations have no right to harm or displace people who exist on a given territory in the name of the supposed antiquity of their national rights. There can be no such thing as ancient national rights because there were no nations before modernity.

This logic has been applied with a vengeance (and sometimes simply with vengeance) by observers of Jewish nationalism, particularly to its Zionist expression. They maintain that Zionism created an apt example of an imagined nation that comprises adherents of the Jewish religion as diverse as Yemenites and Englishmen, who share no language or territory and are as culturally alien to each other as are Arabs and Europeans in general. Zionism conjured up a nation where none existed, in part by inventing 'traditions' which entailed reinterpreting holidays such as Hanukah and Tu Bishvat in nationalist terms, making Hebrew into a spoken language in the name of national renewal, appropriating the Bible to its objectives, and violently contorting the diverse histories of the manifold Jewish communities into a unitary narrative.

Those unsympathetic to Jewish nationalism, then, have attacked it either by charging—if they believe in nationalism—that it does not fit the conventional criteria of nationhood; or—if they belong to the school that is critical of nationalism—by singling it out as a particularly egregious example of artificial nationhood that uses its constructed, imagined, invented collective identity to harm others, by usurping their lands and subjugating them.

Jewish nationalism—and Zionism—has also had its share of defenders, claiming that, as already noted, if nations are in actuality a modern refinement of long-existing ethno-religious groups, then the Jews are one of the oldest nations. All that Zionism did was to recast their already existing historical narrative as a modern national history. The Jews are not, therefore, an imagined community, but a re-imagined one. Jewish traditions are not invented, but reinvented. It is not the substance of Jewish existence that has changed, only the idiom for expressing it appropriately in modern society.[31] Jewish pretensions to national rights are no less urgent than those of other groups. Denying them such rights is a tactic of their enemies who, having been defeated on the military battlefield, seek victory on the political one by depriving Jews of their collective history and through the use of specious moral arguments.

Be that as it may, the acrimonious and unresolved debate over Jewish nationalism and the fact that many—especially non-Israeli—Jews have been, and remain until today, uncomfortable with a national Jewish identity makes this a problematic way to define the Jews. As Rabbi Milton Steinberg said, for example, 'If nation is taken to mean a political entity, and to embrace notions of sovereignty and citizenship, then it [Jewish nationhood] is totally inappropriate to American Jews who owe political fealty only to the American commonwealth.'[32]

An alternative to the category of nation was 'people'. In the English language since the fourteenth century, one sense in which this word has been used is 'nation'. The 'British people' or the 'American people' can denote the British nation or the American nation. In line with this, one might well argue that the Hebrew terms *am* and *goy*, used in the Bible to define Israel, might best be translated as 'people', which has the force but not the modern overtones of 'nation'.

In modern and postmodern *Jewish* discourse, however, the term 'people' seems to have gained in popularity as a surrogate for 'nation', precisely because it can carry a subtly different connotation. I think this was well expressed by Steinberg as long ago as 1945:

The Jews are a *people*. This is the third ingredient in Jewishness. A people is a body of persons who partake together in a social past and its heritage, a present and its problems, a future and its aspirations. To outsiders it appears as a distinct, identifiable historic entity. Viewed from within, it is marked by a sense of kinship and shared interests among its members. It is in sum a *Kultur und Schicksalsgemeinschaft*, a fellowship of tradition and destiny. 'People' then expresses a broad reality, yet political sovereignty and allegiance are not essential to it. Wherefore, both in what it says and leaves unsaid it fits the Jews.

This is the element which goes with religion and culture in Jewishness—the peoplehood of Israel. And this is the motif that persists when the others have been dissipated. By virtue of this a Jew may renounce the Jewish faith and repudiate

---

[31] Conforti, *Past Tense* (Heb.), ch. 5.
[32] Steinberg, *A Partisan Guide to the Jewish Problem*, 149.

Jewish culture, and remain both subjectively and objectively a Jew by identity. He is still part of the Jewish people.[33]

In other words, 'people' is an attenuated form of the nationalist definition—'nation-lite'—adopted by those who wanted to assert their belonging to the 'nation' of their country of citizenship and yet retain a sense of Jewish identity that was not necessarily religious.[34] Moreover, since 'people' may also be a synonym for nation, it provides a convenient ambiguity under which nationalists, especially the Zionists, and those uncomfortable with Jewish nationhood can together take refuge when they need or want to relate to each other positively. They can use the same term, meaning different things, yet appear to be in agreement.

A fascinating example of such usage is connected to the English translation of the standard Zionist summary narrative of Jewish history 'from Tanakh to Palmach' (i.e. from the Bible to the State of Israel), written by scholars of the Hebrew University of Jerusalem and published in Hebrew (in three famous red volumes) in 1969. In Hebrew the title is *Toledot am yisra'el* which in accord with Zionist nationalist doctrine would rightly be translated as 'History of the Jewish *Nation*'. The translation given on the supplementary title page in English is, however, 'History of the Jewish *People*'. The English edition of this work[35] used the latter title for the book, and deleted the introduction to the original Hebrew edition by the editor, Hayim Hillel Ben-Sasson, an essay that stressed the national character of the Jews and their history. In fact, there is no attempt in the English edition to explain what the Jews are beyond the word 'people' in the title. This shift in terminology, unaccompanied by elucidation of the term used, appears to be an uneasy compromise between the Israeli perception of Jewish nationalism that informed the Hebrew, and the less politically fraught peoplehood concept likely to be in the mind of the potential English-language reader. The Israelis could legitimately think of 'people' as meaning nation; the others probably understood it differently.

Like the modernist social-constructivists, postmodernists also consider the Jews to be one of the infinite 'constructs' that culture creates. To them,

---

[33] Ibid. 151

[34] Ironically, definition 1c of 'nation' in the *Oxford English Dictionary* reads: 'A group of people having a single ethnic, tribal, or religious affiliation, but *without a separate or politically independent territory*' (emphasis added). It then gives the following example: 'Freq[uently] used of the Jewish people in the Diaspora'.

[35] Ben-Sasson, *History of the Jewish People*.

however, the construct is not 'nation' but 'minority'. Wherever they lived, Jews were a minority, usually a colonized one, whose identity depended on being defined apart from the majority while in truth they were more a part of the society in which they lived than separate from it. Although there are numerous ancestors to this approach, its father is, I think, Jean-Paul Sartre, who argued in *Anti-Semite and Jew*:

Failing to determine the Jew by his race [which Sartre believed existed in physiological terms but was inconsequential in behavioural and moral ones], shall we define him by his religion or by the existence of a strictly Israelite national community? . . . A concrete historical community is basically *national* and religious; but the Jewish community, which once was both, has been deprived bit by bit of both these concrete characteristics . . . It is neither their past, their religion, nor their soil that unites the sons of Israel. If they have a common bond, if all of them deserve the name of Jew, it is because they have in common the situation of a Jew, that is, they live in a community which takes them for Jews . . . The Jew is one whom other men consider a Jew: that is the simple truth from which we must start.[36] . . . The Jews have neither community of interests nor community of beliefs. They do not have the same fatherland; they have no history. The sole tie that binds them is the hostility and disdain of the societies which surround them.[37]

Denying any substantive historical, religious, or national content to Jewish identity, considering that no behaviour was conditioned by Jewishness, holding that 'the Jewish community . . . keeps a memory of nothing but a long martyrdom, that is, of a long passivity'[38] (i.e. victimhood), insisting that it was the attitudes of, and treatment by, the Other that determined Jewish collective identity, Sartre paved the way to what, in Chapter 4, I call the 'Jew as trope'. This is the idea of Homi Bhabha and others that the Jew is *anyone* who is colonial, victim, subaltern, and oppressed. Conversely, and with Sartre's position in mind, Yuri Slezkine could propose a theory that implies that once the Other has decided to valorize, and even adopt, the behaviour patterns which were traditionally ascribed to the Jews (such valorization being Slezkine's way of hypostasizing modernization), then real Jews are an anachronism.[39]

---

[36] Consider the infamous quip of the antisemite mayor of late 19th-century Vienna, Karl Luegar, in response to accusations that he actually favoured certain Jews: 'Wer ein Jude ist, bestimme ich' ('*I* decide who is a Jew'): see *The Papers of Dr Karl Luegar*.

[37] Sartre, *Anti-Semite and Jew*, 64–9, 91.   [38] Ibid. 67.

[39] Slezkine was probably influenced by a fellow Russian from a previous generation, Lenin, who referred to Jews as an 'economic caste' and claimed that it was hatred and

Another view of 'what' the Jews are is to contend, not that Jewishness is bereft of content, but that its content comes in so many varieties, and is contingent on so many conditions, that it is nearly impossible to speak of 'the' Jews as a subject at all (see the Introduction and the discussion of 'metahistory' below). Although I am well aware of the myriad expressions of Jewishness that exist, to me this implies that Jews have no collective identity and therefore no history. Such an approach ultimately implies atomization of the subject to the point of dissolution and disappearance.[40]

We can conclude this survey of the ways in which Jews have been taxonomized with what is paradoxically both the most precise and the most inclusive definition; that is the demographer's 'operative definition' of 'all those who, when asked, identify themselves as Jews'.[41] Although this definition is similar to that of Sartre in failing to recognize any positive content to Jewish collective identity, it differs in that it is agnostic about such content rather than in denial of it, leaving it to Jews to define themselves rather than being subject to the criteria set by outsiders. Some applications and ramifications of this approach are presented in Chapter 3.

This review of the ways in which Jews have been classified is hardly exhaustive, but it does indicate how difficult our subject is to define. The interplay of genealogy, religion, common history, and other factors makes classifying the Jews in some conventional category virtually impossible.[42]

---

the pressures generated by economic and social forces that lent the Jews a collective identity; see Lumer, *Lenin on the Jewish Question*. The theses of Bhabha and Slezkine are discussed in greater detail in Chapters 3 and 4.

[40] See Jonathan Webber's comments in his edited volume, *Jewish Identities*, 25–6, and Chapter 3 below.

[41] DellaPergola, *World Jewry Beyond 2000*, 9; cf. Baron, 'Who Is a Jew?', in id., *History and Jewish Historians*, 19–22.

[42] Cf. Ben-Rafael, *Jewish Identities*, esp. pp. 3–7. In the context of criticizing any attempt to define an 'essential' Jewish identity, Silberstein has maintained: 'All efforts to impose a dominant category such as religious group, race, nation, transnational people, or ethnic group on the heterogeneous world Jewish population ultimately fail. Moreover, such efforts have the effect of excluding some Jews' (*Mapping Jewish Identities*, 13). Drawing on the work of the feminist critic Judith Butler, he proposed 'reconfigur[ing] such essentially contested terms like *Jew*, *Judaism*, and *Jewish* into a site of "permanent openness and resignifiability"'. The problem with making collective identity so protean is (as Silberstein admitted, and in my opinion had no good antidote for) the 'weakening of a group's integrity as well as struggles on its behalf'. Moreover, it makes historical identification of a given group theoretically anomalous. For further discussion of Silberstein's notions of anti-essentialist, or constructed, identity, see Chapter 3.

Historians' attempts to contend with this instability of definition have been legion. For the Zionist 'Jerusalem school' of Jewish historiography, 'history was understood . . . as it had been by non-Jewish researchers in nineteenth-century Europe—as the story of the nation'.[43] Yosef Hayim Yerushalmi, following the lead of his teacher, Salo Baron (who emphasized the reciprocal relationship of the Jewish religion and the Jewish nation), considered the Jews to be 'a unique fusion of religion and peoplehood'.[44] Anna Foa, one of the voices of new European postwar Jewish scholarship, termed the Jews both 'nation' and 'people', but seemed to imply that the content of Jewish identity might best be expressed not as an instance of a standard general category, but as a collection of elements: 'the elements of this strong [Jewish] identity are concrete and well documented: community and family organization, the sacred texts and their study, separateness, and a complex relationship with the outside world. The law and its rabbinic interpretation, the halakhah (literally, "way of proceeding"), are the most important elements of all.'[45]

In *Cultures of the Jews*, David Biale was certain that the term 'people' was the correct one to apply to the Jews. He was not sure, however, if 'the Jews' are a unitary entity. He attempted to resolve this dilemma by positing 'a dialectic between, on the one hand, the *idea* of one Jewish people and of a unified Jewish culture, and, on the other, the history of multiple communities and cultures . . . The Jewish people were, at once, one *and* diverse.'[46]

Such multiplicity of approaches is usually a sign not only of the difficulty of definition but also of the indispensability of the concept, because common experience lends it great resonance in people's lives (compare, for example, such fundamental—and fundamentally contested—notions as beauty, culture, social history, Europe, terrorism, and martyrdom). In Chapter 3 I will try to point the way towards the development of a 'polythetic' or 'disjunctive' definition of Jewish culture, which may also be useful in getting closer to a historically valid definition of the Jews.

A Unified, Coherent History?

However a historian defines the Jewish collectivity, the history of which is the subject of study, a further question that must be confronted is the question of the unity of Jewish history. This putative unity might have two

---

[43] Myers, 'Between Diaspora and Zion', 95–6.   [44] Yerushalmi, *Zakhor*, p. xvi.
[45] Foa, *The Jews of Europe after the Black Death*, 51; cf. the polythetic definition of Jewish culture suggested in Chapter 3.   [46] Biale (ed.), *Cultures of the Jews*, p. xxv.

dimensions: vertical, whether the events connected to Jews in different ages, from biblical to contemporary times, can be construed as one continuous, interconnected, integral narrative; and horizontal, whether all the Jews everywhere in any given era—and throughout history—represent a unified entity and are part of the same story.[47] In other words: is Jewish history coherent from biblical times to the present? Do all Jews share a common history?

In both of its dimensions, this problem is not unique to the Jews. With regard to coherence through time, if one's objective is to narrate the history of the American nation, how far back does that history stretch? Does American history begin with the migration of tribes from Asia to Alaska some 14,000 years ago, or with the coming of the Europeans in 1492, or with the settlement of English colonists in the seventeenth century, or with the founding of the Republic in 1776 (Declaration of Independence) or 1787 (US Constitution)? If one seeks to write the history of the Chinese people, does that include the Chinese diaspora in South-East Asia, North America, and many other places? Can Poland—with borders, political organization, and ethnic and religious composition in continual flux over the past thousand years—be the subject of a continuous historical narrative? Should such a narrative include Poles dispersed in many other countries?

Some may conclude that these problems demonstrate that 'nation' or 'people' are simply no longer viable frameworks for the writing of collective history. I maintain that whatever the collective history on whatever scale one sets out to document and describe, the question of demonstrating its unity, coherence, or continuity asserts itself. There is no objective criterion for deciding a priori what should be included under the rubric of the history of X; X can be defined in many ways. However, once a community or collective entity is imagined or, better, *conceptualized* through time, and the definition based on such conception stands the tests of rationality and source corroboration, it is valid—at least to those willing to practise what I called in the Introduction 'reformed positivism'. This approach governs my response to one of the most famous and perhaps most trenchant formulations of the problem at hand, that of Jacob Neusner:

---

[47] For a clear statement on the unity of Jewish history in both dimensions, see Baer and Dinaburg, 'Our Purpose' (Heb.), their introduction to the first issue of the Israel Historical Society's journal of Jewish history, *Zion*, in 1935. For analyses and critiques of this view, see Conforti, *Past Tense* (Heb.), ch. 5; Raz-Krakotzkin, 'The National Narration of Exile' (Heb.), chs 3 and 4.

The fundamental question . . . is whether the Jews from Abraham to the present constitute an entity capable of presenting a single, unitary history. By the criteria to be adduced from the data conceived to form a normal historical unit, they do not. For that long period of time, the Jews have not occupied a single geographical area, have not spoken a single language, have not formed a single society, have not produced a single harmonious culture . . .

Historians normally are able to proceed on the assumption, whether based upon geographical, or political, or sociological, or cultural grounds, that they deal with a single entity which has had a unitary history, a history which an objective outsider as much as a contemporary participant is able to discern. Can an observer discern the elements of a common history among groups, called, to be sure, by a common name, from China to Britain, from the United Monarchy of David and Solomon to the United Jewish Appeal of New York?[48]

Neusner appears to have assumed that only a 'normal historical unit' (presumably a 'nation' or a 'people'), whose claim to a unitary history is based on geographical, political, sociological, or cultural grounds, can have a history, and there are difficulties fitting the Jews into such a category. Moreover, he believed that there are 'objective observers' who can detect the objective data that qualify an entity for such a history.

Postmodern consciousness has cast doubt on these suppositions. As I intimated in my comments about America and Poland, virtually no nation or people can claim a stable geographical, political, sociological, or cultural past. Continuity and coherence are always a construct resulting from a process of 'retrodiction' (see Introduction). The 'normal historical unit' is always defined by its members, not by some 'objective observer', and could be defined differently and then matched with a different history. In this spirit, it seems to me that Jewish historians have as much right as the historians of any other collective to conceptualize the historical community they write about in terms that make sense to them, on two conditions: first, that such a construction fits the evidence; second, that the coherent story they arrive at is a de facto interpretation and not a teleological one. That is, they are explaining what happened, and perhaps even why it happened, without claiming that it *inevitably* happened.

If, then, Jewish historians can find rational bases for linking the history of biblical Israel with that of the State of Israel, this is no less valid than

---

[48] Neusner, 'Ideas of Jewish History', 213–14. For a different view of the problems of the unity and continuity of Jewish history, see the book Neusner was reviewing, Meyer (ed.), *Ideas of Jewish History*, 5–6, 23–42. See another, less eloquent, formulation of Neusner's denial of Jewish history, cited in Chapter 3 at n. 65.

twenty-first-century Americans finding continuity with seventeenth-century English colonists, or contemporary Poles finding their roots in the tenth-century reign of King Piast. To be sure, alternative interpretations are possible; that is not the issue. What is germane is whether this particular interpretation is among the plausible, defensible, source-corroborated ones? If no interpretation yielding a Jewish collective history is deemed tenable, then Jewish collective existence itself is deniable. As developments in post-Second World War politics and historiography have demonstrated, only those with a history can claim a present and a future. Groups seeking to ground their present-day demands for recognition and rights invariably turn to history for legitimation. Without a history, Jews disappear.[49]

With regard to the horizontal dimension of continuity, the problem here is one of continuity versus context. On the one hand, Jewish historians have traditionally emphasized the transnational unity of the Jews in every age. Wherever they are they constitute a cell of the larger Jewish 'nation' or 'people'.[50] On the other hand, sophisticated historians readily recognized that, as Shmuel Ettinger put it, 'At no period in their history have [the Jews] barricaded themselves against the social and cultural development of other nations, nor cut themselves off from the influence of other civilizations, but they have confronted them, both resisting their influence and absorbing their riches'.[51] In other words, Jews were always part of the social, cultural, and political context in which they lived. Recently, in

---

[49] Cf. Novick, *That Noble Dream*, 469–521; Iggers, *Historiography in the Twentieth Century*, 143; Bentley, *Modern Historiography*, 148. Perhaps aware of the dangers of relinquishing the idea of a Jewish collective history altogether, Neusner advanced the idea that 'while there is no single, unitary "Jewish history", there is a single (but hardly unitary) history of Judaism' ('Ideas of Jewish History', 218). Later, in his more than voluminous writing, he seemed to retreat even further, referring for example to 'the whole of the history of the Jewish people', as distinct from the history of Jewish religion, in his *Understanding Seeking Faith*, 11.

[50] Myers, *Re-Inventing the Jewish Past*, 30–1, both pointed to this postulate and questioned its validity: 'The nationalist historian of a diaspora people must arrange the experiences of diverse communities into a unified whole . . . to create, or fabricate, national unity out of communal diversity.' I would argue, in line with the above discussion of the 'imagined' nature of all historical subjects, that 'communal diversity' is no less of a construct than 'national unity', and therefore both can be equally valid—or invalid—matrices within which to portray Jewish history.

[51] Ben-Sasson, *History of the Jewish People*, 732. In fact, there is evidence for such recognition on the part of Jewish historians as early as the 16th century; see Yerushalmi, *Zakhor*, 63.

contrast to the older Jewish historians who saw the context in dialectic with the forces of continuity and unity, but secondary to them,[52] postmodern historians have contended that the context is supreme. For them, Jews' primary connection is with the people they live among and not with Jews elsewhere. I will return to this viewpoint in my discussion of metahistory below, and in analysing the idea of cultural hybridity in Chapter 3.[53]

Galut: Good for the Jews?

Another primary issue in Jewish historiography is the status of the Exile (*galut* or the *golah*), or Diaspora. In traditional Jewish theology *galut* was conceived of as punishment for failure to fulfil God's commands properly and all of Jewish history was interpreted as manifestation of this punishment. The official Christian position concurred that the Jews' exile was punishment. To Christian theorists, however, the Jews' offence was rejection of Jesus and the true religion. Jewish historians, looking back on what constituted — according to most periodization schemes — the bulk of Jewish history, offered a secularized evaluation of what was in Jewish religious theory a 'temporary' state of affairs until redemption would come.

Heinrich Tsevi Graetz, the greatest of nineteenth-century Jewish historians, summed up the nearly 2,000 years after the destruction of the Temple in Jerusalem as an era of

unprecedented suffering, of uninterrupted martyrdom without parallel in world history. But it is also a period of spiritual alertness, of restless mental activity, of indefatigable inquiry . . . The external history of this era is a *Leidensgeschichte*, a history of suffering to a degree and over a length of time such as no other people has experienced. Its inner history is a comprehensive *Literaturgeschichte*, a literary history of religious knowledge, which yet remains open to all the currents of science, absorbing and assimilating them.[54]

For Graetz, *galut* meant unending suffering for the Jewish social, political, and communal body. The Jewish soul, however, never ceased to flourish; 'study and suffering—these fill the long stretch of this era'.[55] Since only an

[52] See discussions of this issue in Conforti, *Past Tense* (Heb.), ch. 5; Myers, *Re-Inventing the Jewish Past*, 184–5; and Raz-Krakotzkin, 'The National Narration of Exile' (Heb.), ch. 3.

[53] A possible test-case for examining the relationship between continuity and context is the Shabatean messianic episode, especially its acute phase from Shabetai Tsevi's declaration of his messianism in May 1665 until his conversion to Islam in September 1666. Cf. the account in Scholem, *Sabbatai Sevi*, with that in Barnai, *Shabateanism* (Heb.).

[54] Meyer (ed.), *Ideas of Jewish History*, 229–30.   [55] Ibid. 230.

elite among the Jews engaged in serious study, but virtually all suffered, Graetz's perspective did not suggest a very sanguine overall assessment of life in *galut*.

This pessimistic vision was carried to an extreme by some Zionist ideologues. One of the pillars of classic Zionist ideology is often said to be *shililat hagolah*, rejection of the Exile. This means that the long years between the destruction of the Second Temple (70 CE) and the establishment of Israel (1948 CE), a time when the Jews were neither concentrated in their own land nor rulers over it, was a historical aberration. It was a time when the Jews led an abnormal, anomalous existence as a powerless minority, which could not be an agent of its own history, but only a marginal object in the history of others. The conditions of exilic existence cultivated in the Jews many attributes that were nothing to be proud of: physical weakness, detachment from the soil and physical labour, (pre-)occupation with money and commerce rather than 'productive' pursuits such as agriculture and manufacture that created 'real' wealth, political chicanery, moral ambiguity, and, most of all, passivity, fatalism, and accommodation to suffering.

This was a history to be overcome, perhaps forgotten; not to be carefully researched, recorded, and celebrated. The classic statement of this attitude was contained in a story by Hayim Hazaz, 'Haderashah', the sermon, in which the protagonist, Yudka, declares:

We have no history at all . . . for we did not make our own history; the *goyim* made it for us. Just as they put out the lamp for us on Shabbat and milked the cow for us on Shabbat and lit the fire, so they also made history for us as they wanted and in their way; we just received it from them . . . What does it have? Massacres, libels, persecutions and martyrdom. And again, massacres, libels, persecutions and martyrdom. Again and again, more and more with no end . . . It has no exploits and escapades, no heroes and conquerors, no rulers or men of action or great sovereigns; only a depressed and dejected crowd, sighing, crying, begging mercy.[56]

A less caustic, but more official, expression of this view is the 1948 Israel Declaration of Independence. After lauding the political strength and

---

[56] There are different versions of this story. I translated from the one contained in Hazaz's collection, *Boiling Stones* (Heb.), 227–44. In 'Another Reading of "Haderashah" ' (Heb.), Parush and Dalmatzky-Fischler have suggested that careful reading of Hazaz's story reveals that it was really more a critique of Zionism than of the *golah*. Moreover, one did not need to be a Zionist to take a jaundiced view of *galut* history; see Wisse (ed.), *A Shtetl*, 272.

cultural creativity of the Jewish nation in Erets Yisrael in antiquity, this text moved quickly to the achievements of the Zionist nationalist movement from the late nineteenth century on, mentioning the period of *galut* in passing, and then only as a time when Jews maintained their loyalty to Erets Yisrael, prayed for their return there, and never ceased to try to do so. There was no strength, no creativity, no achievement worthy of mention outside the Land.

Zionist historians, as opposed to Zionist ideologues, were more ambivalent, even positive, about *galut*. Ben-Zion Dinur valued 'the continuation of collective Jewish life in the Dispersion and in spite of the Dispersion', and made prodigious efforts to document that life. In his inaugural lecture at the Hebrew University, Yitzhak Baer asserted categorically:

> There is no point to our history if we are supposed to erase from it some one or two thousand years; if there is such a long period that it is impossible to fit in except as an appendix to the ancient period . . . or even as a transition period and preparation for our new life . . . Every period is connected to the periods preceding and following in a historically evolutionary way.[57]

Led by Salo Baron, Diaspora historians were unambivalently positive about the legacy of *galut* history. Baron pointed out that, as opposed to the picture presented by Graetz and others of a lachrymose history filled with blood and tears, Jewish life viewed historically was more peak-dotted plateaus than valleys. In medieval Europe, Jews actually enjoyed a better legal and cultural status than the majority of the population, the serfs. Whereas sporadic episodes of persecution were a fact of life, most of the time Jews lived neither as quaking cravens nor as cowering sycophants. They made a significant contribution to the structure and functioning of society and culture wherever they were. Jewish cultural achievements and institutional innovations in *galut* were truly something to boast about.[58]

By the late twentieth century such positive, but sober, evaluation had turned into rapturous praise. Daniel and Jonathan Boyarin wrote an

---

[57] Dinur, *Israel and the Diaspora*, 4; Baer, *Studies in the History of the Jewish People* (Heb.), ii. 11–12. For thorough discussions and differing interpretations of the attitudes of Zionist historians towards *galut*, see Conforti, *Past Tense* (Heb.), ch. 4; Myers, *Re-Inventing the Jewish Past*, ch. 6; Raz-Krakotzkin, 'The National Narration of Exile' (Heb.); and Rein, 'The Historian as a Nation Builder' (Heb.).

[58] Baron, 'Ghetto and Emancipation', and 'The Jewish Factor in Medieval Civilization'. For discussion and analysis of Baron's 'anti-lachrymose theory', and other topics relating to *galut* life, see Liberles, *Salo Wittmayer Baron*; Engel, 'Crisis and Lachrymosity'.

influential article, in which they came to the conclusion that the Diaspora experience of the Jews, when it included strong identity and 'Promethean Jewish creativity' that could be 'synergistic with a general cultural activity', was so successful (to be sure, excepting incidents of persecution) that they proposed Diaspora as 'a theoretical and historical model to replace national self-determination'.[59] In semi-opposition to this view, the feminist critic Aviva Cantor stressed the corrosive effects of Exile, and considered that 'calling Exile "diaspora" and prattling about its advantages while ignoring its dynamics is very dangerous'.[60] Yet even she saw a distinct benefit to *galut*. Using functionalist analysis, Cantor came to the conclusion that 'traditional Jewish society [in *galut*] was a reformed patriarchy standing on three pillars: the female value system, Halacha and the community'. Gender roles were significantly and positively altered, with Jewish manhood redefined 'from macho to *mentsch*'. For the 'new Jewish man' of the Exile, power lay in the brain and not the muscle. As a result, 'this was arguably the closest any society came to fulfilling Plato's ideal of the philosopher-king'.[61]

The most enthusiastic embrace of the *galut* experience was Yuri Slezkine's *The Jewish Century*. Slezkine conceived modernity as the apotheosis of the stereotypical *galut* Jewish profile (given the appropriately positive spin):

Modernization is about everyone becoming urban, mobile, literate, articulate, intellectually intricate, physically fastidious, and occupationally flexible. It is about learning how to cultivate people and symbols, not fields or herds. It is about pursuing wealth for the sake of learning, learning for the sake of wealth, and both wealth and learning for their own sake. It is about transforming peasants and princes into merchants and priests, replacing inherited privilege with acquired prestige, and dismantling social estates for the benefit of individuals,

---

[59] 'Diaspora', 711. On their assertion that diaspora, and not monotheism, was the most important Jewish contribution to civilization, see Chapter 4 at n. 45.

[60] Cantor, *Jewish Women/Jewish Men*, 16–32; quotation from p. 32.

[61] Ibid. 4–6, 79–98; quotations from pp. 4, 79, and 98. Daniel Boyarin's book *Unheroic Conduct* is also largely devoted to lauding the superiority of the supposedly feminized Diaspora Jewish male over the macho 'new Jew of muscle' that was so much a part of Zionist mythology. As part of their reconstruction of Diaspora Jewish gender-role alteration, both Cantor (p. 5) and Boyarin (p. 156) made the unhistorical assertion that in many traditional Jewish communities, predominantly women were the primary family breadwinners. For my evaluation of this claim, see Rosman, 'To Be a Jewish Woman', 426–31, and 'History of Jewish Women', 38–40.

nuclear families, and book-reading tribes (nations). Modernization, in other words, is about everyone becoming Jewish.[62]

With 'everyone' in the modern world seeking to turn into '*galut* Jews' (behaviourally speaking), political Zionism—born precisely when *galut* Jewishness was on the cusp of being transvalued—was spitting into the wind of history:

Zionism, the most eccentric of all nationalisms, argued that the proper way to overcome Jewish vulnerability was not for everyone else to become Jewish, but for the Jews to become like everyone else . . . Did they really want to transform themselves into thick-skulled peasants now that actual peasants had, for all practical purposes, admitted the error of their ways? . . . Zionism belonged to the integral-nationalist wing of the twentieth-century revolution against modernity.[63]

By this logic, Zionism (or at least the variety one might surmise from a Jewish National Fund publicity film, circa 1950)—which originally set out to be an antidote to the 'abnormality' that distorted Jewish life in the Exile—actually and ironically attempted to de-modernize the Jews, the originators of modernity! It sought to attach them to a certain territory, to get them to work the soil and become sedentary peasants, to cultivate in them manliness and militarism, and to encourage them to value ethnic purity. And so, in a period beginning circa 1990, after a time—especially following the Six Day War in 1967—during which Zion and *galut* seemed to be reconciled and even mutually reinforcing,[64] diasporists paid Zionists back in their own coin. Compared to *galut*/Diaspora, Zionism and Israel were negated as the 'abnormal' form of Jewish existence.

More irony: none disparaged Zion as a venue for 'normal' existence more than post-Zionist theorists, the great majority of whom live or lived in it. These children of the Zionist dream (most of whom believed in Zionist mythology in their youth) were convinced that their parents and teachers, who represented Zionism to them as humane, progressive, and liberal, 'had distorted and lied about the essential features of Israeli society and history'. With the anger and zeal of a betrayed lover, they pounced on contradictions in Zionism's rhetoric and Israel's existence— socialist vs. nationalist, Jewish vs. democratic, progressive vs. religious, mono-ethnic vs. multicultural, egalitarian vs. hierarchical, peace-seeking vs. conquering/occupying, nativist vs. immigrant, populist vs. elitist, Universal

---

[62] Slezkine, *The Jewish Century*, 1.   [63] Ibid. 2, 74, 269.

[64] A good description and expression of this rapprochement in all of its ambivalence, intricacies, and permutations is Eisen, *Galut*, pt 2.

Jewish (*kelal yisra'el*) vs. Ashkenazi (the list goes on)—and some applied postmodern and postcolonial critiques to these contradictions. Rather naively, even disingenuously, presuming Israel to be virtually unique in its entrapment in rhetorical conundrums as well as in its tense suspension between rhetoric and reality, their conclusion was that these contradictions are inherent in Zionism, a modernist enterprise that exhibits all of modernism's flaws (*pace* Slezkine); they cannot be resolved within Zionist discourse. To these people, the continued effort to frame life in Israel in terms of Zionist discourse, then, renders it unstable and eventually unsustainable. To save itself, Israel must cease to fashion itself as the Zionist-envisioned Jewish state. The Jews, if indeed such a collective exists (see above), will best be Jews in Diaspora—which may even include a significant community in the area between the Mediterranean Sea and the Jordan river, whatever political arrangements happen to be in place there.[65]

How Do the Jews Fit into History?

The fourth a priori issue for our discussion is the relationship between Jewish history and history in general. In 1592, in Prague, David ben Solomon Gans published *Zemah david*, a historical chronicle that reviewed all of the events the author considered to be significant from the creation of the world 5,392 years earlier (according to conventional rabbinic chronology) until his own times. Gans organized his book in two sections, one covering the history of the Jews, the other that of everyone else. In this and other ways he signalled his belief that Jewish history was governed by different rules and was headed for a different destiny from the rest of humankind's history. The Jews had a special relationship with God and, while He managed all history, He situated theirs in the reward-and-punishment and exile-and-redemption matrices that were delineated long ago in the Bible.

Such an attitude towards 'Jewish history' as a special subset of 'history', which, in addition to whatever general rules there were, was bound by the

---

[65] The 'post-Zionist' label has been applied in an imprecise way to a wide variety of critics of Zionist theory and praxis. For an attempt to survey the field, create a typology, and delineate the distinctions, see Silberstein, *Postzionism Debates*. The quotation above and others with similar import appear there (p. 92). While Silberstein's survey is helpfully wide ranging, Penslar, 'Narratives of Nation-Building', is much more rigorous, critical, and contextualized. For a sampling of essays in English by both leading post-Zionists and some of their critics see Arad (ed.), *Israeli Historiography Revisited*. The Hebrew journal *Teoryah uvikoret* (Theory and Criticism) is the key publication venue for the views of the more theoretically oriented post-Zionists.

terms of God's covenant with Israel, continued to echo when Jewish historiography became a modern secular pursuit. Cecil Roth, for example, concluded the 1954 edition of his popular, oft-published, variously titled, and frequently revised single-volume summary of Jewish history thus:

The preservation of the Jew was certainly not casual . . . Time after time in his history, moreover, he has been saved from disaster in a manner which cannot be described excepting as 'providential'. The author has deliberately attempted to write this work in a secular spirit; he does not think that his readers can fail to see in it, on every page, a higher immanence.[66]

Some other historians, who in addition to writing in a secular spirit were profoundly imbued with one, also insisted that Jewish history was a special case—or at least that it was primarily the result of 'internal Jewish' factors. Yitzhak Baer, who considered 'release of historical research from the yoke of theology' to be an imperative, still allowed himself to speak of 'the special character of Jewish [historical] development', and to say that this development was 'uniquely different from that of all the nations'.[67] However, as Yisrael Yuval has observed, Baer appeared to be ambivalent on this point. He could write about 'our central task, to understand the historical foundations of our religious tradition by the historical interpretation of the internal sources themselves . . . In order to promote research, one should reinforce and stress the weight of internal criteria', but he immediately added: 'Judaism is one of the forces of general history, it is influenced by them and influences them. Today there is no more room for Wissenschaft des Judentums without continual attention to the relations between Israel and the nations.'[68] Looking at Baer's work in its totality, I think that his and

[66] Quotation from the Schocken Books paperback reprint (New York, 1961), p. 424. The book was first published in 1935 by the official organization of American Reform Judaism, the Union of American Hebrew Congregations, as *A Bird's-Eye View of Jewish History*. Later editions, published by other publishers, were called *A Short History of the Jewish People* or *A History of the Jews*. The book was translated into other languages and last revised in 1970, the year of the author's death. Not all editions concluded with the text quoted here. For example, the 1948 edition (London: East and West Library) concluded: 'The Providence that guides the process of history had ensured that the Jewish future was safe' (p. 444). Editions appearing after the Sinai campaign left out the reference to Providence entirely.

[67] Baer and Dinaburg, 'Our Purpose' (Heb.), 1; Baer, *Studies in the History of the Jewish People* (Heb.), ii. 12–13; cf. Dawidowicz, *What Is the Use of Jewish History?*, 19.

[68] Quotations translated in Yuval, 'Yitzhak Baer', 84, 78. On Baer's ambivalence and ambiguity on the relationship between Jewish history and history, see Conforti, *Past Tense* (Heb.), chs 1 and 5, and Raz-Krakotzkin, 'The National Narration of Exile' (Heb.), ch. 4.

like-minded historians' conception of Jewish history was not that it was somehow independent of the rest of history, but rather that it was a circle with a central focus that determined its circumference. That central focus was fixed by internal, or immanent, Jewish structures and dynamics (that is, structures and dynamics that were associated with past Jewish experience, whatever their origins may have been).[69] The Jewish circle certainly came into contact with other circles. They frequently collided and intersected, affecting each other's shapes and even overlapping each other's spaces. The point was that, notwithstanding interaction with the multitude of historical factors around them, the Jews, even when lacking political power, were the primary agents of their own history, not passive subjects. Yudka, Hazaz's anti-hero, was wrong.

A corollary of this circle-with-central-focus approach was: who better to study Jewish history as the history of Jewish agency than modern Jewish nationalist scholars whom the State of Israel had liberated from the 'What will the *goyim* say?' mentality? As their leading light, Gershom Scholem, declared:

There took place that fundamental change of perspective which accompanied the national movement . . . We no longer saw our problems from without . . . The new slogan was: to see from within, to go from the center to the periphery without hesitation and without looking over one's shoulder! To rebuild the entire structure of knowledge in terms of the historical experience of the Jew who lives among his own people and has no other accounts to make than the perception of the problems, the events and the thoughts according to their true being, in the framework of their historical function within the people.[70]

An alternative view, usually attributed to the Israeli Baer's American counterpart and counterpoint, Salo Baron,[71] was that Jewish history is not a

---

[69] In his introduction to *The Jewish Past Revisited* Myers questioned the appropriateness of the 'immanent factor' category: 'can we speak intelligently of immanence as a category of historical (as opposed to metahistorical) causality?' (p. 11). Certainly the distinction between 'internal' (or 'immanent') and 'external' loses meaning the more that Jews are seen as part of their context and less as having a separate collective identity. However, if it is possible to maintain the tension between continuity and context discussed above, then it would seem that 'immanent factors' are those more closely tied to the continually aggregating heritage than the 'external' ones that derive primarily from the present context. On externalist vs. internalist causative explanations, see Novick, *That Noble Dream*, 9.

[70] Scholem, 'Reflections on Modern Jewish Studies', 66.

[71] Baer wrote two critical reviews of the first edition of Baron's *Social and Religious History*. He especially took issue with Baron's positive evaluation of *galut* life. For a full discussion, see Liberles, *Salo Wittmayer Baron*, 156–61.

circle, but an ellipse, whose shape is determined by two foci, one internal, one external; that is, Jewish history is always a result of the co-action of immanent, inherently Jewish factors with other factors. Moreover, unlike Scholem, Baron—being a professor at Columbia University in the United States—could not claim to be at Scholem's 'centre', a Jew living among his own people with no other accounts to make. Yet, based on the elliptical conception and in the Diaspora, Baron dared, twice, to write a comprehensive multi-volume history of the Jews, something no other single Israeli scholar has ever attempted.

A different way to conceptualize the relationship between the history of the Jews and history is as an environment full of chemical reagents that are constantly reacting with each other: sometimes mixing, sometimes making new compounds, sometimes inertly bouncing off each other. Thus events and processes involving Jews may have a 'Jewish nature' that ranges from primary, to distinct, to discernible, and finally to indistinguishable. Practically speaking, to a contemporary sensibility it seems beyond question that in every period and place Jews were participants in the general social, cultural, economic, and religious environment. However, as a result of their particular history and circumstances, the effects of general conditions and processes on the Jews may have been different from their effects on others. Jewish history is often distinctive.

An example of this is demography. From the early eighteenth century until the early twentieth, there was general population growth in most of the regions of the world where the Jews lived. Also, in the period 1880–1914 some 35 million people migrated across borders in Europe. Jewish demography was intimately linked to the general processes at work, and the Jewish population both grew and migrated. At the same time, however, because of the particular history and circumstances of the Jews, Jewish demography displayed distinguishing characteristics. Jewish growth far exceeded the general rate, and Jewish migration was disproportionately high and characterized by some different features and objectives. By the same token, as birthrates in the countries Jews inhabited (outside Israel) tended to go down after the post-Second World War 'baby boom', the Jewish birthrate reduced much more.[72]

With its distinctiveness, the *study* of Jewish history, in addition to what it has to tell us about the Jews, can also serve other functions. As Yerushalmi observed: 'Although, as an historian of the Jews, I am concerned primarily

---

[72] DellaPergola, *World Jewry Beyond 2000*, 7–8, 13–14, 25–8, 38–43, 50–1.

with the Jewish past, I do not think that the issues to be raised are necessarily confined to Jewish history. Still, it may be that this history can sometimes set them into sharper relief than would otherwise be possible.'[73] The study of the Jews, then, can lend deeper insight into issues of general concern.[74] This is utilizing the Jews as illustration.

Elliott Horowitz has suggested that the study of Jewish history and history best interrelate in another way. In reviewing the English edition of the memoirs of the seventeenth-century Venetian rabbi Leon Modena, *Life of Judah*, he noted how the introductory essay, by Mark R. Cohen and Theodore Raab, asserted that 'the experience of the Jews deserves to be incorporated into the broader picture of early modern European history "even though they often exhibited distinctive behavior and specifically Jewish modes of response to the forces acting upon them" '. This seems to imply that the Jews are part of the story, but frequently as a subplot or tangent. Horowitz differed: 'Some might rather assert that it is precisely their distinctive behavior and modes of response that make the Jews most interesting to the historian of early modern Europe. How one relates to "difference" can sometimes make all the difference.'[75]

So the Jews can be a test case. Their difference may highlight the fault-lines inherent in what were taken to be stable structures. By probing these one can better understand the basis, function, and dynamics of these structures.

Which Metahistory to Choose?

At the beginning of this chapter I maintained that a historian's position on a priori issues of the type raised here determines the framework within which he or she conducts research and composes a narrative. This framework of beliefs and assumptions about history is sometimes called 'metahistory'. If, for example, you are convinced that *galut* is Diaspora, you will likely accentuate the positive in its history and certainly not privilege the history of the Jews in Erets Yisrael in any post-biblical period. You may omit, gloss over, or explain away details that do not support your overall thesis (sincerely believing that they are of minor importance), while emphasizing those that illustrate it. This need not entail playing fast and

[73] Yerushalmi, *Zakhor*, 6; see also pp. 87–9.

[74] See Chapter 4 on the contribution of Jewish studies to academia and Chapter 7 for Jacob Katz's opinion on this issue.

[75] Elliott Horowitz, review of *The Autobiography of a Seventeenth-Century Venetian Rabbi*, 460–1.

loose with the sources, nor distorting the facts you provide as part of the description. It does, however, weaken the cogency of your presentation and your argument. So something might be lost; but something else may be gained. Your metahistory will probably sensitize you to aspects of the historical picture that someone with a different metahistory will fail to notice, and in that way it is enriching. In any case, in the process of selection and interpretation one's metahistory will play a significant role. Every historian has a metahistorical point of departure, conscious or not, and this is the fifth a priori issue to be addressed here. I will briefly describe a few of the major metahistories that have served as frameworks for writing Jewish history.

First is the nationalist—not necessarily Zionist—metahistory. This originated with Simon Dubnow, who believed that the Jews are a nation who, as noted earlier, had reached the highest stage of nationhood, anchored in history and culture rather than territory. Diaspora was and is the permanent condition of the Jews, but in dispersion the Jews always maintained continuity with the past and solidarity with other contemporary communities. In each era continuity, solidarity, and the relationship with the surrounding non-Jewish environment were mediated primarily by a dominant community which, in its age, put its stamp on the culture of the Jews. This role of hegemonic centre shifted from place to place: Babylonia in late antiquity, Muslim Spain in the High Middle Ages, Ashkenaz–Poland in the early modern period, eastern Europe in Dubnow's own time. With regard to the modern period, Dubnow established a paradigm whereby Jewish history was continually oscillating between two poles:

On the one hand, there was the Jewish nation which had tenaciously survived almost two millennia of exile and dispersion by dint of its internal solidarity, faith and inventiveness. On the other, there were the combined forces of change which, unless creatively absorbed and organically integrated by the nation, could only set in motion a process of inexorable erosion and a process of self-destruction.[76]

Each phenomenon—Haskalah, hasidism, emancipation, religious reform, modern politics—was to be evaluated in terms of its affinity to one pole or the other. Did it further Jewish survival, or contribute to disintegration?

This metahistory offered a simple, powerful means for imposing order and meaning on the jumble of events in the past. Identify the hegemonic centre in each age and everything else could be interpreted as subordinate

---

[76] Frankel, 'Assimilation and the Jews in Nineteenth-Century Europe'; quotation from p. 4.

to it, conforming to the cultural template that it cast. Classify phenomena as centripetal or centrifugal and their role in history would be virtually self-evident.[77]

Zionist historians, while adopting parts of the Dubnovian schema (especially the dichotomizing of phenomena as either reinforcing or weakening the nation and nationhood),[78] added at least one key ingredient. Rather than see Diaspora as permanent and territoriality as passé, to them national life without territory—even granted its considerable achievements—meant debilitation, struggle, lack of power and agency, distorted priorities—in a word, 'abnormality'. Thus their Jewish metahistory had a clear telos: to establish the Jews' rightful place in the world, where regaining their physical place—Erets Yisrael—would inevitably enable them to take their proper political, economic, cultural and, in the final analysis, metaphysical place. By this standard, developments could be measured by how much they promoted or hindered progress towards this objective.

Religious orthodoxy also spawned Jewish historiography, and it too presumed a certain metahistory. The most rhetorically sophisticated Orthodox modern historiography was written by Rabbi Berel Wein. It was premised on traditional religious belief that God guided the Jewish people to its destiny through history according to a plan revealed in the Bible.[79] Similarly to the Dubnow schema, the Orthodox metahistory had history oscillating between two poles, in this case loyalty to Jewish tradition and rebellion against it: 'Jews would attempt to assimilate and blend into the majority society, and the Lord would always provide the circumstances that would eventually thwart them', but never allow them to be totally destroyed. In this ongoing, epic *Kulturkampf* the heroes—the leaders of the Jewish people, or at least that part of it that counted—were primarily rabbis and scholars.[80]

Methodologically, in principle Wein was willing to consider all kinds of sources (although, in fact, his books derived almost exclusively from secondary sources). One source type, however, always trumped the others: 'There exists within the Jewish people a collective memory of its history. This collective memory operates independently of research materials,

---

[77] Cf. ibid. 6–15.   [78] Ibid. 4–15.

[79] Wein's trilogy of books includes *Triumph of Survival*; *Herald of Destiny*; *Echoes of Glory*. For a clear statement of the idea recapitulated here, see *Triumph of Survival*, pp. xii, 1, 478. The classic example of Jewish Orthodox religious historiography is Yawitz, *History of Israel* (Heb.). For analysis of older Orthodox historiography see Bartal, ' "True Knowledge and Wisdom" '.

[80] Wein, *Echoes of Glory*, pp. xiv–xv; id., *Triumph of Survival*, pp. xiv–xv.

books, and other "acceptable" historical evidence.'[81] Blithely unaware of research that has demonstrated how collective memory tells more about the rememberers than the remembered (see Chapter 6), Wein asserted that tradition is the best source for the true overall story of Jewish history (despite possible discrepancies, inexactitudes, factual errors, and contradictions).[82]

With regard to his attitude towards *galut*, Wein was reminiscent of the Boyarin–Cantor–Slezkine approach. Exile was, of course, punishment, full of calamities and horrific events. Erets Yisrael was always both the centre and of central concern. However, 'the negative exile of punishment slowly became transformed into the more positive challenge of being creative and vital in a harsh diaspora'. Exile preserved the Jewish people by dispersing them. It infused love for Erets Yisrael, nurtured Jewish solidarity, fostered extraordinary Torah creativity. 'The Exile allowed Jews to be cosmopolitan, worldly, relatively well-informed and educated, while at the same time remaining aloof, isolated and tenaciously insular . . . In short, the Exile made the Jew "modern" in the most positive sense of that word long before the general world emerged from the Medieval Era.'[83] This comment, anticipating Slezkine and implying a certain Jewish superiority, or at least leadership, in human affairs, represents Wein's attitude towards the relationship between history and Jewish history. The Jews were very much a part of history; in fact they were its real focus. God manipulated events in

---

[81] Wein, *Triumph of Survival*, p. xi.

[82] Id., *Echoes of Glory*, pp. x–xi. For a critical view of this general approach by an Orthodox scholar, see Schachter, 'Facing the Truths'.

[83] Wein, *Herald of Destiny*, 300–2. Wein's argument that the Jews of the Diaspora combine worldliness with insularity seems to contradict his view that assimilation undermines loyalty to tradition; together with his other explanations of the terms and meaning of Jewish existence, his approach surprisingly parallels that of the Reform rabbis and secular Jewish historians whom he disparages throughout his books. Thus he spoke of the 'unique sense of mission' of the Jewish people and of how 'the exile of Israel would contribute to the dissemination of morals and Torah values throughout the entire world' (*Herald of Destiny*, 301; *Echoes of Glory*, 320); this echoed the Reform rabbi Abraham Geiger and his disciples (see Heschel, *Abraham Geiger*). Wein also pointed to how 'the Jews adopted and adapted what was best in their surrounding society . . . They took everything that the outside world showed them to be valuable, internalized it and Judaized it' (*Herald of Destiny*, 301–2); cf. the approaches of Bickerman, *From Ezra to the Last of the Maccabees*, 178–82 (originally written in 1947); Gerson Cohen, 'The Blessing of Assimilation in Jewish History' (originally written in 1966); Hundert, *Jews in Poland–Lithuania in the Eighteenth Century*, 233–40; and the ideas of Bonfil and Marcus discussed in Chapter 3.

general so as to advance His plan for them, and it was they who bore the 'burden of humanizing civilization'.[84]

Acculturationist metahistory had its roots in nineteenth-century Jewish emancipation discourse, which sought to find a basis for Jewish membership in European society and citizenship in its states. It viewed the Jews as a people (some included the political dimension, others effaced it), the Diaspora as largely positive, and Jewish history as a unity. The key point was the relationship between Jewish and non-Jewish society and, by extension, between Jewish history and history. According to this school, as asserted as early as 1896 by Israel Abrahams, 'Jewish life . . . was freshened and affected by every influence of the time'.[85] That is, Jews were not only 'influenced' by their surroundings, but the context had a main role in positively shaping their identity—and ensuring their survival. Only Jewish communities that interacted dynamically with non-Jewish society and culture flourished and perpetuated themselves. The insular withered away.

The classic illustration of this thesis was Baron's *A Social and Religious History of the Jews*, published in a three-volume edition in 1937, and then in a vastly expanded eighteen-volume second edition between 1952 and 1983. Baron's footnotes were teeming with non-Jewish sources, and his exposition always contextualized developments concerning Jews, Judaism, and the Jewish community in terms of what was occurring in general in their time and place. Many, if not most, of the second edition's chapter titles alluded to this context and its paramount importance: for example, 'The Pre-Islamic World', 'Byzantine World in Decline', 'Mohammed and the Caliphate', 'Eastern Europe', 'Italian Potpourri', 'Age of Crusades', 'Imperial Turmoil', and 'Turkey's Golden Age'.

Baron's magnum opus implied the acculturationist metahistory.[86] His successor as Professor of Jewish History at Columbia University, Gerson D. Cohen (subsequently Chancellor of the Jewish Theological Seminary of America), expounded it cogently and pungently:

[84] Wein, *Triumph of Survival*, 2. In general, in his placing the Jews at the fulcrum of history, Wein is a latter-day example of the ethnocentric variety of expressive hostility practised by minority groups discussed in Chapter 4.

[85] Abrahams, *Jewish Life in the Middle Ages*, 6; cf. Elliott Horowitz, 'Jewish Life in the Middle Ages', 150.

[86] Baron made this metahistory explicit in various places, see esp. 'World Dimensions of Jewish History' (1962), and 'Newer Emphases in Jewish History' (1963), both included in the collection, *History and Jewish Historians*. For analysis of Baron's oeuvre, see Liberles, *Salo Wittmayer Baron*, esp. pp. 338–59.

One cannot understand the history of the Jews . . . without viewing it as part of the larger political, economic, social, cultural, and even religious context in which it evolved . . . Acculturation, adaptation, and even assimilation have been constant features of Jewish history . . . Wherever they have gone, they have refashioned their values and their institutions in accordance with the needs of time and place . . . It is only in those places where the Jews were cut off from contact with the surrounding culture that Jewish culture stagnated and eventually became fossilized.

However, Cohen quickly qualified this assertion:

Jewish history must also be examined in terms of Jewish inner drives. To study one aspect of Jewish life without the other . . . yields an incomplete and unsatisfying story . . . If the history of the Jews can be truly understood only in relation to world history, the shape of world history and culture at least in the Western world and in the world of Islam can be understood only in relation to Jewish history.

In sum:

Our history and our survival are . . . the products of two determinants: of our internal drives and commitments and of the cooperation and toleration of the nations that have been our hosts. One without the other, commitment without toleration, or toleration without commitment, would never have been sufficient.[87]

Unlike the previous views we have examined, this metahistory implied that any purported dichotomy between two poles of 'authentic' Jewish behaviour, institutions, and so on (however defined), and 'alien' ones was artificial. It was the interaction of the traditional and the new that produced authentic Jewishness which was continually being refreshed and renewed and, historically, had come in many iterations.

In a similar way to the others, the acculturationist position implied a teleology to Jewish history, although a more subtle one than shifting centres, solving the Jewish problem, realizing God's plan, or many of the other overall patterns or objectives that were proposed. As Cohen put it: 'Our whole history is fired by the desire for distinctiveness . . . The sheer determination of the Jews to carry on—more, to expand—their legacy,

---

[87] 'Changing Perspectives of Jewish Historiography' (1971); quotations from pp. 162, 163, 164–5, 168, 166, 174. Some of the same themes were sounded in Gerson Cohen, 'The Blessing of Assimilation in Jewish History'. Many years later, Adam Teller put it more succinctly: 'The integration of patterns drawn from non-Jewish society with ideas [I would add: and practices] from within Jewish tradition has always been the way in which the Jewish world has renewed its social structures' ('Hasidism and the Challenge of Geography', 7); cf. Abrahams, *Middle Ages*, p. xxii; see also Chapter 5, the section entitled 'The Influence Model Versus the Polysystem Model'.

constantly to invent new forms through which basic loyalties could forever remain central, is a phenomenon unparalleled in history . . . Jews have always chosen to be Jewish.[88] So Jewish history is the story of the Jews' quest to survive with a distinct collective identity which, paradoxically, was highly changeable and variegated. It is the attempt to understand (or rationalize) this paradox that has been the engine of much of Jewish historical writing.

Postmodernity has led to the emergence of a new, as yet not fully articulated, metahistory that can be termed 'multicultural'. Its proponents view the various historical contexts of Jewish existence as not only significant, but determinative. In each historical context, Jewish society and culture are not seen to be cells of some worldwide Jewish community 'in dialogue' with 'surrounding' or 'host' societies and cultures, as the acculturationist school had it, but to be a 'hybrid' component of the 'hegemonic' society and culture whose frameworks set the templates according to which, and the parameters within which, Jewish identity, culture, and society are 'constructed'—differently—in each time and place. The engine of Jewish self-definition is the encounter with the non-Jewish Other.

While Jews may share certain religious and ethnic markers over time and space, Judaism and Jewishness are always and everywhere primarily local constructs. Jewish collective identity should be understood mainly from a local perspective. Judaism and Jewishness are therefore not monolithic and there cannot be said to have existed one Judaism, one Jewish culture or normative, traditional, or representative types of Jewish communities. Rather, Jews are a hybrid version of whatever identity they live among.[89] Jews in Iraq or other Arab lands were 'Arab Jews',[90] and the term 'German Jews' really means 'Germanized Jews'—not only post-Emancipation, but earlier as well. It is difficult, therefore, to speak of 'the' Jews; even more so of some unified, continuous Jewish history.

The essence of Jewish existence—from ancient times onwards—is diversity; Zion has no special status. It is Diaspora, with the broad range of cultural possibilities it implies, that serves as the paradigm of the Jewish historical experience, virtually from the beginning. To the extent that it is possible to write Jewish history, it must take the form of separate histories

---

[88] Gerson Cohen, 'Changing Perspectives of Jewish Historiography', 176–7, 180; cf. Hundert, *Jews in Poland–Lithuania in the Eighteenth Century*, 233–40; cf. Chapter 2, the section entitled 'Voluntary Community', where the question of whether Jews still 'choose to be Jewish' is raised. [89] Silberstein (ed.), *Mapping Jewish Identities*.

[90] Shenhav, *The Arab-Jews* (Heb.).

of numerous communities, each of which has constructed Jewishness differently. There cannot be one grand narrative that seamlessly integrates the histories of all of these individual communities.[91] The teleology of such a metahistory is a state of affairs where individual Jews can define themselves in whatever religious, political, ethnic, intellectual, social, or cultural terms they desire and be a genuine, contributing element of the societies and countries they inhabit.[92] Concomitantly, religious orthodoxy would be eviscerated and Zion relegated to the status of an interesting, and hopefully safe, Jewish tourist attraction. An adumbration—though not a realization—of this conception is the book *Cultures of the Jews: A New History*, which, in its employment of the plural, cultures, its placing America, rather than Israel, as the subject of the ultimate chapter (and implied climax of the book's 'story'), and the emphasis on cultural hybridity in many of its chapters, signals the coming of the multicultural approach.[93]

Metahistory as Destiny

There is a tendency to dismiss metahistories as mere myth, only tenuously connected to the 'real' past. However, it is important to remember that people often live—and sometimes risk their lives—in accord with what

[91] For example Raz-Krakotzkin, 'The National Narration of Exile' (Heb.), ch. 3 (while mentioning in passing that 'the historical existence of such a collective [Jewish] identity is obvious' (English summary, p. iv), although he never took the trouble to define such identity), stated: 'Judaism was always defined within a context, and therefore it is impossible to talk about Jewish history, but only Jewish histories. The attempt to write a single, unified Jewish history as national is therefore by definition a repressive act, based on the disregard of cultural differences created at different times and in different places' (English summary, p. xiii). Would the members of historical Jewish communities, who lived within various contexts, have viewed attempts to make them an integral part of a single, larger, collective Jewish history as *repressing* them? Might they not rather consider the intent to deprive them of their share in such a collective history as a violation of their rightful identity? Is there, for Raz-Krakotzkin, a 'unified' or collective Jewish history that is not national and not repressive? If Jewish 'collective identity' is 'obvious', what are its features and what kind of history might it have? See also n. 49 above.

[92] Such a teleology is implied in Diana Pinto's work, discussed in Chapter 4.

[93] Biale (ed.), *Cultures of the Jews*. Note the quotation from Biale above (at n. 46) where he attempted to bridge the gap between the multicultural and other metahistories. For a fuller discussion of the significance of this book, the use of the hybridity construct, and the multicultural approach, see Chapter 3.

they believe to be true about their history.[94] Many out of the millions of Jews who have settled in Israel have done so out of a belief in a certain metahistory. Jews in the United States have raised and donated billions of dollars to erect institutions that seek to reify a complex metahistory. There are post-Zionists and Israeli settlers in Judea and Samaria who are willing to brave gaol, bodily harm—even death—by participating in activities that concretize their commitment to their particular metahistory.

It is metahistory, not history, that is inscribed in society and culture; but it is historiography, portraying history, that does the inscribing. Culturally, much is at stake in the historian's work. Historians have traditionally provided the matter that has facilitated the transference of ideal to real. What they write is an important component in the existential foundation of people's lives.[95] 'This day [of the Exodus] shall be to you one of remembrance' (Exodus 12: 14), God commands the Israelites *before* the Exodus actually takes place. Remembering the event is integral to the experience of it. Jewish history has formed the Jews. Only if they believe in it will they continue to exist.

[94] Mali, *Mythistory*, 293.

[95] Beard, 'Written History as an Act of Faith'; Becker, 'Everyman His Own Historian'; cf. Novick, *That Noble Dream*, 252–8.

TWO

The Postmodern Period in Jewish History

❦

Definitions of Jewish Modernity

When Is Modern?

From the end of the Second World War until the 1970s, a recurrent theme of discussion wherever Jewish history was taught was historical periodization, especially the question of when the modern period of Jewish history began. A standard exercise or examination question, then, was to summarize and critique the various periodization schemes or dates that had been proposed for the starting point of Jewish modernity by scholars from Isaac Marcus Jost (1793–1860) through to Shmuel Ettinger (1919–88).

By highlighting this subject, teachers aimed to demonstrate to their students that periodization, in addition to its function of defining conventional starting points and caesuras for historical narratives, is a coarse form of historical interpretation. In picking a certain date or event as indicative of the beginning or end of a historical period, each scholar telegraphed what to his[1] mind was the most significant feature, theme, or process of that period. Periodization is an attempt to capture in shorthand the 'essential nature' of a historical era. For example, Heinrich Graetz believed in the primacy of ideas in history and that the primary idea animating Jewish modernity was Jewish Enlightenment, or Haskalah. He also possessed a 'penchant for reducing historical trends and intellectual currents to personalities'. Thus he dated the Jewish modern period from the late eighteenth-century rise of the figure that symbolized the Haskalah, Moses Mendelssohn, who, to Graetz's mind, did the most to shape the foundations of Jewish modernity.[2] Simon Dubnow thought that the key transformation of the Jews in their attempts to live in the modern world was political integration into their countries of residence and their accom-

---

[1] In those days no scheme suggested by a female scholar was analysed.

[2] Graetz, *Structure of Jewish History*, 37, 41, 119–24.

panying loss of communal autonomy. He therefore dated Jewish modernity from the French Revolution, and specifically from the granting of citizenship to the Jews, that is, political emancipation (28 September 1791).[3]

Another lesson that discussions and exercises on periodization taught was the elusiveness of the 'noble dream' of objectivity. It seemed that one could discover in scholars' definitions of periods—and especially of the modern period in which they themselves lived—their constructions of their own historical experience and their own general metahistories. The Zionist Ben-Zion Dinur consciously attempted to create a usable historical past for what was in his day the new Israeli society and polity, and was active in establishing many important Israeli cultural institutions. He believed that the entire thrust of Jewish modernity was to bring the modern Jewish state into existence. For him, then, the rise of an apparently organized, proto-nationalist movement with Erets Yisrael as its objective (the migration of hundreds of people to Erets Yisrael with Judah Hasid in 1700) marked the starting point of Jewish modernity.[4]

Salo Wittmayer Baron was an immigrant to America and one of the founders of academic Jewish studies in the United States. He placed the start of Jewish modernity in the seventeenth century when, by his lights, the migratory, demographic, socio-economic, cultural, and technological trends that eventuated in American society—and led to the formation of American Jewry—had their genesis.[5] Examples such as these suggest that there are certainly no objective criteria for determining the boundaries of periods. All is interpretation based on personal convictions that can be argued, but never proven.

Although never completely abandoned, by the end of the 1970s the consideration of periodization greatly declined in intensity. The students had learned their lessons well. As they became teachers, they saw limited value in investing much time in an irresolvable debate; especially as the interpretative nature and necessary subjectivity of historiography were rapidly becoming commonplace notions.[6] They also learned that history is made up of particulars that do not necessarily form a pattern. As Eli Lederhendler

[3] Dubnow, 'The Sociological View of Jewish History'. For analysis of Dubnow's historiographical theory and its ramifications and applications, see Frankel, 'Assimilation and the Jews in Nineteenth-Century Europe', and Chapter 1 above.

[4] Dinur, *Israel and the Diaspora*, 90–5; cf. Benayahu, 'The "Holy Brotherhood" of Rabbi Judah Hasid' (Heb.), which eroded the foundation of Dinur's argument.

[5] Baron, *Social and Religious History of the Jews*, 2nd edn, vol. v, p. ix.

[6] Novick, *That Noble Dream*, 522–629.

observed: 'The trim lines of a unified history are undermined by the "heaviness" and sheer volume of discrete data.'[7]

With the fashioning of postmodern consciousness there also came a retreat from the attempt to essentialize. Internalizing our teachers' criticisms of the classic historians, my generation of historians has exhibited profound scepticism for grand schemes and broad generalizations.[8] Our Jewish historical writing has tended to take the form of narrowly focused studies analysing individual subjects,[9] rather than sweeping surveys that attempt to make sense of the big picture. Having ourselves unmasked the unhistorical foundations of the grand structures conceived by the greatest lights of our profession, as well as having been humbled by the amount of information that is there for the processing, we are chary of venturing pronouncements on subjects outside our immediate specialty, of risking reduction and oversimplification by widening our scope, of pretending to an understanding that explains more than those details we have thoroughly mastered. We willingly submit to the tyranny of specialization, trusting it might protect us from the types of critiques that we ourselves were so effectively taught to formulate. (Of course, given the easily demonstrated connection of any historical interpretation—no matter how constricted the scope—to some metahistory, this is no more than a vain hope.[10])

Meyer Ends the Discussion

In my opinion, a major facilitator of the decline of the preoccupation with periodization was a short article written in 1975 by Michael A. Meyer, 'Where Does the Modern Period of Jewish History Begin?'. Meyer summarized the theories of the beginning of Jewish modernity as proposed by Jost, Zunz, Krochmal, Graetz, Dubnow, Scholem, Ettinger, and Baron (mentioning in passing Philippson, Mahler, Shohat, Toury, and Katz). He then explicated the problems with the entire endeavour.

First came the fact that periodization was rooted in metahistory (although that word had not yet gained currency): 'All-embracing schemes

---

[7] Lederhendler, *Jewish Responses to Modernity*, 194.

[8] See Introduction, esp. the quote from Eli Lederhendler at n. 38.

[9] My own monographs, *The Lords' Jews* and *Founder of Hasidism*, are examples of this. It remains to be seen if Jonathan Sarna, *American Judaism*, chronicling 350 years of Jewish religious life in America, is an exception or the harbinger of a new trend as those trained in the 1970s enter the sixth and seventh decades of their lives.

[10] See Introduction, and Berkhofer, 'Challenge of Poetics to (Normal) Historical Practice'.

of periodization, nearly everyone now acknowledges, rest more on stipulation than on inference.' Such stipulation was based on 'religious and ideological motivations' and 'shifting conceptions of Jewish existence'.[11] Scholars' differing metahistories ('from Marxist economic determinism to an idealism which largely ignores the relevance of societal change'[12]) also create the impossibility of agreeing on the causes or components of Jewish modernity. Even if a consensus could be reached that, say, 'economic, political and cultural integration be taken together as representative of Jewish modernity, the question as to when they became constitutive must still be settled'.[13] What is to be made of apparently 'modern' characteristics that appeared in earlier periods (such as the cultural integration of medieval Spain or Renaissance Italy)? How does one dispose of 'pre-modern artefacts' (for example, traditional religious beliefs) that persist into the modern period? Finally, who counts as representative of 'the Jews'? If Sephardim in western Europe exhibited 'modern' characteristics but Ashkenazim didn't, had Jewish modernity begun? If the upper and lower classes were 'integrated' but the middle class was 'traditional' was the Jewish people modern? If Diaspora Jews are living as heirs to the Enlightenment and Israelis to modern nationalist ideology, are both in the same period of history?[14]

By asking whether there is any value in setting a definite date for the beginning of modern Jewish history, Meyer came to the pessimistic conclusion that 'There is not . . . Any endeavor to mark a borderline which will be meaningful for all Jewries and embrace the origin or rise to normative status of all—or even most—of the characteristics of Jewish life as it presently exists seems to me bound to fail.' Meyer's solution was to skip the debate over the beginning of Jewish modernity and concentrate instead on 'the process of modernization', that is, to trace the economic, social, and intellectual transformations of Jews, community by community, class by class, region by region.[15]

Meyer's article took much of the tension out of the debate over Jewish historical periodization. It seemed that after Meyer there was little interesting or novel to say on the subject. Rather than have the periodization question surface again and again, continually rehearsing the same—and post-Meyer—stale arguments, one could assign Meyer's article to students, discuss it, summarize its conclusion, and change the subject.

---

[11] Meyer, 'Where Does the Modern Period of Jewish History Begin?', 329–30.
[12] Ibid. 335. [13] Ibid. [14] Ibid. 335–8. [15] Ibid. 336.

However, Meyer did point out that 'one must begin somewhere'. There had to be a conventional date for beginning courses in modern Jewish history and writing surveys of the subject. Meyer suggested that this should be the seventeenth century, because this was when, 'according to nearly all views today, many of the elements that became constitutive of later Jewish life first made their appearance to any degree'.[16] This might be termed the lowest-common-denominator approach to periodization. At least one could point to adumbrations of 'modern' political, cultural, social, economic, intellectual, geographic, and demographic trends in the seventeenth century. Each of these developments had been nominated at some point as an indicator of Jewish modernity. It was the seventeenth century, then, that could serve, even if imperfectly, as the point of origin of the greatest number of processes defining the modern period in Jewish history.

Intriguingly, despite his insistence on the futility of searching for a single date to mark the onset of Jewish modernity, Meyer contended that there is a need to formulate a description of modernization that 'could meaningfully be used to characterize a basic process which has led to both of the forms of Jewish existence today: that of the Diaspora and that of the State. The conceptual unity of Jewish history would thus be preserved even down to the present'.[17] Here, it would seem, Meyer implied his own metahistory; one that postulates the unity of Jewish history both vertically through the past, and horizontally today, with Israel and the Diaspora being two closely related components in a shared world Jewish experience.

After Meyer, treatments of Jewish historical periodization—especially in comparison with such elaborate schemes as those of Krochmal, Dubnow, Dinur, and Baer[18]—have been mostly unoriginal and even perfunctory. They either adopt one of the standard dates,[19] or the lowest-common-

---

[16] Meyer, 'Where Does the Modern Period of Jewish History Begin?', 336–7.

[17] Ibid. 338.

[18] For Dubnow and Dinur see above nn. 3–4; see also Krochmal, *Writings of Rabbi Nahman Krochmal* (Heb.), 112; Baer, *Studies in the History of the Jewish People* (Heb.), esp. i. 19–46, ii. 9–59.

[19] Some recent examples: in the spirit of Dubnow (although limiting their periodization to European Jewry), Vital, *A People Apart* (cf. p. vii), declared: 'All turned, therefore, in the final analysis, on the matter of emancipation'; similarly, Malino and Sorkin, *Profiles in Diversity*, stated: 'Emancipation, the granting of equal civil and political rights, came both to epitomize this period and to define its history' (p. 1). Apparently giving Graetz his due too, Rubinstein et al., *Jews in the Modern World*, ch. 2, considered 'Enlightenment and Emancipation' to constitute 'the roots of modernity'. Gartner, *History of the Jews in Modern Times*, 25, adopted the 1650 date of his teacher, Baron.

denominator approach,[20] or try to finesse the problem of periodization.[21] Perhaps, taking up Meyer's challenge to 'focus on the process of *modernization*', there have been new interpretations of the nature and varieties of Jewish 'modernity' or Jewish 'modernization';[22] but no new periodization scheme, with one signal exception.

Jonathan Israel's New Periodization

In 1985 Jonathan Israel published *European Jewry in the Age of Mercantilism, 1550–1750*. He noted the need to draw 'a firm dividing-line between the medieval and early modern epochs' because, beginning around 1570, 'a freer, more flexible [European] society, and cultural system' allowed for the 'reintegration' of the Jews into the mainstream of European culture, society, and economy, with Jews being freed from many traditional restrictions; so they in turn 'exerted, especially in the period 1650–1713, the most profound and pervasive impact on the west'. Had Israel merely brought the starting date of Jewish modernity forward to the late sixteenth century? No, because he also maintained that the reintegration beginning at that time did not evolve smoothly into the Jewish emancipation and assimilation/acculturation of the nineteenth century. Israel asserted that, for the Jews, the eighteenth century was 'an era of stagnation, decay, and impoverishment, both economic and cultural'. There was no continuity between the integration process pre-1700 and that post-1789. In addition, the earlier process was marked by the Jews' retention of 'a large measure of social and

[20] e.g. Mendes-Flohr and Reinharz, *The Jew in the Modern World*, 4: 'What is, however, manifest in all of these conceptions [of Jewish modernity], despite their often extreme variation, is the conviction that the last two hundred years or so have witnessed a radical transformation of Jewish life'. In practice the earliest documents in the collection, pointing to the first steps in the transformation process, date from the mid-17th century.

[21] A recent important survey of Jewish history, Biale (ed.), *Cultures of the Jews*, does not offer a theoretical explanation for the periodization chosen: 'Mediterranean Origins' (biblical times to the formative period of Islam), 'Diversities of Diaspora' (the 'Golden Age' of Islam through to the 18th century) and 'Modern Encounters' (19th and 20th centuries). To me this implies recognition that there can be no better reasons than convention and convenience for dividing up historical time.

[22] e.g. Berkovitz, *Rites and Passages*; Dubin, *The Port Jews of Trieste*; Endelman, *Jews of Georgian England*; Feiner, *The Jewish Enlightenment*; Hundert, *Jews in Poland–Lithuania in the Eighteenth Century*; Hyman, *Emancipation of the Jews of Alsace*; Yosef Kaplan, *Alternative Path to Modernity*; Ruderman, *Jewish Enlightenment in an English Key*; Zipperstein, *The Jews of Odessa*.

cultural cohesion . . . a recognizably national character . . . the emancipation of the seventeenth century ushered the Jews into the western world as
a tightly cohesive group'. Later emancipation required the Jews to become
'uprooted individuals stripped of their former political and social autonomy and culture'.[23]

Israel, in effect, re-periodized Jewish history in three ways. He defined a
new period of (European) Jewish history,[24] the early modern period,
*c.*1550–1750. A time when Jews were 'emancipated' and 'integrated', but still
traditionally Jewish, both individually and collectively, this era was distinct
from both the 'Middle Ages' and the 'modern period'. Next, he felicitously
synchronized Jewish historiography with general European historiography,
which had been treating the early modern period as a discrete era for decades.
Finally, he proffered a new date for the Jewish modern period, beginning it
from the decline of Jewish economic success (something none of the standard treatments had suggested) and the dissolution of traditional Jewish religious and communal life from around the mid-eighteenth century.[25]

While Israel did attract some criticism,[26] his singling out of an early
modern Jewish period parallel to the general European one has gained a
large measure of acceptance.[27] Still, like his predecessors, Israel defined his
period on the basis of an 'essential' characteristic: integration combined
with tradition. The integration he highlighted, however, was political and
economic—not cultural or social—in nature, and he did not offer a very
profound analysis of Jewish tradition at the time beyond its political, institutional and obvious religious aspects. Moreover, as Meyer (and others
since) had pointed out, much of what has been associated with Jewish
'modernity' (for example, population growth, migration westward, geo-

[23] Israel, *European Jewry in the Age of Mercantilism*, 1–3, 252–3. Israel refined his argument for the discrete identity of this period in *Diasporas Within a Diaspora*.

[24] In his book, Israel succeeded in integrating the history of Jews in western and
eastern Europe and the Ottoman Balkans primarily by demonstrating the economic and
family links among them. He also mentioned ties with Jews in Turkey and the Levant,
but he did not quite produce a comprehensive portrait of world Jewry at the time (nor
did he intend to).

[25] Israel, *European Jewry in the Age of Mercantilism*, 253–8.

[26] Ruderman, 'Israel's *European Jewry in the Age of Mercantilism*'; Levine, 'Jews and
Judaism in the Age of Mercantilism' (Heb.).

[27] For example, beginning in August 2004 the Mellon Foundation sponsored a
workshop at Wesleyan University on early modern Jewish history which subsequently
became an annual event. Such institutionalization bespeaks the belief of scholars that
the idea of an early modern period is useful for teaching and research.

graphic expansion, weakening of traditional institutions, cultural and social integration) did begin in the seventeenth century and—with due respect to Israel—continued through the eighteenth century and after. Israel's period definition, appealing as many have found it, still does not account for all variables, sharing at least part of the weakness of other attempts to impose period divisions on history.

Meyer wanted the historical description of Jewish modernization to yield an understanding of what led to the formation of 'Jewish life as it presently exists'.[28] This might be accomplished, as Meyer came close to saying, by formulating a constellational definition.[29] That is, rather than emphasize a single process (and the date on which it began) that epitomizes Jewish modernity, we might posit that all of the thoughtful suggestions have merit and highlight a constellation of processes that were important and worked synergistically in forming modern Jewry: demographic growth and geographic spread, nationalism, political and legal emancipation and Western-style citizenship, cultural and social integration (traditionally termed acculturation/assimilation), economic integration, enlightenment and secularization, the decline of religion as a force governing people's lives, the breakdown of traditional sources of authority and traditional institutions, the reorganization of the Jewish community on a voluntary basis, and modern Jew-hatred and antisemitism. Moreover, these processes were not necessarily present simultaneously, and modernization in a given community might occur even in the absence of some of them. We may not be able to pinpoint a date that marks the beginning of Jewish modernity, but we can enumerate the constellation of processes that interacted during the modern period. Where and when we find them—or at least many of them—in operation and in interaction, we know we are observing people of modernity.

If this is so, it is my contention that by now this constellation has broken down; Meyer's review no longer delineates the modernization processes that constitute 'Jewish life as it presently exists'. Nearly all the processes the constellation contained have either come to final realization, disappeared, reversed, or been transformed to the point where they are unrecognizable. It is no longer their interaction that establishes the matrix of Jewish existence. In addition, some new processes and issues have

[28] Meyer, 'Where Does the Modern Period of Jewish History Begin?', 336. Cf. Meyer, *Origins of the Modern Jew*, esp. pp. 8–10, 181–2.

[29] Compare this to what in Chapter 3 I call a polythetic or disjunctive definition.

appeared that were not on the modern agenda. It follows that the modern period of Jewish history ended some time ago. We are now in a new period that began in the wake of the Shoah and the establishment of Israel. Influenced by the zeitgeist, we call it the 'postmodern period of Jewish history'.[30]

Jewish Postmodernity Differentiated from Modernity

Let us consider the conventional constituents of the constellation of criteria of Jewish modernity and how the status of Jews has changed in the postmodern period.

Demographic Growth

Between 1700 and 1939, the world Jewish population grew from approximately 1.1 million to 16.5 million people.[31] Like the cities in which they were

---

[30] Dinur (see n. 4) was the first to assert that the modern period had ended and that a new period had begun. Believing the essence of the modern period in Jewish history to be the struggle for relief from the vicissitudes of minority status and for the re-establishment of Jewish political nationhood, he saw the creation of Israel as the climax of Jewish modernity and what followed as the onset of a new era. I adopt a similar date, not because of some teleology, but because I think that all of the changes I describe below either began or became manifest in the period that commenced in the late 1940s. However, I fully realize that, as with Meyer's choice of a starting date for the modern period, this is no more than a convention whose main utility is to provide a convenient platform for focusing attention on the transformations that occurred. By speaking of periods of Jewish history, I do not wish to imply that Jews are not subject to the conditions and processes that affected the people among whom they lived. As is perhaps most easily seen in the case of demography (see n. 31), in every period Jews have participated in the general social, cultural, economic, and religious environment. However, because of their particular history and circumstances, the effect of general conditions and processes on the Jews may be different from their effect on others. Jewish history is often distinctive. For some suggestions as to the possible relationships between Jewish history and history, see Chapter 1 above.

[31] DellaPergola, *World Jewry Beyond 2000*, 13. (This booklet is a felicitous summary of results of the fundamental demographic research DellaPergola has been conducting for over thirty years. For the specialized studies behind the statements quoted here, please consult his notes.) This was a period of general population growth in most of the regions of the world where the Jews lived and Jewish demography is intimately linked to the general processes at work. At the same time, however, Jewish demography featured distinguishing characteristics; see ibid. 7–8, 13–14, 25–8, 38–43, 50–1.

located, Jewish communities grew in size exponentially. For example, around 1600 Constantinople was by far the largest Jewish community in the world, numbering between 30,000 and 40,000 Jews.[32] In 1764 the largest Jewish community in all of Poland was in the town of Brody and its outskirts, with somewhat more than 7,000 Jews.[33] In contrast, by the time of the period between the world wars, 'provincial' Jewish communities such as that of Pinsk numbered in the tens of thousands,[34] while in Warsaw, London, Budapest, and Vienna there were hundreds of thousands of Jews, and in New York nearly 2 million.[35]

Since the Shoah, however—and bracketing off the catastrophic demographic loss of those years[36]—the world Jewish population, outside Israel, has been shrinking almost consistently. In 1950 it was 10,170,000, in 1980, 9,557,000, in 1996, 8,457,000, and in 2005, 7,800,000. Even counting Israel, the number of Jews in the world grew only modestly, from 11,373,000 to 13,025,000, in the last half of the twentieth century. In the postmodern period the trend has been modest increase, due primarily to Israeli population growth, while most other Jewish communities decreased.[37]

[32] Baron, *Social and Religious History of the Jews* (2nd edn), xviii. 200; Barnai, 'Jews in the Ottoman Empire' (Heb.), 81.

[33] Stampfer, 'The 1764 Census of Polish Jewry', 91, gives the raw data number 7,357. According to the adjustment criteria for this census proposed by Mahler, *History of Jews in Poland* (Heb.), 231–3, the real number may have approached 9,000.

[34] Shohat, 'The Jewish Community of Pinsk', 205.

[35] Friesel (ed.), *Carta's Atlas* (Heb.), 15, fig. 8.

[36] For interesting speculation on what might have occurred to the world Jewish population had 6 million Jews not been murdered between 1939 and 1945, see DellaPergola, *World Jewry Beyond 2000*, 14–16.

[37] Ibid. 16–18, 66–70; JPPPI, *Facing a Rapidly Changing World*, 12. There were non-Israeli Jewish communities that grew during this period, notably in the USA. While there is no agreement over how many Jews there were in the USA at any given time, the maximum possible growth between 1950 and 2000 could have been from 4.5 million to 6.15 million, i.e. 1.65 million or about 37% (Sarna, *American Judaism*, appendix, 375; cf. DellaPergola, *World Jewry Beyond 2000*, 21, 24, 69). This number is less than half of the 85% increase in the overall American population (1950: 152,300,000; 2000: 282,400,000; increase: 130,100,000); and pales next to Israeli growth of 3.4 million (1.2 million to 4.6 million: 280%) during the same period. It should be remembered that the numbers reported by DellaPergola represent the 'core Jewish population', i.e. those people who self-identify as Jews. This probably inflates the number of Jews as compared to pre-Holocaust figures; see DellaPergola, *World Jewry Beyond 2000*, 9–12 and below, the section entitled 'Who Is a Jew?'.

The conclusion is that the modern period was a time of Jewish population growth; the postmodern period seems to be a time of population stability and even decline.[38]

Geographic Spread

From the seventeenth century to the early twentieth century the Jewish presence in the world was spreading. Beginning with a core of Jewish settlement in Europe, North Africa, and western Asia, new Jewish communities were established in the Americas and the Caribbean, Southern Africa, Southern and South-East Asia, Australia, and Oceania. The number of Jewish communities in both new and old regions of Jewish settlement multiplied and most of them grew in size, although many remained small in absolute numbers.

Since the Shoah and the establishment of the State of Israel, the number of Jewish communities in the world has contracted sharply. Those in Ethiopia and in Muslim lands in Africa and Asia have virtually disappeared. In Western countries Jews have abandoned rural and provincial locales for large metropolitan areas even more rapidly than the general population. By the end of the twentieth century, almost 60 per cent of world Jewry was concentrated in only ten metropolitan areas worldwide; and only one of those—Paris—was outside North America or Israel. The number of viable Jewish communities in outlying areas is much lower than it was in 1939. In central and eastern Europe and the former Soviet Union, most of the communities destroyed during the Shoah were never re-established, and emigration and ageing demography have doomed many of those that remained.

In short, post-1939 there were progressively many fewer places in the world where significant numbers of Jews could be found. The Diaspora has been reduced in number of people, in number of communities, and in number of major groups of communities. There are at most three major centres of Jewish life: North America, Israel, and Europe (with the last getting progressively smaller[39]). Moreover, by the middle of the first decade of the twenty-first century, a plurality (soon likely to be a majority) of the Jewish people are to be found in Israel, where already the majority of Jewish children in the world are being born and reside.[40]

---

[38] Cf. Vital, *Future of the Jews*; Wasserstein, *Vanishing Diaspora*; Dershowitz, *The Vanishing American Jew*; Gitelman, 'Decline of the Diaspora Jewish Nation'.

[39] DellaPergola, 'Demographic Trends of European Jewry'.

[40] DellaPergola, *World Jewry Beyond 2000*, 28–9, 48–53, 66–72. As of March 2006 the Jewish population of Israel was officially 5,326,700 and rising (according to a personal communication from Aliza Peleg of the Israel Government Central Bureau of Statistics,

If the modern period was typified by 'Diversities of Diaspora',[41] it seems that the postmodern period is characterized by a process of redistribution of the Jewish population among two or perhaps three large centres and scattered small nuclei. This may ultimately lead either to competition between the centres, with each attempting to establish primacy, to a nearly complete rupture of relations among them, or to a new version of homeland and diaspora.[42]

Political and Legal Emancipation and Western-Style Citizenship

Today the overwhelming majority of Jews lives in lands governed by, at least formally, democratic regimes, and Jews are fully fledged citizens of the countries in which they live. There is no legal discrimination or official political disability. This last sentence is an amazing statement in light of the history of the modern era in which Jews suffered notorious discrimination and persecution, and expended tremendous energy fighting for legal and political equality. Most historians have treated the quest for full political emancipation as one of the main themes of Jewish modernity. In the postmodern period this appears no longer to be an issue. In no place where they live in appreciable numbers are Jews in danger of being relegated to an inferior official legal status, or of being deprived officially of political rights. Jewish political equality is politically correct.

The fundamental political problem for Jews in the postmodern era seems to be the extent to which their politics should be 'Jewish'. That is, should Jews participate in the political process *qua* Jews, as an identified collective interest group, and work for or against certain issues in areas such as educational policy, Middle Eastern policy, welfare policy, economic policy, and so on, based on perceived Jewish interests; or should Jews regard their Jewishness as politically neutral and behave politically in accord with other facets of their personal identity and status?[43]

---

11 June 2006), while by 2005 the USA Jewish population was under 5.3 million and shrinking, with the world Jewish population set at about 13 million (JPPPI, *Facing a Rapidly Changing World*, 12). Of course, relative size of Jewish communities depends in part on the definition of who counts as a Jew; see below.

[41] See n. 21.   [42] Cf. Friesel's foreword to Webber (ed.), *Jewish Identities*, p. x.

[43] This was an issue during the process of the formation of modern Jewish political consciousness in the 19th century as well (see Lederhendler, *Road to Modern Jewish Politics* and Mendelsohn, *Modern Jewish Politics*). Then, however, it was subsumed to the larger question of how the Jews might best attain political equality. Currently, the larger question is moot.

Related to this is the question of Jewish political liberalism. In the pre-modern period Jews tended to be politically conservative, preferring the status quo, which included time-tested arrangements enabling them to live, rather than support revolutionaries who might bring with them new obstacles to Jewish survival. This changed, however, with the revolutions of 1848 that demonstrated that it was liberal and even radical ideology put into practice that could bring the Jews equality and opportunity.[44] Thus the long identification of modern Jewry with liberalism apparently began with the events of 1848.

Here, too, there are signs that in the postmodern period Jewish political behaviour has changed. The association of Jews and Jewish organizations with the rise of neoconservatism in the United States and with various conservative political movements elsewhere, as well as the tenure of conservative governments in Israel, all imply that liberalism as a peculiarly Jewish tendency ran its course in the modern period, but that postmodern Jewish political proclivities are becoming more pluralistic.

Nationalism

Zionist and other Jewish national movements arose in the modern period advocating nationalism as the solution to 'the Jewish problem', that is, the modus vivendi by which Jews could survive and flourish under the conditions of modernity. Connected to general nineteenth-century notions of nationalism, Jewish nationalist ideology was dedicated to the propositions that the world was organized according to nation-states, that the Jews are a nation, and that the only way the Jews will be able to live in the modern world is by organizing as a political nation. Some believed that this needed to be based on a self-governing, territorial, Jewish-majority state. According to the Zionist version, there should be a Jewish state in Erets Yisrael that would be as Jewish as England is English, France is French, and Poland is Polish.

In the postmodern period, aside from the intellectual challenges to nationalism described in Chapter 1, the status of nationalism has become ambiguous as a practical matter. Smaller and smaller collections of people have claimed national rights, and in recent years such countries as Slovenia, Estonia, and East Timor (Timor Leste) have been (re-)created with populations of under 2 million or even 1 million. European nationalism and European-style nationalism elsewhere is not dying. To the contrary, it has

---

[44] Baron, 'Impact of the Revolution of 1848'.

undergone radicalization, with terrorism becoming the tactic of choice for small minority nationalities who seek to break off from larger political entities and gain independence in their own sovereign territory. Such terrorism has, to some extent, kept their nationalist claims on the world political agenda.[45]

However, all the major, long-established countries in Europe—for example, England and France—are becoming less and less English or French or whatever traditionally they have been, with large and growing immigrant populations of people whose ethnicity is much different from that of the founding majority. The modern Western state is becoming ever more pluralistic—or even multicultural[46]—with a multiplicity of religions, racial groups, and ethnic identities, along with their multiple histories, rituals, social customs, institutions, and cultures.[47] The establishment, expansion, and continuing articulation of the European Union is facilitating this process. The homogenizing tendencies of the EU are one strong indicator that it is the American model that keeps gaining momentum: that is, the essence of the postmodern state is shared political commitments and not ethnic identity.

Israel, the culminating expression of modern Jewish nationalism, has been forced to turn its attention to a raft of challenges to its declared objective to be a 'Jewish state'. Its growing Arab and other non-Jewish populations, originating mainly in the former Soviet Union, demand that Israel become a 'state of all of its inhabitants'. Even without official concessions in this regard, the immigration of tens of thousands of church-going Christians, for example, surely has an effect on the tenor of Israeli culture.[48]

For postmodern Jews, the problem of nationalism is no longer whether the Jews are analogous to other nations and therefore deserve political sovereignty of one type or another. The new issue is how nationalist the Jewish sovereign state can be, given its demographic, social, and cultural composition. Can a modern democratic state maintain a dominant ethnic identity? Is a Jewish state a viable concept in a multicultural world?

[45] For analysis of the connection between modern nationalist struggles and war and terrorism, see Van Creveld, *Transformation of War*.

[46] For a discussion of the differences between pluralism and multiculturalism see Chapter 4.

[47] See e.g. Waddy, *Shaping a New Europe*; Gerholm and Lithman (eds), *New Islamic Presence*; Joly, *Britannia's Crescent*; Lewis and Schnapper, *Muslims in Europe*.

[48] Asher Cohen, 'From Arranged Democracy to Crisis Democracy' (Heb.), and 'Israeli Assimilation' (Heb.); Kemp, 'Christian Zionists in the Holy Land'.

Furthermore, has Israel 'solved' the Jewish problem? While Israel has, indeed, gained the Jews a place at the table of world politics, and thus guaranteed that Jews will have a say in how their own fate is determined (one of the main planks in the classic Zionist platform[49]), Israel has been, since its inception, a focus for controversy. It is certainly not a 'normal' country, if by normality is meant routine acceptance on the world stage, peaceful existence, and lack of involvement in major political and military conflicts. Being the lightning rod for so much animosity, has Israel improved Jewish status in the world, or has it further problematized it? Is world Jewry drawn into unnecessary confrontations and existential complications by virtue of its association with Israel?

Another issue for Jewish nationalism has been the growing realization on the part of Jews during the postmodern period of the competition between Jewish and Arab, specifically Palestinian, nationalism. For most of the history of Jewish nationalism in the modern period, Arab or Palestinian nationalism was not a main focus of most Jewish nationalists. As Walter Laqueur contended in a chapter entitled 'The Unseen Question':

A minority of Zionists and Palestinian Jews were aware from the beginning of the crucial importance of relations with the Arabs. Some of them thought that the national aspirations of the two peoples could be reconciled, while the pessimists early on reached the conclusion that conflict was basic and unavoidable. The majority of Zionists were less concerned with the Arab question. Only gradually did they face it . . . it seemed almost insignificant in view of the need to save European Jewry.[50]

In the postmodern period, and especially after the consequences of the Six Day War, 'The Arab Question' has moved to the centre of Israeli and Jewish concern. More and more Jews have been willing to concede the existence and even the legitimacy of Palestinian nationalism, the ramifications of which are that Jewish nationalism must limit itself. The debate over this position and the actions taken by both its proponents and opponents have become one of the central loci of postmodern, organized Jewish discourse and activities.

Economic Integration

During the modern period, Jews struggled to penetrate all sectors of the modern economy. Their objectives were to be fully economically integrated

---

[49] See the discussion of Hazaz's story 'Haderashah' (Heb.), and the Israel Declaration of Independence, in Chapter 1.   [50] Laqueur, *History of Zionism*, 268–9.

and prosperous wherever they lived. Like political and legal emancipation, this has been largely achieved. Postmodern Jews can potentially occupy virtually any economic niche they set their sights on, and there is no longer official discrimination against Jewish economic endeavours. There are poor Jews, particularly among the elderly, in the former Soviet Union, and in certain sectors of the Israeli population, but from the collective perspective Jews worldwide have achieved a high degree of economic success. The postmodern goal is not so much the attainment of economic success as the maintenance of it.[51]

Voluntary Community

A commonly cited hallmark of Jewish modernity was the decline of the Jewish community organized as a medieval-style corporation that wielded coercive power over its members. In pre-modern times rabbinic-led courts enjoyed the backing of the non-Jewish authorities and could impose sanctions to enforce their decisions. Taxes and laws imposed by the communal leadership were mandatory for all Jews. The only alternative for someone who did not want to accept Jewish communal authority was to convert and join the Christian or Muslim community. During the modern period, with considerable trauma, the Jewish community became a voluntary organization whose members freely chose to join and support it materially and morally.[52]

In the postmodern period, the voluntary nature of the Jewish community has been taken for granted. However, what was assumed almost universally by Jews throughout the modern period—that Jews need an organized community to provide essential services such as political and economic defence, religious and educational services, and welfare functions—is no longer automatically understood. The question for postmodern Jewry is not the basis of authority for the Jewish community, but how to convince Jews that a Jewish community is worth preserving and supporting. It is the very existence and not the nature of the Jewish community that is at issue.[53]

[51] DellaPergola, *World Jewry Beyond 2000*, 25–30, 38–40, and 'Demographic Trends of European Jewry', 66–8.

[52] Baron, 'Aspects of the Jewish Communal Crisis in 1848'; Goren, *New York Jews and the Quest for Community*; Liberles, *Religious Conflict in Social Context*; Robinson, 'Foundation Documents of the Jewish Community Council of Montreal'.

[53] More than half of Diaspora Jews are not affiliated to the organized Jewish community: DellaPergola, *World Jewry Beyond 2000*, 55–6; Waxman, *Jewish Baby Boomers*, 66, 92–3, 123–4, 127, 154, 159, 161.

Moreover, if Jews question the need for an organized Jewish community where they live, they are even less convinced about their membership in, or even the existence of, *kelal yisra'el*, a worldwide Jewish collective, however it may be defined.[54]

Cultural and Social Integration

During the modern period, the integration of Jews into majority society and culture was considered to be a central process, and one that presented both challenges and dilemmas. Such integration was usually represented by historians as negative ('assimilation') because the absorbing non-Jews expected a concomitant effacement of signs of Jewish identity as the price of acceptance.[55] Hence the dilemma: integration into the majority, or loyalty to Jewishness?

More recent scholars spoke of good integration ('acculturation'), which entailed adapting aspects of non-Jewish culture and even 'judaizing' them in an effort to ensure Jewish survival—and sometimes actually to reinforce Jewish identity—in a non-Jewish context.[56] However, this approach also recognized the threat that integration posed and the need to carefully control it if Jewish identity were to survive.

In the postmodern period, the nature of the integration process has changed significantly. The majority in most places where Diaspora Jews live now espouses a commitment to social inclusiveness, cultural pluralism, and sometimes even multiculturalism.[57] To a significant extent, though not universally, Jews, Judaism, and Jewishness have gained respect and become culturally attractive. Conversion to Judaism is no longer a rarity. In most formal social situations Jewish identity is not something to be apologetic about, and is frequently something to be proud of and to celebrate.

In practical terms, postmodern Jews, both inside and outside Israel, rarely need to choose between identities; they, like many other minorities, can assume the markers of multiple identity. For example, an individual can work in a high-salaried job, shop in the best stores, drive the flashiest car, be the most loyal fan of professional sports teams, play the most popular

---

[54] Steven Cohen and Wertheimer, 'Whatever Happened to the Jewish People?'.

[55] Frankel, 'Assimilation and the Jews', 5–15.

[56] Ibid. 1–37, and see many of the other essays in Frankel and Zipperstein (eds), *Assimilation and Community*. Note also the discussion in Chapter 1 of 'acculturationist metahistory' and the historical relationship between Jewish and non-Jewish culture as analysed in Chapter 3.   [57] See Chapter 4.

music, vacation at fashionable resorts, have non-Jewish friends, and still, if he or she chooses, strictly observe the sabbath and the dietary restrictions of *kashrut*, pray regularly, dress 'Jewishly', send children to a Jewish school, have Jewish friends, be active in Jewish organizations, promote Jewish political positions, contribute to Jewish philanthropies, and marry a Jewish spouse. If they desire, Israelis can be loyal to their country and their Jewish identity and still feel themselves to be culturally fully fledged members of the 'Western world'.[58]

Furthermore, even what was once considered the penultimate form of assimilation, exogamous or 'mixed' marriage (the ultimate was conversion), has become so common (surpassing the 50 per cent mark[59]) that Jewish institutions, including many religious ones, seek methods of keeping the Jewish partner actively identified as Jewish, as well as ways of involving mixed couples and families in their activities. This legitimizes what in the modern period was usually viewed by endogamous Jews as betrayal; but, more portentously, it offers the previously unavailable option of a syncretistic identity.[60]

Postmodern integration, then, is not a zero-sum game. It need not be a dilemma or a threat. Even when it results in exogamous marriage it can be compatible with some configurations of Jewish identity. The problem is no longer the perceived demands of non-Jewish society for Jewish 'cultural conversion', but rather the lack of desire of Jews themselves to maintain a Jewish identity, even when it is not an obstacle to full participation in the general society and culture.

Enlightenment, Secularization, and Breakdown of Tradition

The modern period was witness to a progressive weakening of traditional forms and institutions accompanied by ever more intensive secularization. By the late 1940s, with European Jewry virtually destroyed, Orthodoxy in general was in retreat, hasidism seemed to be in its death throes, liberal versions of Judaism ruled the Jewish street in the Diaspora, and secularism was triumphant in Israel. This appeared to be the outcome of some two hundred years of Enlightenment, rationalist inroads, secular critiques, and

---

[58] Cf. Sharot, 'Judaism and Jewish Ethnicity'; Eisen, 'The Problem Is Still Very Much with Us'.　　[59] DellaPergola, *World Jewry Beyond 2000*, 45–8.

[60] The ramifications of this for the Jewish future can be viewed in different ways; see Mayer, *Love and Tradition*; Miller, Marder, and Bayme, *Approaches to Intermarriage*; Phillips, *Re-examining Intermarriage*; Fishman, *Double or Nothing*. See also a website dedicated to issues concerning intermarried families: <www.interfaithfamily.com/>.

religious reform. The evident winners of the modern *Kulturkampf* between those who believed Jewishness to be dependent on religious tradition and those who championed a secular basis for Jewish identity were the secularists. Even those who maintained a commitment to tradition tried to make it more rational, reflective of modern values, and responsive to modern sensibilities.[61]

The postmodern recrudescence of fundamentalism and mysticism (mirroring more or less simultaneous trends in other religious cultures) therefore seems surprising. As the period has progressed, Orthodoxy has turned triumphalist, hasidism has been thoroughly reconstituted, and tens of thousands of people from secular backgrounds have decided to become *ba'alei teshuvah* (literally, penitents), devoting themselves to various versions of Orthodox belief and practice.[62] In Israel there is still but minimal separation of synagogue and state, and traditional sources of authority such as rabbis and mystics sometimes pose a threat to the authority of the Knesset, the courts, and the government bureaucracy. Secular culture is far from collapse, but the often successful challenges to it from religion and tradition is something that was not foreseen in the modern period and would have seemed out of place then. The balance of forces in the *Kulturkampf* appears to have shifted, and the anticipated modernist demise of tradition has not been realized.[63]

Continuities

Some features of the modern period have continued into the postmodern. One example is Jew-hatred or antisemitism. This did not begin in the mod-

---

[61] See e.g. Levinson, 'Transmitting *Yiddishkeit*', and Feiner, *The Jewish Enlightenment*, 13, who has observed that the *Kulturkampf* between modernists and fundamentalists did indeed start in the 18th century and has continued until today.

[62] Demographers seem to dismiss the significance of these developments because they account for only a relatively small proportion of all Jews, and the overall trend is still a net flow away from religious lifestyle (DellaPergola, *World Jewry Beyond 2000*, 57, 75; Waxman, *Jewish Baby Boomers*, 58). However, given demographic predictions, it is logical to assume that the demographic weight of the traditionalists will progressively increase; cf. Webber (ed.), *Jewish Identities*, 27–8; Lamm, 'The Jewish Jew and Western Culture', 102–6.

[63] Danzger, *Returning to Tradition*; Davidman, *Tradition in a Rootless World*; Waxman, *Jewish Baby Boomers*, 129, cites the common view that renascent fundamentalism is but a confirmation of the ascendancy of secularism. As fundamentalism gains strength and momentum, this may prove to be, at best, a description of the early stages of the process.

ern period, but there was a modern version. In ancient times Jew-hatred was based on Jews' purported arrogance, xenophobia, superstition, and unwarranted political privileges. In the medieval world, anti-Jewish animus was primarily a function of the Jews' religious alienation. In the modern period, Jew-hatred was secularized and dubbed antisemitism. It targeted Jews as possessing traits, even racial ones, which resulted in their behaving in ways that undermined civilization in the service of their own nefarious interests.

While traces of both medieval and modern-style antisemitism continue, particularly in some Muslim countries,[64] there has appeared a postmodern version of Jew-hatred, one that avoids the racism of the modern period, but that insists that, in their efforts to advance their questionable political agenda, Jews as a group violate the human rights of others and the interests of their countries of residence. It complains, for example, about inordinate and detrimental 'Jewish influence' over politics and policy-making in the United States. It raises the spectre of dual loyalty of Diaspora Jews, and identifies all Jews with the policies and actions of Israel, which are often equated in terms of their motivation, cruelty of execution, scale, objectives, and results with those of Nazi Germany. It considers Israel and Jews to be aligned with the reactionary and oppressive forces in the world and to bear great, and even primary, responsibility for many serious problems, such as terrorism, racism, the negative effects of globalization, clashes of Muslim individuals, groups, and states with people and states in the West. If only Israel and/or the Jews would 'go away', it is claimed, these evils would be greatly ameliorated, perhaps even disappear.[65]

Another example of a modern trend that continues into postmodernity is the process of altering the gender structure of Jewish society and culture

[64] *Pew Global Attitudes Project*, 14 July 2005: 'Predominantly Muslim countries have mixed views of Christians and strongly negative views of people of the Jewish faith . . . Throughout the Muslim world, opinions of Jews are highly unfavorable. Dislike of Jews is universal in Jordan and Lebanon, with 99% of the publics in both countries saying they have a very unfavorable view of Jews (the remaining 1% in Jordan takes a "somewhat unfavorable" view, while in Lebanon 1% offer no response). Similarly, 76% of Indonesians, 74% of Pakistanis, and 60% of Turks have an unfavorable opinion of Jews' (p. 811).

[65] Finkielkraut, 'Reflections on the Coming Antisemitism'; Iganski and Kosmin (eds), *A New Antisemitism*; Foxman, *Never Again?*; Wistrich, 'Dangers of Antisemitism in the New Europe'; Brearley, 'Possible Implications of the New Age Movement'. Cf. Chapter 4 on why Jews are rejected from the multicultural academy.

(again, with obvious parallels to what has occurred in other contemporary cultures and societies). Although not usually noted by conventional portrayals, the Jewish modern period was characterized by the continual, if very slow, transformation of Jewish women's role from that of cultural bystanders to that of participants, and from social facilitators of the activities of their menfolk to performers who engage in the most socially valued activities.[66]

Beginning in the sixteenth century, a Yiddish literature was created that counted women, as well as men, in its audience. It included translations and reworkings of the Bible based on rabbinic interpretation; manuals that instructed women in the observance of the commandments especially incumbent upon them; morality anthologies and behaviour manuals incorporating admonitions illustrated by didactic anecdotes; and pious story anthologies. There also appeared prayer collections containing *tekhines*, petitionary prayers, intended for women. Throughout the modern period, women took a progressively more active role in synagogue life, beginning with sixteenth-century halakhic rulings that made it easier for women to attend synagogue services, and the seventeenth-century spread of women's sections (*ezrat nashim*) that were architecturally integral to the synagogue building; the eighteenth century saw an increase in women's *tekhines* to be said during the synagogue service; in the nineteenth-century gender-segregated seating in some Reform congregations was abolished (such abolition to be adopted in the twentieth century by the Conservative movement and even by some Orthodox synagogues); and the twentieth century saw the institution of confirmation and, later, bat mitzvah rituals for girls, and the admission of women to the governing bodies of synagogues.

This process of increasing women's Jewish cultural and social capital has continued at a much more rapid pace in the postmodern period, with some significant additions: it has become more consciously aimed at blurring gender distinctions in the name of equality; it has revolutionized Jewish education; it has been embraced, albeit hesitatingly, by certain Orthodox elements. Emblematic of the change that has occurred is that women rabbis, who were barely even a curiosity in the modern period, are now commonplace (even showing signs of appearing among the Orthodox).

New Challenges in the Postmodern Period

The postmodern period has also brought with it some new questions, challenges, and processes. The following sections give some examples.

[66] Rosman, 'History of Jewish Women'.

Israel–Diaspora Relations

From the Muslim conquest until the establishment of Israel (or, at the earliest, the founding of the new Zionist Yishuv (the Jewish community established in Erets Yisrael in the late nineteenth century), the question of relations between Erets Yisrael and the Diaspora did not loom very large from a practical point of view. In theory, if not always in practice, Diaspora Jews saw it as their duty to support economically (and, in the case of important Ottoman communities such as Alexandria and Istanbul, sometimes politically) the Jews who were in the Holy Land; a small number of them aspired to move there; and a still smaller number actually did.

Political Zionism, and especially the establishment of Israel, changed the relationship profoundly. Israel resolves to be the centre of world Jewish life, to represent the Jewish People, and to lay claim to the loyalty of Jews everywhere. During the postmodern period many Diaspora Jews have enthusiastically seconded these aims, and more than 2.5 million of them have moved to Israel and become Israeli.[67] Many, however, have not seen the relevance of Israel to their lives, and have not allotted it a significant role in their actions. A sizeable number have regarded Israel's ambitions towards them as pretentious or worse. They resent being associated with its policies and actions, and view Israel as an albatross rather than a source of inspiration and pride. In and around these three positions there are many nuances, and it seems clear that one of the great themes of postmodern Jewish history has been, and will continue to be, the dialectic between the State of Israel and Israeli Jews, on the one hand, and Diaspora Jewries as organized entities and Diaspora Jews (including former Israelis) as individuals, on the other.[68]

The Economics of Jewish Identity

Through to the modern period, a large majority of Jews in the world probably maintained a standard of living that was not too distant in either

---

[67] DellaPergola, *World Jewry Beyond 2000*, 32–5.

[68] Eisen, *Galut*, 117–80; id., 'The Problem Is Still Very Much with Us', 24–5; Ben-Rafael, Gorny, and Ro'i (eds), *Contemporary Jewries*; Mittelberg, *The Israel Connection and American Jews*; Seliktar, *Divided We Stand*; Kosmin, Lerman, and Goldberg, *Attachment of British Jews to Israel*; Cesarani, 'The Dynamics of Diaspora', 62; Weinberg, 'Between America and Israel'; Bodemann, *In der Wogen der Erinnerung*, 164–84; Sheffer, 'From Israeli Hegemony to Diaspora Full Autonomy'; id., 'A Nation and its Diaspora'; Schweid, 'Changing Jewish Identities in the New Europe'; Webber (ed.), *Modern Jewish Identities*, 78–9; Solomon, 'Judaism in the New Europe', 94; Gutwein, 'The New Europe and the Zionist Dilemma', 275–82.

direction from some theoretical poverty line. This was virtually irrelevant to their Jewish identity, except to the extent that in some areas, such as eastern Europe, poverty and Jewishness were highly correlated, and often the former seemed, subjectively at least, to be an intrinsic aspect of the latter. There certainly was no bar to poor people feeling identified as Jews.

As I have observed, in the postmodern period the majority of Jews live far above the poverty line. Yet, outside Israel, maintaining ties with the institutions of the organized Jewish community, providing one's children with the experiences considered basic to a sophisticated Jewish identity, and just being part of the general Jewish ecosphere impose a significant financial burden. It is interesting that a prime tenet of Jewish fundraising has become the equation of the need to preserve Jewish 'continuity' with the need to raise money. In practice, synagogue and Jewish club memberships, 'normal' charitable contributions, school and camp tuition, financial requirements of Jewish organizations, kosher food, and housing in most Jewish neighbourhoods all represent a hefty slice of family income that often must come at the expense of some of the essentials of middle-class life. If there is a lifestyle dilemma for postmodern Jews that has replaced, 'Can we be Jewish and culturally integrated?' it is 'Can we afford to be Jewish?'[69] When coupled with doubts about the necessity of maintaining a Jewish community and the very existence of *kelal yisra'el*, the answer often enough is 'Why bother?'.

The New Hebraism

Notwithstanding the persistence of antisemitism, there are many contexts in the postmodern world where Jews, Judaism, and Jewishness have enjoyed a new, positive re-evaluation and acceptance.[70] This goes beyond mere tolerance. Jews are 'establishment'. Jews are high government officials and leaders of political parties, captains of industry, and presidents of universities. Culturally, in a world premised on the ideals of pluralism or multiculturalism, virtually every major university has a Jewish studies programme (most of them financed by Jewish donors) where many non-Jewish scholars also specialize in Jewish studies; the holiday of Hanukah has begun to be publicly marked by kindling a special candelabrum or *ḥanukiah* at the White House in the presence of the US President; the Holocaust is a subject on many school curricula; Jewish museums and

[69] Meir and Hostein, *The High Cost of Jewish Living*.

[70] e.g. The Pew Forum, Survey, 'Views of Muslim-Americans': 'The [American] public continues to express overwhelmingly favorable opinions of Jews (77%)' (p. 7).

monuments are architecturally and culturally prominent in many of the world's great cities; Jewish community leaders are routinely consulted by politicians on appropriate issues; one can even order kosher meals at Disneyworld.

Older Jews, with a consciousness formed by the modern period, rub their eyes. Is this more than condescending philosemitism or Holocaust guilt? Can it last? How does it relate to the 'new' antisemitism? When dealing with non-Jews, do Jews dare take 'Yes' for an answer? Postmodern Jews, more sanguine, are willing to believe. This time there really seems to be a neutral society where all meet equally, where one's Jewishness is purely a personal matter, where minority status is irrelevant.[71] More than that, they know that Jewish culture can both benefit and benefit *from* the general culture. They make earnest arguments that such cardinal elements of postmodern sensibility such as egalitarianism, ecology, pluralism, tolerance, self-determination, and even feminism and multiculturalism, have roots in Jewish tradition, and they welcome the chance to explore these together with non-Jews; reciprocally learning no less from the heritage of others. The development of a new relationship with non-Jewish society and culture has been and will be a major factor in shaping Jewish existence in the postmodern period.

Who Is a Jew?

In the sophisticated demographic research work that has been done on the world Jewish population since the latter part of the twentieth century, the data are usually based on the 'core Jewish population', defined by an 'operative definition': 'all those who, when asked, identify themselves as Jews . . . This is a comprehensive approach that reflects both subjective feelings and community norms and bonds.'[72]

The alternative to an operative definition of who is a Jew would be a 'normative definition' derived from the halakhic maxim that a Jew is someone whose mother is Jewish, or who has formally converted to Judaism. In

---

[71] Slezkine, *The Jewish Century*: 'Surveys of public opinion in the Russian Federation as a whole suggest that the majority of non-Jewish Russians have a favorable opinion of Jews and Israel' (p. 361). This is in contrast to developments in late 18th-century Germany, which Katz, *Out of the Ghetto*, 42–56, termed a '*semi*-neutral society'.

[72] DellaPergola, *World Jewry Beyond 2000*, 9–11, 25. There is also something called the 'enlarged Jewish population' that includes the core Jewish population, plus Jews by birth or parentage who do not currently identify as Jews, plus non-Jewish household members living with Jews (p. 10).

the postmodern period such a definition would obviously include significantly fewer people than the operative definition resting on self-
identification.[73] This is because the operative definition recognizes as Jews
not only formal converts, but also those who 'have decided to join the
Jewish group informally'. It also accepts the common usage in the former
Soviet Union and eastern Europe, and the controversial (from a normative
point of view) decision by the Reform movement whereby those with a
Jewish father (but a non-Jewish mother) are counted as Jews. In addition
it includes many Israelis who profess to Jewishness, although they are not
halakhically qualified.[74]

It is very probable (although it needs to be proven) that in the modern
period the gap between the two approaches was much smaller. The reason
for this is that the possible permutations of a person's relationship to
Jewishness then were more limited. It was relatively rare for a person who
was not halakhically Jewish to want to claim that status (probably the
opposite was much more frequent). In the postmodern period—with
the breakdown of traditional nuclear and extended family structures, the
dramatic increase in the percentage of mixed Jewish–non-Jewish marriage,
the Israeli Law of Return enabling many types of 'non-normative Jews' to
become part of Israel, and the positive re-evaluation of Jewishness on the
part of the majority culture—there are more ways, often not coextensive
with halakhah, for an individual to see herself or himself as associated with
Jewishness than in the past.

Many religious leaders, especially Orthodox ones, are fighting hard to
retain (or perhaps to re-establish) the primacy of the normative, halakhic
definition. However, the sheer numbers of 'non-Jews' seeking to be identified as Jews, especially in Israel, and the problems implied by the Jewish
demographic decline outlined above, are powerful forces opposing their
efforts. It seems, given the postmodern impracticality of imposing the policy of the biblical Ezra (Ezra 10: 11, ordering the Jewish men of ancient
Judea to separate from their foreign wives), that they may eventually have
to choose between the policy of Zerubbabel (Ezra 2: 59, who included in
the returnees to Jerusalem from Babylonian exile those who 'were unable
to tell whether their father's house and descent were Israelite') and outright
schism.

---

[73] DellaPergola, *World Jewry Beyond 2000*, 45.

[74] For an ideological defence of this definition of Jewishness, see Yehoshua, 'Who Is
a Jew?', 73–5.

That struggle goes on. In the meantime 'the Jewish People' in the post-modern period is a somewhat different entity from what it was in the modern period (which raises the issue of the comparability of the numbers of Jews in the two periods). Its genealogy, the historical heritage of its members, their collective consciousness and collective objectives, their family relationships, the kinds of ties they seek and maintain with each other, their conceptions of what it means to be a Jew, their modes of Jewish identification—all are much more variegated than they were in 1950.[75] This, combined with the changing political and economic configuration of the general world context, and the expiration or transformation of most of the primary issues that preoccupied the Jews during modernity, suggests that in the postmodern period Jewish history will be as different from the modern as the modern was from the Middle Ages and antiquity.

An Unphilosophical Postmodernity

When in contemporary discourse we say that ours is a 'postmodern age', we are usually using that expression in a heedless, unrigorous manner. It is much the same as the application of Freudian terminology to everyday events by people who have never read Freud. In the Introduction I explored the term 'postmodern' as denoting a set of theoretical concepts; in this chapter I have used it to code a new set of circumstances and processes interacting to mark the period in which they became operative as substantially different from the preceding time. What I have argued here is that, at least in terms of Jewish history, the 'postmodernity'—in the literal sense of succeeding modernity—of the current era is demonstrable.

Does my schema share the weakness of all 'grand structures'? To be sure. Critics will find inconsistencies, counter-examples, additional criteria to consider, more inclusive paradigms. By proposing this periodization am I revealing my own metahistory? Doubtless. Nevertheless, I offer this construction in the hope that it will be part of a process of reconsideration of how we configure, organize, and present the Jewish past, as well as how we understand the Jewish present. If Jews are no longer modern, what does that say about modernity? What does that say about the Jews?

---

[75] See the following in Webber (ed.), *Jewish Identities*: Friesel's foreword (p. ix); Webber's introduction (pp. 16–17, 21); DellaPergola, 'Overview of the Demographic Trends of European Jewry' (pp. 57–8, 74–6, 130–4).

THREE

Hybrid with What?
The Relationship between
Jewish Culture and
Other People's Cultures

꩜

WHEN READING CONTEMPORARY scholarship on Jewish cultural history, it often seems to me that it has developed two 'meta-
solutions' that are applied to virtually any question. These are 'influence'
and 'pluralism'. That is, if the question is why Jewish family life is organized
in a particular configuration, or why Jews eat specific foods, or how certain
institutions of communal governance evolved, or what is the basis for
Jewish prayer rituals, or any of a multitude of issues, the answer almost
invariably relates to the influence of the surrounding culture, the existence
of competing and co-operating Judaisms, or both.[1]

Later in this chapter I will examine some problems posed by the Jewish
pluralism paradigm. With regard to the metasolution of influence, there is
a firm article of faith shared by practically all of today's Judaica scholars
that, in all times and places, pre-modern or 'traditional' Jews lived in inti-
mate interaction with surrounding cultures to the point where they may be
considered to be embedded in them and, consequently, indebted to them
in terms of culture. This contrasts with an older conception of Jewish culture which represented Jews as living in at least semi-isolation from the
non-Jewish world, animating their lives with an original, autonomous and
authentically Jewish culture that functioned according to its own dynamic.[2]
In the following sections my first objective is to demonstrate, by using the

---

[1] See almost all of the chapters in Biale (ed.), *Cultures of the Jews*, and the critical,
somewhat tendentious, review of this work by Roskies entitled 'Border Crossings'. Cf.
Silberstein, *Postzionism Debates*: 'Ahad Haam's discourse, like all zionist discourse and all
other Jewish discourse, was a multiplicity' (p. 28).

[2] e.g. Ben-Sasson, *History of the Jewish People*; Finkelstein (ed.), *The Jews*, vol. ii: *Their
Religion and Culture*.

example of Polish Jewish cultural history, that there are more than these two possible approaches to the history of Jewish culture, and that these two themselves should be understood in a more sophisticated way. I will assert that the first approach (universal cultural influence, in its incarnation as hybridity theory), when applied mechanically, unimaginatively, and uncritically can be as ideological, dogmatic, and inappropriate as the second (Jewish cultural autonomy) often has been. Next I will contemplate the metahistories implied by the various approaches to Jewish cultural history and their relationship to intellectual presuppositions for engaging in Jewish studies in the academy.

Conceptions of Polish Jewish Culture

There have been four distinct historiographical approaches to writing the Jewish cultural history of the Polish–Lithuanian Commonwealth in the early modern period.[3] The first was characteristic of the classic Jewish historians of pre-Shoah Poland, Majer Bałaban, Ignacy Schiper, and Mojzes Schorr, and to some extent the generation that followed them, Emanuel Ringelblum and Raphael Mahler. Perhaps surprisingly, although conversant in Jewish and especially Polish sources, these scholars gave only cursory acknowledgement to both the traditional nature of Polish Jewish culture—its derivation from and its continuity and coherence with medieval Ashkenazi (that is, German Jewish) and other versions of traditional Jewish culture. They also paid scant attention to the influence of Polish culture on Polish Jewish institutions and its parallels with their mores, customs, and so on. These historians chose instead to emphasize, indeed to celebrate, the lush flowering of Jewish culture in Poland: new-style yeshivas, the Council of Four Lands, *kehalim* (self-governing communities), taxation regimes, charity arrangements, synagogue architecture, Jewish clothing and jewellery, Jewish language, music, and theatre.

Despite the fact that, like us, these early Polish Jewish historians easily rejected the postulate that Jewish culture existed in splendid isolation, the issues of origins, precursors, influences, and precedents were, at most, of secondary importance. These men were all accomplished scholars of Polish history and worked primarily with Polish material. They indubitably recognized the background intimacy, embeddedness, and indebtedness of Jewish culture relative to Polish and other European cultures. However, unlike today's scholars, they detected no overriding significance in this. It was a fully

---

[3] Cf. Bacon, 'Polish–Jewish Relations in Modern Times'.

expected mundane detail, not a novel insight worthy of elaborate research and presentation. For them, the central point—the exciting discovery—was the vibrancy, comprehensiveness, and power of Polish Jewish culture, irrespective of its possible genetic links to non-Jewish culture.[4] These scholars dwelt on what Polish Jewry had wrought through an ingenious resourcefulness, often in the face of legal and other obstacles. The conclusion implied by their depiction was that Polish Jewish culture was a unique array of cultural institutions and behaviours that outstripped its Ashkenazi progenitors in quality and quantity; matched or outmatched other Jewish subcultures in authenticity and integrity; and compared favourably with Polish culture in terms of originality, creativity, vitality, and sophistication.

While, in describing in loving detail the values, symbols, and institutions of Polish Jewry, this approach has much to teach us, it begs the question of the extent of the cause-and-effect connections between Jewish culture and Polish culture. For the pre-Shoah Polish Jewish scholars, the key question was not one of cultural genesis, but of *juxtaposition* and *comparison* of the two cultures. Rather than utilizing the three metaphors of intimacy, indebtedness, and embeddedness (the latter two implying hierarchy and dependency) to conceptualize the relationship between the two cultures, they recognized two distinct, intertwined, but independent and functionally equal, entities. For them, it was important to understand that the Jewish as configured in Poland could hold its own vis-à-vis the Polish; outside or mutual influences were taken for granted and largely beside the point.[5]

---

[4] See e.g. comments made in passing, such as Bałaban, *Historja i literatura*, iii. 188, 205–6, 232 (Hebrew version in Halperin (ed.), *Jewish People in Poland*, i. 45–6, 50, 55, 69). Also Mahler, *History of the Jews in Poland* (Heb.), 74, 188–9, 191, 202, 360–1, 381. See also references in n. 5.

[5] Bałaban, *Historja i literatura*, iii. 183–259 (Halperin (ed.), *Jewish People*, i. 44–80). Schiper, *History of Yiddish Culture* (Yid.); Schiper, Tartakower, and Hafftka (eds), *Żydzi w Polsce odrodzonej*, i. 81–110, 213–374, with various sections written mainly by Schiper, but also by Bałaban and Frenkel. Schiper devoted much of his attention (not always to the best advantage) to Jewish language, arts and literature; see e.g. *History of Jewish Theatrical Art and Drama* (Yid.) on Jewish theatre in Poland from earliest times; and chapters on Jewish language, folk literature, plastic arts, music, theatre decoration, graphic arts and sculpture in Poland in *Żydzi w Polsce odrodzonej*, i. 225–35, 308–36; ii. 114–47; also Mahler, *History of the Jews in Poland* (Heb.), 50, 188–215, 357–95. It should be noted that Mahler's presentation of Jewish life in the Polish–Lithuanian Commonwealth was much less sanguine than that of his predecessors. There are similarities between the evaluation of Polish Jewish culture presented here and the views of Shlomo Dov Goitein on Arabic-Jewish culture; see Libson, 'Hidden Worlds'.

The second approach to the description of Polish Jewish culture was that of Jewish nationalist, Zionist, and what might be termed 'intellectual historians' (where these groups are not mutually exclusive). This began with Simon Dubnow[6] who, based on his master narrative of shifting culturally hegemonic centres of the Diaspora, crowned Polish Jewry as the co-hegemon (together with the rest of Yiddish-speaking Jewry in Ashkenaz) of world Jewry in the early modern period.

This notion of a worldwide, interconnected, nationally self-conscious, transnational Jewish people with a common history, culture, and fate was continually cultivated by such historians as Hayim Hillel Ben-Sasson, who termed the Polish–Lithuanian Commmonwealth 'a *province* of Jewish Society and Culture', the 'outside' influences on which came from other *Jewish* communities.[7] Jacob Katz's classic work *Tradition and Crisis* took it

[6] Dubnow's master-narrative, first published in Russian in 1924, went into many editions and was translated into German, Hebrew, and English (see bibliography). Note the subtle differences between the Russian original and the various translations: Russian, 'Periodizatsia i raspredeleniye materiala' (literally, 'Periodization and Distribution of the Material'), (vol. i, pp. xx–xxv, and see esp. p. xxii on the period of joint Ashkenazi–Polish hegemony; German, 'Periodisierung und Stoffverteilung' (vol. i, pp. xxiii–xxx, and see esp. p. xxv); English 'Periodicity and System of Hegemonies' (vol. i, pp. 33–8, and esp. p. 35); Hebrew, 'Keviat hatekufot vesidur haḥomer' ('Setting the Periods and Organizing the Material') (vol. i, pp. 6–11, esp. p. 8). For an introduction to the development of the nationalist school in Erets Yisrael, see Yuval, 'Yitzhak Baer'; Myers, 'Between Diaspora and Zion', and id., *Re-Inventing the Jewish Past*; Conforti, *Past Tense* (Heb.); Raz-Krakotzkin, 'The National Narration of Exile' (Heb.); Rein, 'The Historian as a Nation Builder' (Heb.).

[7] Ben-Sasson, *Trial and Achievement* (Heb.), 144. As to the influence of other Jewish communities, see id., *Theory and Practice* (Heb.), e.g. pp. 14–16. At times, like the generation of Polish Jewish historians before him, Ben-Sasson did emphasize the uniqueness of Polish Jewish culture and how it broke with Ashkenazi precedents (e.g. *Theory and Practice*, 152–3, 155–6). Nevertheless, he announced: 'In the end the western Ashkenazi culture became dominant' (*Trial and Achievement*, 144), and 'In the sixteenth and seventeenth centuries Poland–Lithuania became the main center of Ashkenazi culture' (ibid. 162). In *Theory and Practice* he was even more emphatic that Polish Jewry was the direct cultural descendant of Ashkenazi Jewry, and especially Hasidei Ashkenaz (see e.g. ibid. 11–13; but cf. Soloveitchik, 'German Pietism', 484–8). Note that Ben-Sasson was well aware of Polish sources and knew that some individual Jews were subject to Christian intellectual influences. He lent this little significance (e.g. *Theory and Practice*, 30, 38–9, 78); he took non-Jewish parallels with Jewish culture not as evidence of a cause-and-effect impact of Polish culture on Jewish culture, but merely as proof of correlations reflecting common factors that acted on both cultures and subjected both cultures to some of the same conditions, pressures, and demands (e.g. *Theory and*

as axiomatic that 'all Jews, whether in Poland or Yemen, Holland or Palestine, saw themselves as members of a single nation'.[8] However, this nation was geographically divided into various centres, and one of them, stretching from the Loire to the Dniepr, was in Jewish terms an expanded Ashkenaz (in the early modern period no longer just the Germanic areas, but also including Poland–Lithuania), a single cultural domain.[9] Jacob Elbaum highlighted the profound effects of non-Ashkenazi Jewish sub-cultures on Polish Jewish culture in the wake of the spread of printing, and implied that Polish culture itself impinged on the Jews barely at all.[10]

All of these scholars, and many others, presumed that Polish Jewish culture was, at base, an elaboration of a traditional, authentic, autonomous Jewish culture that had developed organically at least from talmudic times and probably even beginning with the first writing down of the books of the Bible. It was a culture that was continuous and coherent over time and geography; its essential core recognizable through all of its myriad permutations. This culture was, of course, subject to alien influences, but these were insignificant, ultimately eschewed, or so Judaized as to make the question of origins moot. Here is the concept of an isolated culture with a dynamic of its own, which, as remarked above, was abandoned a genera-

---

Practice, 52–4, 60, 65, 89, 101, 117, 150, 240, 249, 250). Ben-Sasson believed that, for Polish Jews, non-Jews represented a halakhic problem but not a cultural one (e.g. ibid. 56, 60, 104). There might be a question as to how to deal with them on their holidays, but they did not pose any challenges to Jewish lifestyles.

 [8] Katz, *Tradition and Crisis*, 5, see also pp. 6–8. Cf. Biale's remarks quoted at n. 47 below.   [9] Katz, *Tradition and Crisis*, 6.

 [10] Elbaum, *Openness and Insularity*, esp. pp. 30–2, 63–4, 179–80. Many others contributed to this school of study, including some of the classic Jewish historians of the past as well as some more recent ones: e.g. Simha Assaf, Ben-Zion Dinur, and Israel Halperin. The latest example of this approach is Breuer, *Tents of Torah* (Heb.). Tellingly, this book is not organized geographically or chronologically, but thematically by aspects of the yeshiva as an institution (curriculum, methodology of study, administration, etc.), as if to say that the yeshiva embodies and symbolizes a universal Jewish culture, the individual expressions of which, in various times and places, are but specific examples of an abiding, timeless—even essential—Jewish culture. On Polish and Jewish mutual cultural alienation, see Shmeruk, *Esterke Story* (Heb.), and my discussion in Chapter 5. Several younger scholars, such as Elchanan Reiner, Edward Fram, and Zeev Gries, have kept to the basic idea of Polish Jewish culture as developing, cultivating and further articulating general Ashkenazi, and earlier, Jewish culture, but have tried to explain the mechanisms of this process and explicate the resultant differences between the progenitors and the filiation in an inflected, sophisticated, and complex way.

tion or more ago. Interestingly, however, just as this view was losing favour with many Jewish historians of the pre-modern periods, it was reinforced from unexpected directions. In his 1988 essay 'Jewish Continuity in an Age of Discontinuity: Reflections from the Perspective of Intellectual History', the modernist intellectual historian Paul Mendes-Flohr attempted to define the universal, if variably inflected, ingredients of Jewish culture that made for an unambiguous, self-evident, and unproblematic Jewish continuity up until the age of secularization, and that everywhere resisted co-optation. These he archly dubbed the seven Cs: Creed, Code, Cult, Community, Culture, Cognitive, and Covenant.[11]

A more historical, detailed, and closely argued claim appeared in *European Jewry in the Age of Mercantilism* (a book that served us in Chapter 2 as an example of Jewish historical periodization), where Jonathan Israel, theretofore primarily a historian of early modern Holland and Spain, boldly asserted that there was

a distinctive Jewish culture within Europe . . . Hispanization of Levantine, and Germanization of east European Jewry . . . imparted a remarkable degree of cohesion to a people scattered in small groups over vast distances in a score of lands. What is more, the two spheres, the Hispanic and the Germanic, were now brought into a high degree of interaction . . . at a deeper level the two spheres developed intellectually and spiritually largely as one.

Moreover with respect to influences from the surrounding cultures, the 'unified and integrated Jewish culture . . . was increasingly remote from that of the peoples among whom Jews lived'. However, Israel said nothing about the eras preceding the sixteenth century, and regarded this 'maximum cohesion in the history of Jewish culture' as a product of the early modern period. Still it is striking how his evaluations, and those of Mendes-Flohr, lend credence to the idea of an early modern traditional, coherent Jewish culture standing as an equal among and apart from other cultures; not embedded within one or another of them; certainly ever *less* indebted to them; and, while itself modulated into various subcultures, still laying claim to be an integral, continuous whole. This notion was further refined by David Ruderman, who proposed five elements as composing this transnational early modern Jewish culture: (1) mobility, social mixing, and hybridity; (2) communal cohesion and laicization of communal authority; (3) knowledge explosion; (4) crisis of authority, heresy, and enthusiasm;

---

[11] Originally appearing in the *Journal of Jewish Studies*, 39 (1988), 261–8, this piece was reprinted in Mendes-Flohr, *Divided Passions*, 56–9.

(5) the blurring of religious identities.[12] (In line with Mendes-Flohr and Israel, one might add a sixth element explicitly acknowledging the continuing relevance of classical Jewish texts and many traditional Jewish forms.)

Whether propounded by nationalists or others, this approach has the virtue of proffering a reasonable explanation for two seemingly fundamental aspects of Polish Jewish culture. The first is that much of early modern Polish Jewish culture is an iteration of earlier Ashkenazi and even talmudic modes which often defies attempts at historicist analysis aiming to identify features that make it a specific product of its Polish milieu.[13] The second basic aspect is that on numerous counts the mutual cultural alienation between non-Jews and Jews in Poland is patent. As is illustrated by their respective legislative systems and economic activity, Poles and Jews both regarded the members of

---

[12] Israel, *European Jewry in the Age of Mercantilism*, quotations from pp. 31, 33, 184; see also the introduction and p. 71; Ruderman, 'Jewish Cultural History in Early Modern Europe'. One might also infer the existence of a coherent, worldwide Jewish culture in the early modern period, in dialogue with local Jewish cultures or subcultures, from Miriam Bodian's description of the 'rejudaization' of the 'Portuguese Nation', i.e. the descendants of the Portuguese *conversos*, who emigrated from the Iberian peninsula in the 17th century, settling in Amsterdam and elsewhere. These people worked towards the objective 'of a collective "return" to mainstream Jewish life and historical experience . . . integration into the wider Jewish world' while still cultivating an Iberian-informed way of life. See ead., *Hebrews of the Portuguese Nation*, 19 (where the previous quotation appears), 30, 45, 47, 89–92, 96–131, 132–3, 138, 146, 148, 152, 155–6. Perhaps the strongest case for the existence of an autonomous Jewish culture in the early modern period juxtaposed to the non-Jewish 'outside' culture was made by Bonfil in *Jewish Life in Renaissance Italy*, although his argument was limited to Italy. Bonfil variously asserted: 'I have tried instead to point out the component elements of the subject's [i.e. the Jews] *different* culture and the implications of that *difference* for the complex process of the insertion of the Jew into the sociocultural fabric of the Italian cities of the period' (p. xi); 'the structural opposition between the two societies was absolute and fundamental' (p. 123); 'the *importation* of elements of the outside culture must be understood as the adoption and manipulation of contents considered as "neutral" as far as their potential impact on their consciousness of a Jewish identity—perceived as different from, or better yet, *opposed* to Christian identity—was concerned' (p. 151); see also pp. 3, 103, 104, 108–9, 110, 115, 124, 151, 152, 284. In a similar spirit Hundert, while seeing Polish Jews as both insular and integrated into the society in which they lived, maintained that 'Polish society held no attraction for Jews' (*Jews in Poland–Lithuania in the Eighteenth Century*, 238), and that Jews' insistence on determining their own identity and their refusal to be defined by others is the 'defining . . . element in the modern Jewish experience' (p. 240).

[13] See Chapter 5, the section entitled 'The Elusiveness of Historicist Analysis', for a more detailed discussion of this problem (including the Esterke myth).

the other group as most definitely 'Other', to be suspected, feared, and often demonized or worse. They had no real common language. Boundary markers, such as differently structured calendars, food restrictions, and various distinguishing religious rituals, carefully delineated the respective cultural space of each group. Contact between cultural elites was limited and, where it existed, was usually negative. Although living physically intermixed to a significant degree, each group had its own institutional infrastructure that functionally, and—one might argue—redundantly, duplicated the other. Even ostensibly shared cultural possessions, such as the Esterke myth, proved to have different origins. In general, it is fair to say that to a great extent the cultural creations of Poles and Jews stemmed from different sources and usually developed along different lines.[14]

Both the difficulty of historicist analysis and the mutual cultural alienation of Jews and their neighbours are much easier to understand and contend with historiographically if Polish Jewish culture is viewed as primarily Jewish, deriving from Jewish antecedents outside Poland and in constant dialogue with contemporary Jewish cultural communities all over the world. Such a conception clashes, however, with the now conventional belief that Jewish culture was always embedded in and indebted to the local culture in which it was found.

Approach number three to Polish Jewish culture is what we might call the 'early American school'. This was espoused by ex-Europeans, in particular, Salo Baron and Bernard Dov Weinryb, who made their home in the United States and adopted its ways. They took Baron's general paradigm for Jewish history—which can be characterized as an ellipse whose contours are determined by two foci, one internal, one external[15]—and applied it to the Polish case. As Weinryb put it:

[14] See Chapter 5, the section entitled 'The Influence Model Versus the Polysystem Model', for a more detailed discussion of this problem. See also Rosman, 'Innovative Tradition', 523–5, 527; id., 'Jewish Perceptions of Insecurity and Powerlessness in 16th–18th Century Poland', 21–5; id., 'A Minority Views the Majority', 36–9; Hundert, *Jews in Poland–Lithuania in the Eighteenth Century*, introduction, afterword, and *passim*. Cf. Roskies, 'Border Crossings', 65. Overt Polish cultural influence on Jews can be detected in the areas of dress, diet, music, and book illustrations; see Shulman, *Authority and Community*, 80; Shmeruk, *Illustrations in Yiddish Books*; Assaf, *World of Torah* (Heb.), 93–9.

[15] Baron explicated his view of the relationship between Jewish and general history in two articles republished in his book *History and Jewish Historians*, 'World Dimensions of Jewish History', 34–42, and 'Newer Emphases in Jewish History', 100–5. For more detailed discussion of his position see Chapter 1 at nn. 71, 86 and 87.

As a minority[16] [the Jews] absorb elements of their environment, but they are also conditioned by the heritage of their own history, religion, and culture, as well as by the possibility of contacts with their places of origins and kindred Jewish groups. This leads to a distinctive Jewish existence, which in the case of Polish Jewry embodied elements of both Jewishness and Polishness. Jewish history in Poland thus deals with these two processes: Polish history and Jewish life, often with emphasis on the latter.[17]

Although Weinryb claimed to privilege what he called 'Jewish life', in his book he gave Jewish heritage short shrift while focusing on the importance of the Polish setting in determining the circumstances of Jewish existence in many ways. He devoted most of his efforts to describing how, thanks to the structures of Polish society and culture, the Jews were largely well situated, comfortable, and successfully adapted in Poland.[18]

'Embedded' would certainly be a fair epitome of Weinryb's characterization. However, his discussion largely omitted any systematic consideration of Jewish culture. Glaringly missing are Polish Jewish halakhic development, rabbinic culture, and the educational system. He managed to treat the hoary, and to most scholars cardinal, subject of Jewish autonomous communal organization in the shortest chapter in the book (numbering but eight pages); and denied that Shabateanism exercised a significant influence in Poland, thus undercutting what for Zionist historians was the classic proof for the existence of a world Jewish culture.[19]

Baron, for his part, gave so much weight to the Polish focus of the Polish Jewish ellipse that in many places the reader of his book will be forgiven for thinking that he is reading a textbook on Polish history which happens to

---

[16] Hundert, *Jews in Poland–Lithuania in the Eighteenth Century*, 21 ff., contends that applying the term 'minority' to Jews in early modern Poland is inappropriate.

[17] Weinryb, *The Jews of Poland*, p. ix.

[18] Ibid., e.g. pp. 156–76. This approaches the notion of 'Jewish–Christian synthesis' as exemplified in the work of Cecil Roth and others on the Jews in Renaissance Italy (see Ruderman, 'Cecil Roth', 139–40). Some have suggested characterizing the Jewish–Polish nexus as 'symbiosis', which may be a better way to define Weinryb's conceptualization; cf. Rosman, *The Lords' Jews*, 207–12; Bacon, 'Polish–Jewish Relations in Modern Times', 49–53, 65–8; Lehmann, *Symbiosis and Ambivalence*.

[19] Weinryb, *The Jews of Poland*, 71–8, 228–31; cf. Scholem, *Sabbatai Sevi*, who portrayed the Jewish reaction to Shabetai Tsevi as simultaneous, similar and synergistic worldwide; see esp. pp. 591–602 on Poland. Cf. Rosman, 'Reflections on the State of Polish-Jewish Historical Study', 118–19; see also Chapter 1 at n. 24.

highlight the Jewish angle.[20] Moreover, under the rubric 'Extraordinary Creative Elan', where one might rightfully expect a full-blown exposition of the achievements of Polish Jewish culture and how each of the two foci determined the profile of this culture, Baron wrote a bare two and a half pages, devoted mainly to the subject of religious toleration in Poland, while noting merely in passing how Polish Jews 'achieved a cultural level which exceeded anything known in Ashkenazic Jewry since the days of the Tosafists'.[21]

As was true of the nationalist approach, the two-foci perspective on Polish Jewish history in the early modern period has been continued by a somewhat unexpected group—Polish-born and trained historians who have chosen to devote their efforts to the elucidation of the history of the Jews in Poland. They have naturally highlighted the Polish focus of the ellipse, and are supplying a steady stream of sources and information that shed an ever brighter light on the conditions of life for Jews in the Commonwealth as shaped by the Polish context.[22]

[20] Baron, *Social and Religious History of the Jews* (2nd edn), vol. xvi: *Poland-Lithuania 1500–1650*. Note headings such as 'Poland's Golden Age', 'The Last Jagiellonians', 'Two Interregna and Bathory', 'Protestant Sectarianism', 'Poland-Lithuania on a High Plateau', 'Poland's Eastern Drive', where there is much to learn about Polish history, irrespective of the Jews. Like Dubnow before him, Baron was convinced that Polish Jewry attained cultural hegemony in the Jewish world: 'In sum: the Jewish community of the dual Commonwealth could now assume the communal and cultural leadership of Ashkenazi, and in some respects of all world, Jewry' (ibid. 163).

[21] Baron, *Social and Religious History of the Jews* (2nd edn), xvi. 75–7.

[22] The pioneer in this regard was Jacob Goldberg, trained in Poland, but who settled in Israel; see e.g. his collection of articles, *The Jewish Society in the Polish Commonwealth* (Heb.). For a bibliographic discussion about renewed Polish interest in writing Jewish historiography, see Rosman, 'Historiography of Polish Jewry' (Heb.), 718–21 and esp. nn. 28–30. In the 1990s a new generation of Polish historians dealing with the history of the Jews in this period emerged, including such scholars as Adam Kaźmierczyk, Hanna Węgrzynek, Michał Gałas, and Magda Teter (although her doctorate was earned at Columbia University in the USA). Also in this group is Anna Michałowska, whose book *Między demokracja a oligarchia* is, however, atypical of the trend in that it utilizes mainly Jewish sources and explains the working of the autonomous Jewish community in a way that is reminiscent of the approach of Bałaban et al., discussed at the beginning of this chapter, although the audience today is obviously Polish and not Jewish. For later periods one might add Natalia Aleksiun, Alina Cała, and Marcin Wodziński. Also noteworthy is Andrzej Kamiński's book, *Historia Rzeczypospolitej wielu narodów*, which stresses the multi-ethnic character of the Polish–Lithuanian polity and regards the Jews as one of its bona fide constituent groups. Cf. Davies, *God's Playground*, i. 32.

Intuitively—for our consciousness is still similar to theirs, Baron's, Weinryb's, and their successors'—assertion of the importance of the Polish context seems all too obviously correct. Their views, that Polish policy and actions towards the Jews and the Jews' parameters of existence cannot be understood except within a Polish context and largely on the basis of Polish sources, are convincing. However, they did not, and have not, successfully tackled the question of the relationship between Polish and Jewish cultures. The conclusion of Baron's discussion of the effects of Polish culture on the Jews is that there was a lack of significant impact, certainly no relationship of either embeddedness or indebtedness. He even intimated that the Jews made more of an impression on Polish culture than the other way around.[23] Baron and his intellectual heirs failed to solve the problems of elusive historicist analysis and obvious mutual cultural alienation in a way that makes Polish culture seem to be a significant element in the shaping of Jewish culture, let alone serve as the soil which gave it life. Because our intellectual convictions predict such a solution, this failure rankles.

In response came the fourth approach to the Polish Jewish cultural nexus, which we might call 'late (North) American'. This demonstrated an abiding belief in Baron's basic assumption, and was determined to get around the problem with it by evaluating cultural contact more subtly. If culture is defined, not as the fruit of creative production—as in all of our previous examples—but in Geertzian terms as meaning and the ways in which it is expressed, then on the level of meanings taken for granted—the unspoken assumptions that served as the substratum for daily behaviour— Jews really could be seen as sharing in Polish culture.[24]

This perspective was dramatically enunciated by Gershon Hundert when he entitled a chapter of his book *The Jews in a Polish Private Town*, 'Jews and Other Poles'. By this he meant that Polish Jewish identity was 'incontestably Polish', differentiated from other Jewish communities, even the rest of Katz's Ashkenaz to the west; and perceived by non-Jews as well as a perma-

---

[23] Baron, *Social and Religious History of the Jews* (2nd edn), xvi. 52–77 and esp. p. 79. Note his comment on p. 89: 'In fact next to the Greek Orthodox and Uniate groups concentrated in the eastern parts of Poland, the Jews remained the principal dissenting minority; and because of their dispersion throughout the country and their economic vitality, they continued to play a role in Polish and Lithuanian affairs far in excess of their ratio in the population'.

[24] See Chapter 5, the section entitled 'The Influence Model Versus the Polysystem Model', for a more detailed discussion of this notion.

nent and integral part of the Polish social landscape.[25] Jews were embedded literally and figuratively in Poland.

In my own work I sought to explore the possibilities of this idea further, claiming that not only was there a distinctive, identifiable Polish Jewish cultural style with regard to such things as Jewish ritual observance and communal organization, but that phenomena such as the Jews' mental universe, aesthetic sensibilities, material culture, and political behaviour all indicate a profound identification with Polish categories and values. In Chapter 5 I will consider a telling example: the various myths that place Jews as kings, king-makers, or 'powers behind the throne' in Poland all signify that, for Jews in Poland, meaningful empowerment had to be legitimate in Polish terms. In general, Jews placed a premium on Polish modes of cultural validation.[26] In addition, Jews and Poles shared a common Western heritage (with roots in late antiquity) in connection with political, civic, economic, gender, scientific, and legal theory and practice, popular ideas about causation and medicine, and principles of theurgy.[27]

This response to the question of the nature of the Polish–Jewish cultural connection acknowledged that many components of Jewish culture were indeed unconnected to Polish culture, that on a conscious level there was unquestionably a significant degree of mutual antagonism and alienation, but that these coexisted with various shared cultural axioms and behaviours. As we have been taught by postmodern mentors, upon close inspection virtually all dichotomies dissolve. Life is rarely either/or. So the issue is not 'Is Jewish culture apart from or a part of Polish culture?', because both Polish and Jewish cultures were polysystems; open, dynamic, *heterogeneous* cultural systems. The origins of their elements are various and in constant interaction with each other in manifold ways at multiple intersections within the systems.[28]

[25] Hundert, *The Jews in a Polish Private Town*, 37–9.

[26] Chapter 5 at nn. 23–5. See also Rosman, 'Innovative Tradition', 525–8; cf. Bar-Itzhak, *Jewish Poland*; Hundert, *Jews in Poland–Lithuania in the Eighteenth Century*, 8–11.

[27] Rosman, 'Innovative Tradition', 528–30; see also Chapter 5 at nn. 26–30 below. This position was anticipated to some extent by Baer, who wrote of 'the everyday contact of Jewish and Christian society and the mutual ties between them in politics and economics, their sharing of various concepts and methods in the life of the community and the individual, the common root of their religious-historical heritage . . . the surprising affinities between the histories of their religious ideals' (*Studies in the History of the Jewish People*, ii. 238, as translated and quoted in Yuval, 'Yitzhak Baer', 79), and also by Goitein: see Libson, 'Hidden Worlds', 175–7.

[28] For more discussion of polysystem theory and reference, see Chapter 5 at n. 21.

Metaphorically speaking, Polish and Jewish cultures were at times separate, at times intertwined, at times embedded, and at times coincident with each other along broad bands. They each generated multiple vectors that did not need to be consistent with each other.[29] Contradictions (for example, the grant of autonomy to Jewish *kehalim* that were physically part of self-governing towns and cities) put stresses on each polysystem, stresses that could result in creative solutions (for example, multiple arrangements for adjudicating legal cases involving Jews), or, at the other end of the spectrum, frustrations (for example, over the lack of effective political control of Jews) resulting in violence. Non-Jewish consultations on health problems with Jewish *ba'alei shem* shamans or Jewish consultations with their Polish or Ukrainian equivalents posed no challenge to the rarefied discussions of the fine points of talmudic law carried out in the yeshivas far from the eye and understanding of Catholic canon lawyers.[30]

Was Jewish culture embedded? Yes. Was it autonomous? Also, yes. This fourth approach to the relationship between the two cultures appreciates the influences of one culture on another, but recognizes that not all is influence. One facet of the polysystemic quality of each culture is its own autonomous dynamic. Most importantly, the cultural interrelationship is fluid and requires description at various points of contact rather than one all-embracing characterization.[31]

Hybridity and the Jewish Problem

At this point, I shift to slippery ground by predicting the evolution of a fifth approach. I must emphasize that while this seems to be an outgrowth of the 'influence-is-the-answer' view discussed at the beginning of this chapter, it has not yet been articulated explicitly in the scholarly literature. However, judging from what is being written about Jewish cultural history in general and from certain adumbrations,[32] some specifically connected to

---

[29] Cf. Even-Zohar, *Polysystem Studies*: 'in order for a system to function uniformity need not be postulated' (p. 12).   [30] Rosman, *Founder of Hasidism*, 57–60.

[31] For a complement to this analysis see Chapter 5, the section entitled 'The Influence Model Versus the Polysystem Model'.

[32] For example, the monograph and the edited collections by Silberstein, *The Postzionism Debates*, *The Other in Jewish Thought and History*, and *Mapping Jewish Identities*, and especially his introductory and summary essays in those books, and the essays in Cheyette and Marcus (eds), *Modernity, Culture, and 'the Jew'*, discussed below. There are much more cautious treatments of this topic by Hundert, in 'On the Problem of Agency', 82–9, and *Jews in Poland-Lithuania in the Eighteenth Century*, pp. xv, 37–8.

Polish Jewry (although it is still too soon to say how these will turn out), the wave seems to be approaching. I am referring to the school of Jewish historical cultural analysis which, drawing either intuitively or consciously on postcolonial discourse, and in particular on the theories of Homi K. Bhabha,[33] sees traditional premodern Jewish communities as subaltern peoples, and Jewish culture everywhere, like the cultures of modern colonized peoples, as primarily hybrid with the culture of the majority. In other words, Jewish culture develops within frameworks laid down by the hegemonic culture, and is limited by it as well as trying sometimes to resist it.

According to my reading, Bhabha's work[34] is inseparable from the gestalt of modern colonialism and the issues it engenders, such as discrimination, racism, and slavery; intentional, planned, yet disavowed cultural domination; culture as political struggle; the threat that hybridity poses to the colonial power; postcolonial liberation and the contra-modernity or non-modernity that accompanies it; and the proposition that it is the postcolonial process that is the mainspring of *modern* culture.[35] While he does

---

Unlike many Jewish followers of Bhabha, Myers, *Re-Inventing the Jewish Past*, 10, 15–16, 21, 185, and *passim*, judiciously applied postcolonial theory to the Jewish case in what really was the Jewish decolonizing era, the late 19th and early 20th centuries, when the nationalist-oriented Jewish scholars he analysed were 'in search of historiographical empowerment' (p. 185), attempting to cultivate a genuinely national culture for the Jews that would help them perfect emancipation from their 'colonized' circumstances in Europe. In their insistence on European standards and methods, while scouring the past for 'authentic' (i.e. uninfluenced by outside forces) expressions of Jewish culture, these scholars did reflect a Bhabha-like doubling of the colonizing culture; they were continually 'in the process of being made' without ever feeling completely comfortable in a fully formed new identity. Yohanan Petrovsky is currently working on a study of 19th-century Ukrainian Jewry in what he posits as a colonial context.

[33] For example, the call for papers to a conference held in Venice in 2007, entitled 'Interstices: Jewish–Christian Cultures under Venetian Rule (14th–18th Century)' contained the following instruction: 'All speakers should bear in mind Homi K. Bhabha's concept of interstices—the overlap and displacement of domains of difference.' See also Cheyette and Marcus (eds), *Modernity, Culture, and 'the Jew'*, the foreword to which was written by Bhabha.

[34] References here are to Bhabha, *Location of Culture*; cf. Ashcroft, Griffiths, and Tiffin (eds), *Post-Colonial Studies Reader*; Prakash, 'Subaltern Studies as Postcolonial Criticism'; Mallon, 'The Promise and Dilemma of Subaltern Studies'; Cooper, 'Conflict and Connection'.

[35] Bhabha, *Location of Culture*, e.g. pp. 6, 34–5, 38, 55, 110–11, 114, 115, 152, 251.

make an occasional bow in the direction of history, Bhabha's analysis relies predominantly on modern literary, linguistic, and philosophical associations rather than historical ones.[36]

It is not simple to apply Bhabha's theories to early modern Jewish societies (as Bhabha's Jewish epigones are beginning to do), including that of Poland. These were dominated by forms of political-economic organization other than colonialism (early modern Poland was a version of feudalism) and characterized by different types of social structures (Poland was divided into estates, not castes, or colonizers and natives). The exercise of interpreting them from the perspective of colonial hybridity risks anachronism and reductionism.[37]

However, those who do attempt this task are willing to brave these problems, seemingly because of its powerful attraction on one key plane. Bhabha offered an antidote to the 'invented tradition' and 'imagined communities' critiques of nationalism and its cultures.[38] Not that he tried to resurrect the idea of homogeneous, authentic, essentialist, national culture, but he made it possible to pick up the shards the criticism left behind and conceptualize a new way to construe national culture: hybridity. As the Anderson, Gellner, and Hobsbawm triumvirate had asserted, there never is a pre-existent, homogeneous, authentic, essentialist national culture; but Bhabha pointed out that there is a continually evolving hybrid one. More importantly, Bhabha emphasized that cultural hybridity is not 'a third term that resolves the tension between two cultures . . . colonial hybridity is not a *problem* of genealogy or identity between two *different* cultures which can

[36] Bhabha repeatedly cites many fiction writers, such as Toni Morrison, Salman Rushdie, Derek Walcott, and Joseph Conrad, as well as thinkers and critics such as Jacques Derrida, Walter Benjamin, and especially Frantz Fanon.

[37] Cf. Segre, 'Colonization and Decolonization', on the dangers of 'thesis mongering, that is, mixing ideology, political fashion, and academic evidence; differences in historical experiences must continuously be borne in mind. The impact of Europe on the Jews, even on those of Eastern Europe, who kept a separate social identity much longer than did the Jews of the West, was totally different from the impact of European culture on African colonial societies' (p. 219). Segre (ibid. 219, 231 n. 6) points out that comparisons of Jews and blacks are already to be found in the classic works on colonialism of Frantz Fanon and Albert Memmi.

[38] Bhabha, *Location of Culture*, e.g. pp. 5–6, 37, 149, 152, 172–3; see Chapter 1 above on the by now standard treatments of Hobsbawm and Ranger (eds), *Invented Traditions*, Anderson, *Imagined Communities*, and Gellner, *Nations and Nationalism*.

then be resolved as an issue of cultural relativism'.[39] The hybrid is not a compromise between cultures, but a product of domination and discrimination. It is something new, related to the group's pre-colonial history only by, what I would call, a palimpsest.

For our purposes, the first implication of this conception is that—as opposed to the Bałaban–Schiper school, for example—Jewish culture is always in a hierarchical relationship with the culture of the Other, with the Jewish in the inferior position. It is always, even when resisting and subverting the hegemonic culture, both embedded and indebted, owing its evolution primarily to energy supplied by the encounter with the hegemony.

A second implication is that Jewish culture is always a *local* phenomenon. In terms of content, there is no universal, essential, core, authentic, autonomous Jewish culture that informed Jewish life everywhere and that always stood in independent relationship to the hegemonic culture of any given place.[40] The presumption is that there is, rather, a plurality of Jewish cultures, each of which is an aspect of its place of origin—Spain, Poland, Yemen—not of some putative Jewish culture; and certainly more linked to its locale than to other Jewish communities, either contemporaneously or through history. The common Jewishness of these communities tends to be reduced to artefacts of religion.

In short, what animates Jewish culture is the dynamic interplay of minority and majority in each particular place; not vestiges, such as food restrictions or sexual practices that for unexplained reasons have survived in one variation or another over the ages. Probe virtually any aspect of a given Jewish culture and you will find some practice, belief, or value of the majority at its root. Jewish culture is so embedded in the majority culture that it is of a piece with it, distinguished, perhaps, as a subculture coloured by its religious difference. It certainly cannot be understood except in terms of the foundation non-Jewish culture that both helps to unleash its vital forces and subordinates it. Furthermore, being always a locally generated hybrid, it is so pluralist and protean that it defies definition.

Such an approach is implied in Laurence J. Silberstein's 'anti-essentialist, constructivist approach to Jewish identity' (and, by the same token, to

[39] Bhabha, *Location of Culture*, 113–14; see also e.g. pp. 5, 35–6, 38, 54–5, 58, 113–14, 126, 162–3, 172–3, 177, 224, 251.

[40] Cf. Mendes-Flohr, *Divided Passions*, 56–9; Israel, *European Jewry in the Age of Mercantilism*, 31, 33, 71, 184; Bonfil, *Jewish Life in Renaissance Italy*, esp. pp. xi, 3, 103, 104, 108–9, 110, 123, 151–2, 284.

Jewish culture) which opposes the idea of the 'existence of a core, authentic, or essential "Jewish self"' . . . what all Jews, as bearers of a shared history, are said to share in common'. Instead, Silberstein asserted 'the need for new, non-essentialist definitions of Jewish identity . . . that emphasize process over product, multiplicity over unity, and becoming rather than being . . . to reconfigure such essentially contested terms like *Jew, Judaism,* and *Jewish* into a site of "permanent openness and resignifiability" [quoting Judith Butler]'. Silberstein made it very clear that the motivation and objective of this exercise was to 'provide openings for contemporary Jews wishing to free themselves from the prevailing normalizing discourses and develop alternate modes of Jewish becoming' as well as to reveal 'power relations within the Jewish community and between Jews and others, particularly Palestinians', and to promote 'efforts to reevaluate and reconfigure these relations'.[41]

So Silberstein's eye was on the needs he perceived in the present and the future, but his approach also had undeniable implications for the study of the past. Jewish identity and culture have always been contested and under construction to some extent; certainly they have always been in an active relationship with the hegemonic culture. If that means, however, that they have no fixed content whatsoever, no defining—yes, I'll say it—*essential* characteristics, how can we identify what in the past is properly the object of the study of Jewish history. If anything can be Jewish, then is anything not Jewish, or is nothing Jewish?[42]

Silberstein not only recognized this problem,[43] but in another context he argued for a different approach in order to circumvent it. In his book on post-Zionism he contended that, like Jewish identity and culture, Zionism was 'essentially contested'. Yet, in order to define Zionism as a target for attack, he suggested that 'it is possible to identify within its spaces shared premises that all who identify with it accept'. He then proceeded to explore what these might be.[44] If this is the case, why can it not be true of Jewish identity and Jewish culture as well? Rather than dichotomize

[41] Silberstein (ed.), *Mapping Jewish Identities,* 2–3, 8–9, 13–14.

[42] Cf. the Introduction to this book on the problem of constructivism vs. essentialism and the question I asked there: if Jewish can be everything, is it anything? This controversy is in some ways a recycling of the polemics surrounding Scholem's position, expressed in *Sabbatai Sevi,* denying that there is 'a well-defined and unvarying "essence" of Judaism' (p. xi). See Maciejko, 'Gershom Scholem's Dialectic of Jewish History'.

[43] Silberstein (ed.), *Mapping Jewish Identities,* 13.

[44] Silberstein, *Postzionism Debates,* 18–24; quotation from p. 21.

essentialist versus constructed definitions, would it not be more useful to recognize that phenomena such as identity and culture have both constructed (even hybrid) *and* essential components?

Consider Robert Bonfil's summary of the relationship between Italian Jewish culture—often seen to be the most 'embedded and indebted' of Jewish subcultures—and Italian culture:

> it is also possible to read the history of the Jews of the Renaissance in a modern perspective—that of the complex question of the definition of an identity in the context of a nascent awareness of the Self as organically interrelated with the Other, *without for all that being confused with the Other, and still less annihilated by it.* [emphasis added]

Like others, Bonfil also recognized that the encounter with the culture of the Other was an important source of Jewish cultural creativity. As opposed to the hybridity construct, however, he stressed that the Other's culture was filtered and transformed by a strong, vital, self-conscious, and lasting Jewish culture with at least a partially positive and fixed content.[45]

The hybridity construct holds that the key factor is not the people, the Jews—whom, according to Mendes-Flohr, the philosopher Franz Rosenzweig characterized as mastering and melding 'an ensemble of cultures'[46]—but a deterministic cause-and-effect mode. Human choices are, if not preordained, then pushed along certain vectors by the overriding processes of initial embedding followed by hybridization. This proposition is latent in many of the chapters of the award-winning cultural history of the Jews edited by David Biale, *Cultures of the Jews*, and, emblematically, in the plural of its title. As one of the authors of *Cultures of the Jews* I can testify that the 's' in 'Cultures' was the subject of a lively email debate when it was proposed, with the authors deeply divided on the issue.[47] The pros

---

[45] Bonfil, *Jewish Life in Renaissance Italy*, 115, 116, 151, 152; quotation from p. 286. Other scholars who have grappled with this problem are Marcus, *Rituals of Childhood*, 4, 8–13; Biale, in his preface to *Cultures of the Jews*, p. xix; Hundert, *Jews in Poland–Lithuania in the Eighteenth Century*, see especially the introduction and afterword; Sharot, 'Religious Syncretism and Religious Distinctiveness', esp. pp. 23–5; Satlow, 'Beyond Influence'.

[46] Mendes-Flohr, 'The Jew as Cosmopolitan', in *Divided Passions*, 420.

[47] It is instructive to take note of the attempt by Biale, in *Cultures of the Jews*, to coordinate the two positions on this issue: 'Both high literary culture and material culture, from the way Jews dressed to the way they looked and behaved, from their natural landscapes to the architecture of their homes and communal institutions, differed radically from period to period and from place to place. Culture would appear to be the domain

contended that it was cardinal to emphasize that Jewishness was always pluralistic and multivocal. The cons insisted that, by denying the existence of a common Jewish culture at some basic level, the book was denying the existence of a Jewish collective identity and negating the legitimacy of the entire project; for what might define such a collective except its shared culture? As Moshe Idel has proposed:

After all what has unified the disparate Jewish communities was mainly their common cultural heritage, which not only preserved the spiritual specificity of a certain community in a different religious and cultural environment, but also safe-guarded a degree of unity between all remote communities. No less characteristic of Judaism than its cosmopolitanism is its conservatism, considered as another, complementary and basic feature of Jewish culture. If their relative openness has facilitated the adjustment of some Jews to new environments, conservatism has enabled them to maintain and elaborate upon their peculiar culture.[48]

To state the problem slightly differently, if the plurality of Jewish cultures is assumed, one is left with the question of how each separate culture is to be recognized as indeed 'Jewish'. What common characteristics define them as part of that cultural category?

Many have tried to tackle this intractable problem.[49] As one of the 'cons' in the 'Cultures of the Jews' controversy, I dare to suggest, after the jetti-son of the teleology and rigid essentialism of the nationalist approach, how we can still attempt to define a continuing Jewish culture, the variants of which are interlinked by more than the fact that they responded to similar initial categories (by that standard one might plausibly argue that Christianity and Islam are 'Jewish' cultures as well). Such a definition would contain not only ideas and beliefs of the culture about itself, but also

---

of the plural: we might speak of Jewish cultures instead of culture in the singular. And, yet, such a definition would be missing a crucial aspect of Jewish culture: the continu-ity of both textual and folk traditions throughout Jewish history and throughout the many lands inhabited by Jews . . . The Jews throughout the ages *believed* themselves to have a common national biography and a common culture. These beliefs are also an integral part of the history of Jewish culture . . . We can speak of a dialectic between, on the one hand, the *idea* of one Jewish people and of a unified Jewish culture, and, on the other, the history of multiple communities and cultures . . . On both the elite and popu-lar levels, then, the Jewish people were, at once, one *and* diverse' (pp. xxiv–xxv). Cf. Baron, 'Problems of Jewish Identity, 64–5.

[48] Idel, 'Subversive Catalysts', 63–4.

[49] See e.g. the discussions surveyed by Silberstein, in *Postzionism Debates*, 35–45, and Shmueli, in *Seven Jewish Cultures*, 3–7, 12–15.

a constellation of behavioural elements which show up in different numbers, in different permutations, and in combination with elements of other
constellations in each era and location. A constellation of this type might be
termed a 'disjunctive description' of Jewish culture, where all of the elements of the constellation are never present simultaneously in any given
historical example of Jewish culture, but where varying combinations of
them always are. Taking a similar tack, and borrowing from biology,
Jonathan Z. Smith has called this a 'polythetic' taxonomy, in which 'a class
is defined as consisting of a set of properties, each individual member of the
class to possess "a large (but unspecified) number" of these properties, with
each property to be possessed by "a large number" of individuals in the
class, but no single property to be possessed by every member of the class'.[50]
We might argue that the combination of these 'class specific' properties
with new constructions—the challenge posed to them by new contestations, their conflict-filled development in response to new historical circumstances—constitute the most significant aspect of Jewish cultural
hybridization.[51] The Jewish cultural constellation is expressed in myriad
ways, yet maintains a fundamental identifiability. Once a cultural manifestation loses such identifiability, we are justified in excluding it from the
Jewish class. To retain meaning, Jewish culture, while highly variegated,
malleable, and multi-faceted, cannot be infinitely protean. As Jonathan
Webber has formulated it:

a *disinterested* inclusive view that makes no attempt to specify the normatively
essential within the full range of all that is happening in the Jewish world may well
be valid and interesting as an analytic exercise in social description—but perhaps
it reflects a certain moral indifference and lack of genuine concern to develop
more of a global view of Jewish destiny. After all, even though Jews have always
thought of their identities as locally based, and put together some notion of a
community in order to give that identity some flesh and bones, nevertheless at
the same time there was another idea standing behind it—the concept of *kelal yisra'el*, the belief in the ultimate unity of the Jewish people despite all its disparate

[50] Jonathan Smith, *Imagining Religion*, 4–8, 18; cf. Beckner, *Biological Way of
Thought*. However, while I believe that such an approach, allowing for a limited variety,
can lend a measure of stability to the concept of Jewish culture, Smith seems to maintain the opposite (*Imagining Religion*, 14). Compare the concept of a polythetic
definition of Judaism with Michael Meyer's metaphor of the rope ('In a rope few if any
strands run fully from one end to the other yet the rope itself does not pull apart'), *Ideas
of Jewish History*, 40–1.

[51] Cf. Teller, 'Hasidism and the Challenge of Geography', 7.

manifestations in time and space. Without this overriding concept of *kelal yisra'el* and a long view of the spiritual requirements of Jewish survival, is there not a danger in seeing the diversity of the contemporary Jewish experience as being little more than of exotic, ethnological, or antiquarian curiosity?' One might argue, analogously, that if we are interested in portraying a meaningful representation of the Jewish experience through history that 'exotic ethnological curiosities' should be rightfully excluded, or at least demoted to the footnotes.[52]

In other words, unity despite disparity—or, perhaps, beyond disparity.

What might be the elements, then, in this historical Jewish cultural constellation? This is a subject for a full-scale research project, but we can tentatively suggest beginning with Baron's common descent, common history, common faith, common fate; Biale's traditions, ideas and beliefs; Shaye Cohen's intra-Jewish association and ritual sancta; Jacob Neusner's group solidarity and Jewish religion; Diaspora experience and minority status; and variations on Mendes-Flohr's seven Cs.[53]

To return to the issue of applying hybridity to the Jewish case, a historical example that at first glance appears appropriate as an illustration of hybridity is the phenomenon of 'the Men of the Nation', that is, the Portuguese crypto-Jews and their descendants who underwent rejudaization to one degree or another. These people developed an ethnic identity that both doubled and subverted the hegemonic culture and accompanying persecution—both physical and cultural—which they experienced in the Iberian peninsula. The catch is that they did this largely *after* their emigration, once their contact with the hegemonic Iberian culture was reduced to a minimum or severed completely. Moreover, since their 'native culture' was fundamentally non-Jewish, they might be seen as constructing a *hybrid with Jewish culture* at the same time as they were doing so with respect to Iberian culture.[54]

---

[52] Webber (ed.), *Jewish Identities*, 25–6; see also pp. 77–8.

[53] Baron, *History and Jewish Historians*, 12–13, 21–2; Biale (ed.), *Cultures of the Jews*, pp. xxiv–xxv (see n. 46 above); Shaye Cohen, '"Those who say they are Jews and are not"', 1–45, esp. pp. 26–35 (cf. Berkovitz, *Rites and Passages*, the beginning sections of chs 3 and 9). See also the discussions in Cheyette and Marcus (eds), *Modernity, Culture, and 'the Jew'*, and Neusner, below, n. 65. It might be interesting to compare the definitions of Jewish culture proffered by historians who are themselves personally committed to halakhah and those who are not. The question of the problematics of cultural definition is not unique to the Jewish case; see Porter, 'Is the Pope Catholic?'.

[54] Bodian, *Hebrews of the Portuguese Nation*, esp. pp. 20, 77–9, 85–95; and see n. 12 above.

In writing on Poland, the subject that keeps recurring as a candidate for illustrating the idea of Jewish hybridity with the hegemonic culture is hasidism. Beginning with Torsten Ysander in the 1930s, there have been several (thus far wholly unsuccessful) attempts to link hasidism to contemporary Russian Orthodox schismatic sects.[55] Anticipating the future, however, and assuming that there will be numerous attempts to apply at least parts of hybridity theory to Jewish history, I would suggest that hybridity theory can be understood somewhat differently from the way I think it is being brought to bear on the Jewish case in lectures and essays (see below). There can be hybridity that is combination without hierarchy. There can be hybridity of one culture with multiple other cultures. Hybridity is not always at work in every context. Therefore I propose a few caveats to be considered by those preparing to hike the hybridity trail.

First, I don't think we should assume that, to the extent to which there is some kind of partial cultural hybridity in the context of the pre-colonial period, it must always be a function of political subordination and power relationships. For example, hybridity can be 'Western', resulting from the adoption of established cultural models from other places that had no political claim on the Jews. Here I would again call attention to the Western heritage common to Jews and Poles referred to previously.[56] Second, hybridity may be with other Jewish communities. For example, if Israel, Elbaum, Ruderman, and others were correct that the sixteenth and seventeenth centuries marked a high point of Jewish intercommunal cultural cohesion, then why was it not hybridity with Sephardi Jewry that led the Polish Jews to attempt to co-ordinate, compete, or—if the Sephardim be the Jewish cultural hegemons and the Ashkenazim the Jewish subalterns of the era—to mimic and double them in hybrid fashion?[57] In a different vein, as intimated above, might the Jewish culture amalgamated with Portuguese ethnicity, developed by the 'Hebrews of the Portuguese nation' in Amsterdam, be considered

[55] Ysander, *Studien zum B'estschen Hasidismus*. For discussion of this issue, see Rosman, *Founder of Hasidism*, 56–60; Hundert, *Jews in Poland–Lithuania in the Eighteenth Century*, 176–9.

[56] See above at n. 27; Hundert, *Jews in Poland–Lithuania in the Eighteenth Century*, 176–7.

[57] For an example as late as the 18th century of Sephardi claims to superiority over Ashkenazim, see Isaac de Pinto, *Apologie pour la nation juive* . . . (Amsterdam, 1762), translated and excerpted in Mendes-Flohr and Reinharz, *The Jew in the Modern World*, 253–5. Cf. Bodian, *Hebrews of the Portuguese Nation*, 125–31, 133, 158, 195–6 n. 154; Schorsch, 'Myth of Sephardic Supremacy'.

hybrid with 'old Sephardi' or hegemonic rabbinic Jewish culture of the time?[58] Third, as Hundert has already observed, hybridity, or what he called the 'dialectical relationship between Jews and surrounding cultures', might be selectively operative. He argued that with regard to Polish Jewry it applied to economic and political processes, but much less to culture.[59]

If hybridity is to be added to the arsenal of Jewish cultural interpretation, it must be done with due diligence. Scholars may not assume that hybridity is a given that can serve as a standard explanatory framework for virtually any cultural phenomenon. Rather, they should be required to prove its presence in each separate historical circumstance, and to carefully delineate how it functions as a factor and what its limits are.

A possible example is the phenomenon of roughly simultaneous projects of codification of law in the sixteenth century in Europe in general, in Poland, in the Polish Jewish community and among Sephardi Jewry. Research here might offer an instructive example of how codification of the law shows the degree to which these were independent and interdependent, how much they impinged upon each other and how much they were all responding to common impetuses. In other words, this might serve as a test case for the applicability of hybridity theory to the Jewish sphere, testing as well the three caveats I have proposed.[60]

Which Metahistory to Choose?

It does not require much effort to connect each of these five approaches to Jewish cultural history in Poland to more general metahistories which they

---

[58] Bodian, *Hebrews of the Portuguese Nation*, 85–95, 96–131, 152–6; and above at n. 12. There are other examples of early modern intra-Jewish cultural hybridity, such as the Jewish communities in Italy, Safed, and Istanbul.

[59] Hundert, 'On the Problem of Agency in Eighteenth-Century Jewish Society', 89.

[60] See Joseph Davis, 'The Reception of the *Shulhan 'Arukh*', 252–3, and literature cited there, and, in addition, the following. On Polish codification (and its possible links to more general European activity), Lowmianski, *Historia Polski*, vol. i, pt 2, pp. 370–7; Bardach (ed.), *Historia państwa i prawa*, ii. 193–5; Uruszczak, *Próba kodyfikacji prawa polskiego*, 11–70; Voisé, *Andrzej Frycz Modrzewski*, 8, 33–6, 51, 91, 231, 258. On general European codification, see Bellomo, *The Common Legal Past of Europe*, 206, 215–16, 223, 224; Robinson, Fergus, and Gordon, *European Legal History*; Kelly, *A Short History of Western Legal Theory*, 180; Manfredini, 'Codes and Jurists', 17–18. On Sephardi and Polish Jewish codification, see Tchernowitz, *History of the Jewish Codes* (Heb.), iii. 1–191; Twersky, 'The Shulhan 'Aruk'; Ginzberg, *On Jewish Law and Lore*, 180–4; Shulvass, *Jewish Culture in Eastern Europe*, 52–70, 120–2; Reiner, 'The Ashkenazi Elite at the Beginning of the Modern Era', 93–8; id., 'Urban Jewish Community' (Heb.), 13–24.

appear to represent and reinforce. In describing the Polish case historians were and are also making larger claims about the nature of Jewish history and Jewish existence. For the Polish Jewish historians who reached their prime between the world wars the objective was, in a sense, Warsaw: to demonstrate how deeply rooted the Jews were in Poland. They aimed both to give Jews pride and confidence in their rightful claim to Polish citizenship combined with Jewish national consciousness, and to counter antisemitic critics who called for a Polish Poland and for Jews to go to Palestine. As Schiper put it, the historian's task was to 'forge a sword for battle out of knowledge'.[61] Their metahistory was that Jews, while possessing their own national culture and not being ethnically Polish, were still Polish natives whose made-in-Poland culture gave them legitimacy and the right to see themselves as not just in Poland but of it, and the prerogative to make demands upon government and society.[62]

For the nationalist portrayal of Polish Jewish culture it was the nation and its culture fashioned in the once and future capital of Jerusalem that Polish Jewry was cultivating and preparing for the return to Zion. This explains the tremendous emphasis by nationalists on the institutions of Polish Jewish autonomy, and on the legal and literary legacy of Polish Jewry. Autonomy proved that Jews were politically adept long after their formal state was dissolved and this political tradition could easily be applied in establishing a new Jewish political entity. Law codes and elite literature provided ready-made, genuinely Jewish civic culture and elite culture, which could serve as the foundation for a renewal of national collective life. Polish Jews were a key component of an always existing Jewish nation that—as Polish Jewry itself demonstrated—possessed virtually all of the accoutrements of nationhood except territoriality. When the time came to move to the territory, Polish Jewry would be ready to do its part in reconstituting the Jewish nation.

The two-foci approach to Jewish cultural history set its sights, I think, on New York. It assured Jews and non-Jews alike that Jews could be both Jewish and American without jeopardizing either identity. Jewish life in the Diaspora continues because the internal focus of the metaphorical historical ellipse is ever present; but the external focus will always lead Jews to accommodate themselves to the larger environment. The two foci working

---

[61] Quoted in Litman, *The Economic Role of Jews*, 233, from *Księga jubileuszowa . . . Bałabana*, 28–9.   [62] Litman, *The Economic Role of Jews*, 232–5, 251, and *passim*.

together promise not contradiction, but mutual enrichment. Attending synagogue and rooting for the Yankees can be two sides of the same coin. As already observed, Jews have much experience at mastering an ensemble of cultures. Jewish culture has had an unlimited capacity to expand and embrace what is new, while remaining true to itself.[63]

The fourth approach, positing that, despite obvious differences, on the level of deep structures there is shared meaning among contiguous groups, seems best suited to a belief in moderate, liberal, individualist, Western-style moderate multiculturalism as one might find espoused, even if not practised, in many northern European capitals. This approach recognizes that any group, the Jews included, has the right to define an identity for itself that results from a process of recombining the strands of cultural DNA that it has acquired in various ways. The origin of the strands, or metaphorical genotype, is not important; their recombinance and its result-ant phenotype are. Moreover, within each group's cultural DNA are elements that it has in common with all the other groups with which it also shares a territory, a government, and a society. So everyone has a right to a seat at the table, everyone has something to bring to the table that the others can respect, but everyone can also be trusted not to overturn the table. This might be a viable strategy for holding together the culturally ever more variegated countries of the Western world, including Israel, where the disaffections and dissonances among constituent groups are all too obvious, while unifying factors seem to be fading away.[64]

The fifth approach, Jewish culture as a locally evolved hybrid, has its roots, I believe, in Sartre's denial of any positive content to Jewishness.[65] Thirty years later, Jacob Neusner made the implications of Sartre's position explicit with his rejection of what he termed the 'peoplehood-and-history theory of Jewish historiography'. Along with this he opposed the idea that 'a single, clearly defined entity, "the Jewish people"', has produced what he caricatured as 'a unitary and linear history, "Jewish history"', which extends back to the time of Abraham'. For him there was in fact no 'Jewish history', but only 'the history of Judaism'.[66] The latest twist on this I hear in the cor-ridors is 'not Jewish history, but history of the Jews', or alternatively

[63] Cf. Teller, 'Hasidism and the Challenge of Geography', 7.

[64] On the Jews and multiculturalism, see Chapter 4, and for further development of the DNA metaphor, see Chapter 5 at n. 30.   [65] Chapter 1 at nn. 36–8.

[66] Neusner, *History of the Jewish People*, and 'Ideas of Jewish History', 214; cf. discus-sion about Neusner's denial of Jewish history in Chapter 1. As mentioned in Chapter 1, n. 49, Neusner was not consistent in this denial.

'history of Jews'. (If, however, *'the* Jews' don't exist, can 'Jews'?) What we should be writing about is individual Jewish communities in the only context that had meaningful historical reality; and that context is as an integral component of whatever larger society they belonged to.

As discussed in Chapter 1, Neusner—taking a page from Sartre, and anticipating Silberstein—asserted that there is no canonical definition of the traits that define Jews and Jewishness; there is no fixed content to Jewish culture, and Jewish religion is always historicizable. With regard to metahistory this premise, touting a haphazard and absolute Jewish pluralism, facilitates dissociation from what is, to some, a now much more than embarrassing, or merely politically incorrect, Jewish nationalism and, especially, Zionism, while confirming the primacy of the Diaspora experience in the history of the Jews. It also undermines Orthodox triumphalist religious claims to be *the* loyal and true bearers of Jewish heritage, and reaffirms the *essential* variety and multivocality of the Jewish experience.

Some of Neusner's successors have taken his approach to its logical conclusion, as represented by a conference and book devoted to the subject of 'Modernity, Culture and "the Jew" ',[67] which put the last term in quotation marks as a sign of the lack of any determinate content to Jewishness. The editors, however, filled the vacuum caused by this lack with the processes that create the vacuum; what they called the creative disruptiveness and unfixity of Jewishness.[68] For them, the value of Jewish history is that while in all of their diasporas they have undoubtedly been part of the larger civilizations that incorporated them, the Jews always challenged and discomfited those civilizations.[69] In addition, the Jews confound the conventional ways of studying and constructing those civilizations. The value of studying Jewish history and culture is that they 'are able to disrupt and to cross

---

[67] Cheyette and Marcus (eds), *Modernity, Culture, and 'the Jew'*. Strictly speaking, this book treats the modern period and not the early modern period which is my primary subject here. However, just as colonial and postcolonial discourse in general have been imposed on the historiography of the early modern period in various contexts, so will the positions of the authors of *Modernity, Culture and 'the Jew'* probably be transposed to the earlier period. Be that as it may, my critique takes the book as it stands.

[68] Ibid., p. x. Note the depiction and criticism of the position I am advocating penned by Paul Gilroy in his afterword to Cheyette and Marcus (eds), *Modernity, Culture, and 'the Jew'*, 296.

[69] e.g. ibid. 3, 9–10, 287–8. This appears to be an elaboration of a view propounded by Steiner in 'Season in Hell' some thirty years earlier.

received gendered, sexual and racial boundaries . . . the specificity and incongruity of Jewish history and culture will both encourage the critique of an empty western universality and help to break down, on all sides, an increasingly untenable and divisive identity politics'.[70] Evidently Jews are valuable to the extent that they problematize and complicate political and cultural discourse.[71]

The foreword to *Culture, Modernity and 'the Jew'*, written by Homi K. Bhabha himself, catches the spirit of the enterprise when he states:

The 'Jew' *stands for* [emphasis added] that experience of a lethal modernity, shared by the histories of slavery and colonialism, where the racist desire for supremacy and domination turns the ideas of progress into a *danse macabre*. In the half-century since the Shoah, we have had to stand too often with, or in the place of, 'the Jew', taking a stance against the spread of xenophobic nationalism . . . The editors urge their collaborators to represent the 'present history of the Shoah' in the voices of the excluded, written from the margins.[72]

The Jew, representative par excellence of diaspora, of alterity, of dissident culture, of discrimination and exclusion, can serve as the basis 'to build bridges across supposedly different histories of diaspora'.[73] The Jew is the perfect metaphor or allegory for telling the story of what is wrong with modern civilization. The Torah the Jews have to offer the world comes not from Zion but from the location of the ultimate Diaspora experience, Auschwitz.[74]

---

[70] Cheyette and Marcus (eds), *Modernity, Culture, and 'the Jew'*, 2; see also pp. x, 3, 12, 17, 18, 294–6, and *passim*. [71] See Chapter 4 on the 'Jew as trope'.

[72] Cheyette and Marcus (eds), *Modernity, Culture, and 'the Jew'*, pp. xv–xvi, xx.

[73] Ibid. 2; cf. 285–8, 290–1, 294, 295.

[74] e.g. ibid.: 'It is precisely the fraught interrelationship between "the Jew" as metaphor and Jews as historical agents that this collection addresses' (p. x). While many of the writers in the book subscribe to the approach of Jew as trope, allegory or metaphor, it is partially protested against in Silverman's article, 'Re-figuring "the Jew" in France', 197–207; although even he could not refrain from retaining the quotation marks: 'conceiving of "the Jew" neither simply as an open-ended signifier nor as an unproblematic signified but as a real hybrid between the two, a "Jew" in inverted commas but with an upper-case "J" ' (p. 205). For the importance of Auschwitz in promoting interest in Jewish studies, see Richmond, 'The Jews in Medieval England', 1, 3. For 'postmodern' interpretation of the significance of Jewish Diaspora, see D. Boyarin and J. Boyarin, 'Diaspora'; Cesarani, 'Dynamics of Diaspora'; Band, 'The New Diasporism and the Old Diaspora'.

Why Jewish Studies?

The approaches to Jewish cultural history described in this chapter not only have implications for the study of that subject and for its practitioners' larger metahistories, but they can also determine the direction, content, and style of Jewish studies today. My critical evaluation of hybridity should not obfuscate my belief that a syncretistic, pluralistic, non-dogmatic view of culture has something to offer. That said, in my view Jewish studies is at a crossroads. It can, like the hybrid approach of *Modernity, Culture and 'the Jew'*, see the object of its study, Jewish culture, as a subset, appendage, or example of something else that has the potential to shed much light on that entity, or even go a step further, as did the editors of *Modernity, Culture and 'the Jew'*, and regard the most valuable aspect of the Jewish experience to be its utility as an allegory for the circumstances of other peoples and their cultures. To me, this is a postmodern version of the venerable, but discredited, 'contribution approach' to Jewish history.[75] If, however, this be the justification for its study, the usefulness of Jewish studies will soon be exhausted and interest in it will quickly run its course. Soon, more apt examples will be found and more cogent allegories developed. Moreover, this instrumentalist view of Jewish studies implies that it does not require a profound, rigorous, integrated knowledge of the components of Jewish culture, since they are essentially illustrations of something more important, and that larger something is more important to master.

In my opinion, the academic study of Jewish culture should not be primarily instrumentalist, whether for the sake of better understanding other cultures (although such understanding will certainly be a by-product of this study, just as it can be of the study of any particular culture), or for the sake of constructing or reinforcing a contemporary Jewish identity (the exploration of which is beyond the scope of this book). There lies the path to a modern kind of apologetics, seeking to please the dons of the hegemonic culture or of the organized Jewish community, and ultimately to irrelevancy as standards and intellectual tastes shift.

While certainly having the potential to contribute to other fields of knowledge, Jewish studies in universities should be engaged in, first of all, on the basis of the belief that Jewish culture in all of its manifestations has an intrinsic value that requires no justification other than its existence as a constituent part of human culture, equal to all the other constituents and

---

[75] This thesis will be developed in Chapter 4.

therefore deserving of consideration on its own terms, with the knowledge and by the methods most appropriate to unlocking its secrets. When, beginning in the 1960s, Jewish studies programmes at universities multiplied exponentially, both its practitioners and the universities that established the programmes seemed to agree that this, indeed, was the explicit logic for incorporating the subject in the academic curriculum in a serious way. There was also an esoteric objective. As David Biale has phrased it, 'the integration of Jewish Studies into the humanities symbolized the integration of Jews into American society'[76] for the Jews; while for the universities it probably represented a significant fundraising opportunity. The president of Yale, A. Bartlett Giamatti, intimated both of these rationales in his remarks concerning that university's Jewish studies programme:

Ours is a program meant to affirm throughout the humanities that essential third strand in our common culture, the strand that, with classical antiquity and Christianity, made our world, and to build links back to history, across intellectual disciplines, between undergraduates and graduate students, between the University and the Jewish community locally, nationally and internationally.[77]

The esoteric agenda is probably still with us. However with respect to the exoteric agenda, a change occurred once it became difficult to speak of 'our common culture' and 'our world' when the climate shifted from pluralist to multicultural, and from modern to postmodern. This change and its context in Jewish history are the subject of the next chapter.

[76] Biale, 'Between Polemics and Apologetics', 176.
[77] As quoted in Marcus, 'Judaic Studies', 142.

FOUR

The Jewish Contribution to (Multicultural) Civilization

۞

A S A PERENNIAL minority the Jews seem always to need to fit in. One way to do this is to contribute, and to be seen to contribute, to the larger society, culture, and civilization in a meaningful way. The subject of 'the Jewish contribution to civilization', however, is usually thought of as referring to a certain type of Jewish apologetic rejoinder to modern anti-semitism's denial of the possibility or reality of full integration of Jews into Western societies from the late nineteenth to the mid-twentieth centuries, and particularly after the rise of the Nazis to power in Germany.[1] This kind of apologetic concentrated on describing how Jews contributed to or bene-fited the societies in which they lived, or humankind in general. The genre was common enough for the United States Library of Congress to coin the subject headings 'Jews: Contribution to Civilization' and 'Civilization: Jewish Influences'.

It is noteworthy that this 'contribution discourse' appeared *after* the for-mal success of the Jewish political emancipation project, and the incubation of a high degree of Jewish acculturation to general European values and lifestyles. It was a sign of Jewish unease, frustration, and fear in the face of indicators that, despite Jews' 'good faith' efforts to conform to the legal, social, and cultural demands of the emancipating societies, and notwith-standing legal guarantees of civil and political equality, their integration was in reality but partial, contingent, tenuous, and even revocable. The persistence of active antisemitism and unofficial or informal barriers to complete Jewish participation in social, cultural, and economic endeavours

---

[1] One can find Jewish authors touting Jewish contributions to the benefit of the world in the ancient and medieval periods as well; but, as a genre, literature of this type appears to be a modern phenomenon (see n. 2). In fact there are still popular books appearing in this genre, e.g. Cahill, *Gifts of the Jews*. Other minority groups, such as African Americans, have also detailed their contributions to general society as a means of legitimizing their membership in it; see Novick, *That Noble Dream*, 480.

prompted Jews to attempt to demonstrate their worthiness to qualify as fully fledged members of society. Analysis of their contributions would serve this cause. At least it could bolster Jewish self-confidence and stiffen Jews' resolve in continuing their struggle for acceptance. It was paramount that Jews themselves should have a sense of their own value and importance if they were to morally convince or legally coerce others to recognize finally that they really belonged.

Classic Contribution Discourse

The best-known examples of the genre of classic contribution discourse are Joseph Jacobs's *Jewish Contributions to Civilization: An Estimate* and Cecil Roth's *The Jewish Contribution to Civilization*.[2] Neither was reticent about announcing his book's objective. Writing during the First World War, Jacobs subtitled his introduction 'The Higher Anti-Semitism', and spent most of it reviewing the history of antisemitism, especially in its modern racist guise. Jacobs explained his book's purpose thus:

such an estimate of contemporary contributions to the world's progress is an essential part of the Jewish defence. Against the vague anti-Semitic denunciations of Jewish characteristics, which are mainly the results of prejudice and, in any case, cannot be checked or measured, we can here set down the definite results of Jewish achievement. We can even go further and, by the aid of modern statistical science . . . arrive at some measurable comparison between the output of Jewish ability and that of others.[3]

Roth also made the anti-antisemitism objective of his book very clear:

This work is intended as a contribution towards the settlement of a discussion of long standing, which is now once again to the fore. It is alleged by modern Anti-semites . . . that the Jew is essentially a middleman, who has produced nothing; that he is an alien excrescence on European life: and that the influence which he has had on western culture, during the past two thousand years, has been entirely negative, if not deleterious. Such a criticism demands an analysis based not on

---

[2] Many books and booklets of a widely varying nature have been published with similar titles, e.g. Stonehill (ed.), *The Jewish Contribution to Civilization*; Laski, *The Jewish Contribution to Western Civilization*; Feldman, *Contributions of Judaism to Modern Society*; Bevan and Singer (eds), *The Legacy of Israel*; Kirschstein, *The Jew*; Roback, *Jewish Influence in Modern Thought*; Runes, *The Hebrew Impact on Western Civilization*; Maybaum, *Synagogue and Society*.

[3] Jacobs, *Jewish Contributions to Civilization*, 50.

theory but on fact . . . I am making no attempt to evaluate the Jewish genius, or even to decide whether such a thing exists . . . I have tried to assemble and set down in this volume a representative selection (at least) of the contributions made to the civilization, the culture and the amenities of the western world by persons of Jewish lineage.[4]

Whereas Jacobs and Roth approached the subject with at least a nod to critical sophistication, other works were more crass; for example, counting Jewish combat soldiers and casualties or Jewish Nobel prizewinners as methods of 'proving' how valuable Jews were to their countries and to the world.[5]

Ironically, this advertising of Jewish achievements can readily be interpreted as implicit acceptance of racial theory. It virtually grants the validity of antisemites' fundamental assertion that the Jews were a race, differing only by insisting that the Jewish race was in possession of positive traits. Jacobs apparently did believe in a moderate version of racism, 'the notion of Chosen Races, each with its own special characteristics . . . by innate or acquired ability'.[6] Roth, faced with the Nuremberg Laws and early Nazi anti-Jewish depredations, was more sensitive to the ramifications of legitimizing racial theory, and performed rhetorical contortions attempting to distance himself from it, claiming, for example, 'however distinct the Jews may have been from their neighbors ethnologically at the beginning of their settlement in Europe, this distinction has been progressively modified'.[7] The inconsonance was, however, obvious, and after the Second World War, as racial theory was progressively confuted and abandoned, most Jewish contribution boosters took pains to ascribe Jews' achievements to nurture and not nature.

Although contribution literature was apologetically motivated, it still included several works of lasting scholarly value. Especially noteworthy among these are *The Jewish Encyclopedia*, Mordecai Kaplan's *Judaism as a*

[4] Cecil Roth, *The Jewish Contribution to Civilization*, p. vii.

[5] e.g. Adler (ed.), *British Jewry Book of Honour*; Haas (ed.), *The Encyclopedia of Jewish Knowledge*, s.v. Jewish Nobel Prize Winners. This practice continues: see *Encyclopaedia Judaica*.

[6] Jacobs, *Jewish Contributions to Civilization*, 52. In this period 'race' also sometimes bore the connotation of ethnic nation; see Graetz, *Structure of Jewish History*, ch. 4, 'The Rejuvenation of the Jewish Race'.

[7] Roth, *The Jewish Contribution to Civilization*, p. viii. Cf. Mordecai Kaplan's attempts in *Judaism as a Civilization*, written in 1934, to cast aspersions on racial notions of Jewishness; see index, s.v. racialism.

Civilization, Salo Baron's 'The Jewish Factor in Medieval Civilization', Louis Finkelstein's *The Jews*, and Cecil Roth's *The Jews in the Renaissance*.[8]

Contribution Discourse as Expressive Hostility

Although specifically Jewish in its content, in its intent this 'contribution discourse' is related to a more general phenomenon typical of minority groups whose place in society is unstable. Sociologically speaking,[9] ethnic, racial, or other minority groups can be classified as subcultures; that is, groups within society, differing from the larger society in such matters as language, values, religion, and lifestyle, and perpetuating their own normative systems. Simultaneously, however, the minority usually shares many of the values of the larger society, and strives to achieve them. The minority wants to be a *sub*culture, not a separate culture. It aims for inclusion as a component of the total society and culture.

For its part, the majority disapproves of the subculture's separate norms, regarding them as inferior, divisive, and threatening. Historically, in such situations majorities have tended to resort to a mix of two strategies: encouraging the minority to shed its separateness and to assimilate, but also frustrating its attempts to share in the values and culture of the larger society by discriminating against it and making it the victim of various

[8]   Adler, Singer, et al. (eds), *The Jewish Encyclopedia*; cf. Shwartz, *Jewish Scholarship in America*; Liberles, *Salo Wittmayer Baron*; Ruderman, 'Cecil Roth'; Bonfil, 'The Historian's Perception of the Jews in the Italian Renaissance'. Baron consciously tried to separate his study from the apologetic trend: 'the term "factor" still seems preferable to the usual phraseology of "Jewish contributions to medieval civilization" which, without being less ambiguous, has decidedly apologetic overtones' (p. 2). Yet he too utilized the expression 'cultural contributions' (p. 24) and the use of the word 'factor' did not prevent his article from conforming to the conventions of contribution discourse.

[9]   The following analysis is my attempt to adapt and apply the theories presented in Floyd James Davis, *Minority-Dominant Relations*, and Yinger, 'Contraculture and Subculture', as well as his *Countercultures*, esp. pp. 18–50. In the later work Yinger, over-influenced I think by the popular use of the term 'counterculture' in the USA in the 1970s, saw countercultures as 'emergent phenomena not rooted in traditional subsocieties, ethnic communities, occupational groups, or other fairly stable social structures', although he admitted that subcultures and countercultures 'are sometimes empirically mixed' (ibid. 41, and cf. 89–113). The earlier article, with its theorizing less tied to contemporary developments, is more useful for historical application. Cf. Gordon, *Assimilation in American Life*, esp. pp. 38–51, 68–74, 105–9, 126–9; Kurokawa (ed.), *Minority Responses*; Davis (ed.), *Understanding Minority-Dominant Relations*; Kazal, 'Revisiting Assimilation', esp. pp. 439–40, 443–51.

exclusionary practices.[10] The contradiction between these two tendencies is seldom fully resolved, with the ultimate status of the minority within the larger society usually dependent on the balance achieved between them.

When the second tactic, exclusion, is primary and the minority finds itself in constant conflict with the majority, facing frustration in its attempts to realize a comfortable identity as a subculture, the result often is that the *sub*culture becomes a *counter*culture, in which a central element of the normative system of the group is conflict with the values of the majority society it is in. The counterculture defines itself largely by virtue of its contradictions with respect to the majority.[11]

By mutual, if tacit, agreement between Christians and Jews, medieval European Jewry was a marginal group in northern European society. Having been subject to many legal, economic, social, and cultural restrictions in the Middle Ages, one important process of modernity for the Jews was 'emancipation'—their release from these limitations. Simultaneously, Jewish attitudes and cultural devices, such as ritual laws and communal discipline that promoted Jewish segregation, were also eroded by a process of acculturation. Through emancipation and acculturation, Jews in the modern period moved progressively from the margins of society towards its centre, although throughout the modern period Jewish identity never shed all of its distinctive characteristics. One might portray this trajectory of modernity (in my view roughly 1650–1950)[12] as Jews evolving from a counterculture to a subculture.[13]

In the course of the transition from counterculture to subculture Jews adopted more and more of the values of majority society, but they also used various forms of covert aggression to combat continuing manifestations of majority hostility and the desire to keep them marginalized. In the custom of minority groups, one important form of this covert aggression was

[10] The phenomenon of multiculturalism, where society rejects the notion of a core, hegemonic culture to which others are expected to assimilate to some degree, and attempts to arrange intercultural interaction in a non-hierarchical and non-power-related way, is a rather recent and, one might say, experimental development in Western society; for how it has affected historical and sociological analysis of the past see Kazal, 'Revisiting Assimilation', 437–8, 441, 448–62, 470–1.

[11] Yinger, 'Contraculture and Subculture', 628–30, 632–3, 635.

[12] For the rationale behind this periodization of the modern period, see Chapter 2 above.

[13] See e.g. the analysis of how modern German Jewry became a subculture in Sorkin, *Transformation of German Jewry*, esp. his introduction and conclusion.

expressive hostility; verbally denigrating and otherwise casting aspersions on the majority group. One type of expressive hostility is ethnocentric interpretation of both history and current events. Minorities often create myths asserting—appearances to the contrary notwithstanding—that they stand at the centre of events, wield unseen power over the majority, and in some significant measure determine society's fate.[14] Consider, for example, the various Jewish stories about how Jews influenced or controlled royal policy in Poland, or even the monarchy itself; or the Jewish claim that Poland was partitioned by its neighbours as punishment for its Jewish policies.[15]

This kind of ethnocentrism is intended to affirm the minority's importance in society: this society needs us; we make a crucial difference; we are part of you; by discounting us the majority impoverishes itself and works counter to its own interests. Such expressive hostility also subtly indicates the minority's *desire* to be important in a given society. It is an expression of the minority's internalization of majority values as well as an assertion of the minority's right to internalize them; it means minority members believe they should belong. In addition, this ethnocentrism is a counter-reaction to the majority's continued exclusionary practices; its apparent preference that the minority remains a counterculture rather than a subculture.

By stipulating that it is a founder of the culture or that it exercises a determinative influence on events, the minority is declaring that it cannot possibly be excluded; it is an intrinsic, integral component of the whole. This declaration is part of the larger attempt to establish a modus vivendi (or to re-establish one that has been ruptured) between majority and minority that both sides can live with. While implicitly conceding the primacy of the majority culture, the minority members are also trying to bolster their own self-image and to convince the majority of their loyalty and utility so that they might be granted security and acceptance.

Contribution discourse is a form of ethnocentric expressive hostility. By proving how valuable minority members—in this case Jews—were to society, indeed to civilization as a whole, the apologists were trying to convince their non-Jewish interlocutors of the indispensable role that Jews play in

---

[14] Cf. Davis, *Minority-Dominant Relations*, 50, 131–2, 138, 145; LeVine and Campbell, *Ethnocentrism*, 33 (theorem 3.10) and 68 (theorems 5.1, 5.1.2). Like the quasi-racist claims noted earlier, this too was an ironic echo of a primary antisemitic assertion that Jews dominated government, culture, and the economy; see Ettinger, *Modern Antisemitism* (Heb.), 1–12 and *passim*.

[15] See Chapter 5, and Bar-Itzhak, *Jewish Poland*; Birkenthal, *Memoirs of Ber of Bolechow*, 149–51.

society. They were also trying to provide Jews themselves with confidence-building facts that would help them in their fight for fully fledged membership in society (as opposed to mere citizenship). Perhaps, most of all, they were demonstrating to both the non-Jews and themselves how much they really had adopted and internalized general Western categories of value, and how much they believed in the truth of this way of life and wanted to adhere to it.

Older Versions of Contribution Discourse

When viewed as a type of expressive hostility, however, contribution discourse has a much longer history than the period coinciding with the rise of modern antisemitism and the lead up to and aftermath of the Second World War. It is at least as old as the modern period itself, beginning when some Jews first realized that it was possible—and decided that it was desirable—to be an integral component of European or Western society. It has reappeared whenever that desire was obstructed, until the present day.

This discourse began in the early modern period when secularizing and rationalizing trends in Europe undermined the old religion-based evaluation of many cultural conventions, including the status of the Jews in society. Once religion ceased to be the only authoritative guide to formulating an attitude towards the Jews, new possibilities developed. If, for example, it was *raison d'état*, and not Christianity, that was to determine the value of a group or an idea, then Jews who brought economic advantage to the state might be seen as an asset worth cultivating. Rather than remain pariahs to be tolerated that they might provide an object lesson in the consequences of failing to recognize theological truth, or to be relegated to performing socially undesirable functions such as moneylending or high-risk entrepreneurship, Jews might be transformed into constructive, contributing members of society.[16]

The possibility of such a transformation was, to be sure, not a foregone conclusion. All three leading early Enlightenment theorists of toleration, Benedict Spinoza, John Locke, and Pierre Bayle, came to the conclusion that Judaism was 'fundamentally intolerant—and thus inevitably also in some sense intolerable', while adherence to this Judaism and the exceptional historical circumstances surrounding Jewish existence prevented inclusion of the Jews on an equal basis in enlightened society.[17] Though

---

[16] Israel, *European Jewry in the Age of Mercantilism*, 35–69.

[17] Sutcliffe, 'Enlightenment and Exclusion'; quotation from p. 40.

often considered to contain the seeds of Jewish rehabilitation, deist doctrine in general was nonetheless profoundly hostile to Jews and Judaism, supplying, according to Shmuel Ettinger, 'an important link in the development of modern Antisemitism'. Most of the enlightened thinkers of the seventeenth century were still of the opinion that even under the newly formulated conceptions of society the Jews would perforce continue to serve as civilization's nemesis, thwarting its good intentions and undermining its institutions at every opportunity. For its own reasons, the emerging secular state could no more rely on Jews' loyalty or trust their intentions than could the receding religious one.[18]

It was left to Jews to be the first to theorize on the possibilities of the new secularizing world-view for changing the perception of the Jews and making a positive place for them in society. To persuade their non-Jewish readers (all of the famous Jewish tracts on this subject were written in European languages) that Jewish status should be ameliorated, they resorted to contribution discourse. The seventeenth-century Jewish thinkers Simone di Luzzatto, Menasseh ben Israel, and Isaac Cardoso all insisted that the Jews did not need to be improved or reformed; they were already fine, upstanding, noble, even superior people.[19] Emphasizing mercantilist arguments, Luzzatto and Menasseh ben Israel enumerated the myriad ways Jews contributed to the welfare—especially economic—of the places where they resided. Cardoso averred that Jews were actually the best of people. Discrimination against them hurt the discriminators, made no rational sense, and was unjust. Dismantling barriers would enable Jews to make a tremendous contribution wherever they lived.[20]

Even those Christian Europeans who were willing eventually to entertain new attitudes towards the Jews[21] were not as confident as the Jewish

---

[18]   Ettinger, 'Position of the Deists' (Heb.); quotation from p. 224.

[19]   Luzzatto, *Discorso circa il stato de gl'hebrei*; Menasseh ben Israel, *Menasseh ben Israel's Mission*; Cardoso, *Las excelencias de los hebreos*.

[20]   For analyses of these apologia, see Ravid, *Economics and Toleration in Seventeenth Century Venice*, and ' "How profitable the nation of the Jewes are" '; Roubey, 'Simeone Luzzatto's "Discorso" '; Schorsch, 'From Messianism to Realpolitik'; Yerushalmi, *From Spanish Court to Italian Ghetto*, 350–472. To the apologetic works listed here one might add Leon Modena's *Historia degli riti hebraici*, although it was more concerned with defending Judaism as a non-superstitious religion than with the issue of Jews' contribution; see Mark Cohen, 'Leone de Modena's Riti'.

[21]   Ettinger, 'The Beginning of Change in the Attitude of European Society Towards the Jews' (Heb.).

writers that the Jews were a latent, powerful, positive force needing only to be unbound. Their point of departure was that currently the presence of Jews in society posed a problem, but they postulated that the Jews might make a positive contribution if properly refined. The argument was over how to do this, whether by giving Jews maximum freedom, or by supervising their progress through the imposition of restrictions that would be abolished gradually as the Jews proved their worthiness.[22] The basic premise was clear: any improvement in Jewish status, any move to integrate Jews into society was a function of the supposition that they had a positive contribution to make. Early modern Jewish apologists welcomed the opportunity to prove the point.

By the nineteenth century the terms of the argument over Jewish integration had shifted. Romantic, progress-preoccupied, culturally arrogant nineteenth-century Europe virtually dared Jews to demonstrate how they—never feeling at home in a world they did not create, constituting a state within the state, incapable of loving justice, mankind, and truth, and utilizing their privileges in order to exploit their fellow citizens—could be part of the grand projects of its civilization.[23] The Jews responded in several ways. Whether it be internalization and self-application of non-Jewish critiques of Jews and Judaism, development of Jewish mission theory, 'missionizing' European culture to 'uncivilized' Jews, or an impudent insistence that actually it was the Jews who laid the foundations for civilization (which Christianity in many ways subverted), Jewish apologists sought to prove that Jews could be, and had indeed become, contributing members of civilization. They were not only civilized, but forgers of civilized culture.[24]

[22] Compare for example the proposals for Jewish integration made by John Toland in *Reasons for Naturalizing the Jews in Great Britain and Ireland* . . . (London, 1714) and Christian Wilhelm von Dohm, *Ueber die buergerliche Verbesserung der Juden* (Berlin, 1781), conveniently excerpted in Mendes-Flohr and Reinharz, *The Jew in the Modern World*, 13–17, 28–36. Note especially Toland: 'In a word they ought to be so naturaliz'd in *Great Britain* and *Ireland*, as, like the Quakers, to be incapacitated in nothing but where they incapacitate themselves' (*The Jew in the Modern World*, 16) versus Dohm: 'it would even be permissible at least in the beginning, to restrict the number of Jews active in commerce, or subject them to special taxes . . . But impartiality would demand that if a Jewish and a Christian applicant show equal capability, the latter deserves preference. This seems to be an obvious right of the majority in the nation—at least until the Jews by wiser treatment are changed into entirely equal citizens and all differences polished off' (ibid. 33).

[23] See the excerpts from writers of the first half of the 19th century in Mendes-Flohr and Reinharz, *The Jew in the Modern World*, 309–13, 321–31, 334–6.

[24] See the essays in Cohen and Cohen (eds), *The Jewish Contribution to Civilization*.

If I am correct that contribution discourse is part of Jews' efforts, within the new parameters of modernity, to move from the status of counterculture to that of subculture, then discussion of Jews' contribution was also a component in the attempt to formulate a new definition of Jewishness that would be appropriate in the modern world. In the early modern period, people such as Luzzatto, Menasseh ben Israel, and Cardoso saw the Jews as a semi-autonomous ethnos who contributed as a coherent community to the larger society in which they lived. Nineteenth-century German, French, and English Jews held Jews to be members of a different, but vital and essential, religion. This meant that they could contribute by applying the positive religious values and insights of Judaism to social life, and that there was no impediment to their contributing as individuals to general civil life as any other citizen might.

In the second half of the nineteenth century, with the world continually subdividing into nation-states, another definition of Jewishness was proffered as the means by which Jews could lay claim to a place in the developing Western—or world—civilization. Since the world was being organized according to nation-states, it was only within the framework of a political state that Jews could take their rightful place in civilization, and make their dutiful and proper contribution alongside other nation-states to the furthering of human progress and whatever was necessary for the advancement of enlightened civilization. Only as a nation, asserted some early Jewish nationalists, could Jews carve out a role and contribute on an equal basis with everyone else. Thus, although not usually categorized in this way, early Jewish nationalist assertions can also be seen as a version of contribution discourse.

The classic Jewish nationalist theorists Lev Pinsker and Theodor Herzl saw Jewish nationalism as an antidote to the anomalous nature of Jewish existence as a minority, eternally unwanted by its host nations. For them, Jewish nationalism would solve, primarily, the so-called Jewish problem, that is the question of the basis on which the Jews could attain a normal existence in the world. Indeed, they both believed that Jewish nationalism would be enthusiastically accepted by non-Jews as well as Jews because it would alleviate the non-Jews' problem with the Jews.[25]

In contrast, earlier theorists such as Yehuda Alkalay, Moses Hess, Peretz Smolenskin, and Moses Leib Lilienblum, with various individual codicils and qualifications, all saw the Jewish national state as providing a natural platform, in parallel with the other nation-states, for enabling and launch-

---

[25] See Chapter 1 at nn. 19–20.

ing the Jews' substantial contribution to the world order. Organized as a state, the Jewish nation could finally assume its rights as well as its duties in the world.[26] As they saw it, the issue was not the current impossibility of the Jews' circumstances, but the desirability of creating new conditions that would facilitate their reaching their full potential. Hess, for example, vigorously advocated Jewish nationalism as the *sine qua non* for Jewish partnership in a better world:

The contemporary movements for national self-realization do not only not exclude a concern for all humanity but strongly assert it. These movements are a wholesome reaction, not against universalism but against the things that would encroach upon it and cause its degeneration . . . and it is only against these destructive forces that I appeal to the power of Jewish nationalism . . . all political and social progress must necessarily be preceded by national independence . . . The Jewish people will participate in the great historical movement of present-day humanity only when it will have its own fatherland.[27]

Contemporary Contribution Discourse

In recent times academic experts in Jewish studies have tended to disparage the investigation of 'the Jewish contribution to civilization'. Its overt apologetic nature and vulgar ethnocentrism are, they argue, pathetic, embarrassing, and silly in a context where Jews have 'made it' as part of the academic and other establishments. Having gained full acceptance, having assured themselves that they indeed belong to the general culture and society, Jews have no need to prove their worthiness. As if to drive this home, many Jewish academics revel in a new-found capacity to parade Jewish foibles, misdeeds, and mistreatment of others; the display of which testifies, among other things, to Jewish security and self-confidence.

In the mid-twentieth century Jacob Katz, an Israeli scholar safely ensconced in the Jewish state (at the time boasting its ability to allow the Jews to be themselves without regard to 'what the *goyim* might say'), was the first to state unambiguously that traditional Jewish society practised a double standard of morality in its dealings with non-Jews. Even as late as 1958 this threatened to serve as confirmation of a standard antisemitic canard.[28] In the twenty-first century, however, most Jewish scholars feel so

[26] See e.g. the chapters treating each of these figures in Hertzberg, *The Zionist Idea*; also Avineri, *Varieties of Zionist Thought* (Heb.).

[27] Hertzberg, *The Zionist Idea*, 130, 136, 137.

[28] Katz, *Tradition and Crisis* (originally published in Hebrew), 32–4. In his autobiography *With My Own Eyes*, 147, Katz noted that his continued demonstration in his

securely embedded in their social and cultural environments, wherever they may be, that they are convinced that skeletons in the Jewish collective closet will not be held against them, and they certainly do not hesitate to expose blemishes.[29] Conversely, when the subject of 'Jewish contribution' is discussed, it is often placed in quotation marks to emphasize that modern Jewish scholarship has moved beyond apologetics, and to denote the ironic posture preferable for treating a topic whose time has passed.

But has it? As a means for an insecure minority to justify its position, contribution discourse is still very much with us, albeit in a new incarnation. Postmodernism and multiculturalism have once again shaken Jews' confidence that they belong. Multiculturalist critics consistently speak about Jews, Judaism, and Jewishness as conservative, even reactionary and oppressive, aligned with the established powers of hegemony that seek to exclude and disempower people of colour and other minorities.[30] This gives rise to feelings of hurt, frustration, resentment, and anger among Jews. Once again, they have become an anomalous minority: part of the establishment in the eyes of other minorities but still not completely at one with the majority monoculture.[31] Some Jews feel cheated because the goalposts have been moved in the middle of the game. For three or four generations they were taught that they could integrate by adopting a pluralist ethos—assimilating to the majority's monoculture while maintaining, with majority approval, distinctive minority cultural norms in private and within the minority community. Witness to occasional transvaluation of their own culture to the point where it influenced the majority (think of the role of the Holocaust in Western culture, or the popularity of kosher food among healthy-eating advocates), they understood that the price of such acceptance was full internalization of majority monoculture. Recent, if somewhat extreme, statements of both sides of this equation can be found in the writings of Diana Pinto and Yuri Slezkine.

second book, *Exclusiveness and Tolerance*, 'that traditional Judaism upheld neither absolute religious tolerance nor a universalist code of morality' led to hesitations on the part of its publisher because of fears 'that the book might provide ammunition for the enemies of the Jewish people'.

[29] Biale, 'Between Polemics and Apologetics', 176.

[30] Alexander, 'Multiculturalism's Jewish Problem'; Whitfield, 'Multiculturalism and American Jews'; Mitchell Cohen, 'In Defense of Shaatnez', 45.

[31] Biale, 'Between Polemics and Apologetics', 176–7.

Pinto repeatedly urged that European Jews must 'transcend' the Holocaust and 'regard themselves not as victims, but as a vibrant force'. Yet she spoke of 'their inherent "belonging" [to contemporary European culture], *if only through suffering*' (emphasis added), and shared the supposition that it is the Holocaust experience and its incorporation into European consciousness that has largely qualified the Jews to truly 'belong' to the new European society and culture and to assume a central role in fashioning these.[32] Slezkine also saw the Holocaust experience as 'the true source of late twentieth-century Jewishness. In a world without God, evil and victimhood are the only absolutes. The rise of the Holocaust as a transcendental concept has led to the emergence of the Jews as a Chosen People for the new age.'[33] So it was the European and American transvaluation of the Holocaust that entitled the Jews to full membership in Western culture.

The price, however, was the Jews' obligation to prove their dedication to the common monoculture. Thus, despite advocating a pluralist approach to Judaism and the evolution of a protean Jewish identity where Jews can define themselves in whatever—religious, cultural, intellectual, ethnic, social, political—terms they desire, Pinto consistently assigned European Jews an indispensable, 'essential responsibility' (one is tempted to say a *mitsvah* [religious obligation]) for 'promoting historical, national and religious reconciliation and fighting for a tolerant democratic pluralism'.[34] Slezkine, for his part, seemed to regard a continuing Jewish identity in the modern world as pointless. 'The painful transformation of Europeans into Jews was paralleled by the emergence of the Jews from legal, ritual, and social seclusion . . . most simply joined the world created in their image.' With the purported adoption of supposed Jewish values and Jewish-style economic and cultural practices by the societies which shape the world today, the historical destiny of the Jews had, finally, been fulfilled. Slezkine quoted Tevye the milkman from Shalom Aleichem's stories—'What did being a Jew or not a Jew matter?'—clearly implying that it no longer mattered. Those Jews who insist on shaping an articulated Jewish identity with

[32] Pinto, 'The New Jewish Europe', 6–7, 9, 10; ead., 'Jewish Challenges in the New Europe', 242–3; quotation from p. 243; ead., *A New Identity for Post-1989 Europe*, 1–4; quotations from pp. 1, 3; cf. Michman, 'A Third Partner of World Jewry?', 123–35.

[33] Slezkine, *The Jewish Century*, 370.

[34] Pinto, *A New Identity for Post-1989 Europe*, 1, 5, 6, 8; ead., 'The New Jewish Europe', 4–5, 8, 9, 11, 12, 14; ead., 'Jewish Challenges in the New Europe', 247–8.

a strong cultural component are flailing at history, which by transvaluing their contribution to civilization has made them superfluous.[35]

Most Jewish believers in an integrative pluralism would have much more sympathy with Pinto's position than that of Slezkine. They think that some sort of positive Jewish identity (probably more defined than that given by Pinto) has a purpose and is worth preserving. Now Jews need not leave the world stage, their historical destiny supposedly having been fulfilled. However, having successfully negotiated the barriers to the internalization of the majority monoculture and to cultivating a pluralist stance, such Jews have suddenly learned that pluralism is no longer desirable. Having mastered the construct of subculture, these Jews now discover that to gain postmodern legitimacy it is preferable to be a counterculture; precisely the circumstance that was abandoned with so much effort.[36]

Cultural evolution has reached the stage of multiculturalism, defined as, for example, 'pluralism without the element of public conformity and without pluralism's optimism of ultimate inclusion for all . . . a nation of disparate entities sharing public power but existing, immutably, as separate and autonomous units'. Multiculturalism, unlike pluralism, sees no virtue in acculturation. There is no hierarchy of cultures, no majority-minority, no general, and no sub. The only accommodations cultures might make should be pragmatic in order to allow for peaceful coexistence. Substantive accommodation in the form of assimilation is unnecessary and even un-

---

[35] Slezkine, *The Jewish Century*, 46, 370–1. Cf. Edouard Gans's famous prediction dating from the 1820s that in modern times Judaism would live on 'as the current lives on in the ocean' (quoted in Meyer, *Origins of the Modern Jew*, 182) which Meyer interpreted: '[Gans] could justify his act [conversion] by the argument that Judaism's contribution to civilization had already been absorbed' ('Modernity as a Crisis for the Jews', 160). Thus there no longer was a need for Jews to keep their river flowing beside that mighty cultural sea.

[36] For an interesting example of Jewish attempts to adopt a pluralist stance in the past, see Malinovich, 'Orientalism and the Construction of Jewish Identity in France'. See Pinto, *A New Identity for Post-1989 Europe*, 'The New Jewish Europe', and 'Jewish Challenges in the New Europe'; in all of these articles Pinto passionately advocated a pluralist position for Jews in contemporary Europe. In my view, hers is an illustration of the argument put forward towards the beginning of this chapter that 'it was [is] paramount that Jews themselves should have a sense of their own value and importance if they were [are] to morally convince or legally coerce others to recognize finally that they really belonged'. In her writings, Pinto emphasized again and again that the Jews in Europe do now 'belong'. For Pinto's critique of multiculturalism, see *A New Identity*, 13, and 'Jewish Challenges in the New Europe', 248–50.

desirable. As the avatars of pluralism Jews cannot fit easily into the multicultural matrix.[37]

Other Jews are willing to turn their back on pluralism and adopt the multicultural paradigm; they believe that in a world organized as 'a community of communities and a culture of cultures' Jewish culture and the Jewish community can assume a respected place. Jewishness, as the product of so much historical multicultural experience, might even be emblematic of multiculturalism, with 'multicultural theory itself [lying] at the heart of modern Jewish experience'.[38] Responses to this thesis from multiculturalists are often, however, in the nature of: your culture was too complicit in the formation of the oppressive monoculture for you now to claim membership in—much less leadership of—the ranks of the oppressed; however you might construe your history in the past, today you are aligned with the white elite; you are no longer vulnerable (if indeed you ever were); you are not outsiders; contrary to your claims there is no valid multiculturalism inherent in Jewishness.[39]

This is most poignantly and vociferously expressed in the so-called new academy, the stronghold and fountainhead of multiculturalism. Jewish academics who thought that Jewish studies belonged in a framework dedicated to entitling every tile in the cultural mosaic to full visibility are rudely awakened to their exclusion.[40] They are left out and, like Jews legally emancipated but socially discriminated against, they protest that they deserve to belong. In time-honoured fashion, their argument for inclusion

[37] Biale, Galchinsky and Heschel, *Insider/Outsider*, 3–7; Greenberg, 'Pluralism and its Discontents', 55–65, 80–1; quotation from pp. 57–8; cf. David Goldberg (ed.), *Multiculturalism*, 1–42.

[38] Biale, Galchinsky, and Heschel, *Insider/Outsider*, 8–12; quotation from p. 12; Heschel, 'Jewish Studies as Counterhistory', 113; Diner, 'Geschichte der Juden'.

[39] Greenberg, 'Pluralism and its Discontents', 78–9; Newman, 'The Idea of Judaism in Feminism and Afrocentrism', esp. pp. 152, 154, 160, 161, 167, 174, 176; Heschel, 'Configurations of Patriarchy, Judaism and Nazism in German Feminist Thought'; ead., 'Anti-Judaism in Christian Feminist Theology', 25–8, 95–7; Gilman, *Jews in Today's German Culture*, 4, 35–6. On the 'occlusion of Jewish otherness', see Boyarin, 'The Other Within and the Other Without', esp. pp. 430–5.

[40] Sara Horowitz, 'The Paradox of Jewish Studies'; Eisen, 'Jews, Jewish Studies, and the American Humanities'; Silberstein, 'Benign Transmission Versus Conflicted Discourse'; Boyarin, 'The Other Within and the Other Without'. In contrast, what might be termed celebration of Jewish studies' acceptance by the 'old academy' is represented by Schorsch, 'The Place of Jewish Studies in Contemporary Scholarship', 16–20, and Pelikan, 'Judaism and the Humanities'.

in the hegemonic group concentrates on the contribution Jewishness can make to the dominant discourse and ethos, now connected to multi-culturalism. Where other minority groups may use their history to prove that they are 'somebody', that they have a past that entitles them to stand-ing in the present and the future, the Jews use their past to prove that they can contribute to everybody else's future.[41]

This new discourse on the contribution of Jews to multicultural civiliza-tion has two main vectors. One version (popular among non-Jewish theor-ists as well as some Jews) is to regard Jews, whose identity is always in flux, as an allegory, metaphor, or trope representing all of the people sinned against by modern Western civilization and summarizing all of the ways in which they have been harmed. As we learned from Homi Bhabha in the last chapter, the Jewish experience is shorthand for the universal experience of all hybridized, colonized, alterior people who have suffered at the hands of modern civilization because they disconcert it. It is studied as an intro-duction to the need for multiculturalism and for the way in which it prob-lematizes hegemony. It has no intrinsic value, or even significant content, beyond its representative potential and its power to discomfit.

This depriving Jewish identity of particularistic substance (essence?) and converting it into a trope is facilitated in part by the current fashion to dichotomize essentialist versus constructionist approaches to definitions of Jewish identity. The advocates of this approach take whatever 'Jews' might do to be 'Jewish' without, however, being able to tell us how we are to iden-tify prima facie those whose behaviour we should be studying.[42]

Consequently some academics whose main occupation is the study of Jewish texts and Jewish experiences, yet who are committed to a multi-

---

[41] See Biale, 'Between Polemics and Apologetics', 180–4, for a discussion of this new style of apologetics; cf. Yerushalmi, *Zakhor*, 88.

[42] See Cheyette and Marcus (eds), *Modernity, Culture, and 'the Jew'*, pp. xv–xvi, and Silberstein's summary of the 'antiessentialistic, constructionist approach to Jewish identity' in *The Other in Jewish Thought and History*, 11–27, and also in *Mapping Jewish Identities*, 1–36. Silberstein's insistence on dichotomizing essentialist vs. constructionist approaches easily leads into the Jew-as-trope rhetoric. In my opinion one can agree that Jewish culture and identity are constantly under construction, yet still ask if there are not some fixed, if flexible, features that enable all of the various constructions to be grouped under the genus of Jewish; see Chapter 3 above. The Boyarins traced the view of the Jew-as-trope (i.e. the Jew 'as both signifier of unruly difference and symbol of universalism') to Paul and early Christianity; noting that 'once Paul succeeded, "real Jews" ended up being only a trope. They have remained such for European discourse down to the present' ('Diaspora', 697).

cultural perspective, have reacted strongly against this tendency to make Jewishness into a mere trope devoid of positive content. They reject the presumption that Jewishness has no substance valuable in and of itself, or that the attempt to ensure the deracialization of Jewishness requires its deracination as well. Daniel and Jonathan Boyarin, for example, perhaps the most accomplished advocates of Jewish studies before the bar of post-modernism, justified their critique of the Jew-as-trope on the basis of one of multiculturalism's most hallowed precepts, the right to be different:

> Although well intentioned, any such allegorization of *Jew* is problematic in the extreme for the way that it deprives those who have historically grounded identities in those material signifiers of the power to speak for themselves and remain different. In this sense the 'progressive' idealization of *Jew* and *woman*, or more usually, *jew* and *Woman*, ultimately deprives difference of the right to be different . . . We will suggest that a Jewish subject-position founded on generational connection and its attendant anamnestic responsibilities and pleasures affords the possibility of a flexible and nonhermetic critical Jewish identity.[44]

This second vector of the new Jewish contribution discourse sees the Jews, not as trope, but as model; that is, the Jewish experience and Jewish texts have something to teach—to *contribute*—to contemporary, multiculturalist-governed discourse. For the advocates of Jew-as-trope the Jewish contribution lies in 'the Jew' being a background concept for use in interpretation and criticism and not in any specific, concrete Jewish idea or action (except, perhaps, as a special—that is, Holocaust-legitimated—protagonist within the larger struggle for equality and multiculturalism—or pluralism[44]); so the Jewish contribution is rather amorphous. The proponents of Jews-as-model, who contend that Jews and Judaism possess precious and powerful cultural treasures, propose many concrete ways for Jews to contribute (sometimes they actually use the words 'contribute' and 'contribution'). Some examples are:

> Indeed we would suggest that Diaspora, and not monotheism, may be the most important contribution that Judaism has to make to the world.[45]

---

[43] Boyarin and Boyarin, 'Diaspora', 697–701; see also Boyarin, 'The Other Within and the Other Without'.   [44] Cf. the writings by Pinto listed in n. 32 above.

[45] Boyarin and Boyarin, 'Diaspora', 723. For their development of the idea of Diaspora as a theoretical and historical model to replace national self-determination (and especially Zionism), see pp. 706–23. Cf. Jewish claims to have contributed to egalitarianism, ecology, pluralism, tolerance, self-determination, feminism and multiculturalism, noted in Chapter 2 at n. 71.

Both the examples of the Jews and Jewish studies as a field can make a theoretical contribution to the development of the multicultural academy.[46]

What can [Jewish studies] perspectives contribute to a rethinking and reshaping of cultural studies?[47]

By engaging in systematic comparisons of their condition with the analogous conditions of postcolonial diasporas, American Jews may be able both to learn from and to contribute to dialogues of inordinate importance in a time of global population shifts and the thrilling but frightening restructuring of nations.[48]

The presence of Jews and Judaism in the academy, then . . . may contribute to debate within the academy about the nature and purpose of humanistic learning.[49]

Jews, in many ways the prototype of the new European, have the chance to *belong* in Europe as never before . . . The Jewish contribution to the fostering of a tolerant, pluralist, European democratic identity is best fulfilled by drawing the widest possible conclusions from the positive developments of the post-war Jewish experience in Europe . . . Other groups could also profit from the Jewish precedent . . . Jews can make an important contribution in this realm for, in this tragic century, they experienced both the attractions and dangers of acculturation.[50]

I have no doubt that each of the paths of enquiry or action suggested by these scholars has some merit. The point in the present context, however, is not really the fact that Jewish studies can enlighten an array of cognate and general subjects, or that Jews can make a prodigious contribution to the formation of culture, but the perception of the necessity to justify the utility of the endeavour.

Compare the potential 'contributions' of Jewish studies proffered by *fin-de-siècle* academics to the value of Jewish studies suggested a generation before them by the teacher of some of them, Yosef Hayim Yerushalmi, and

[46] Heschel, 'Jewish Studies as Counterhistory', 112.

[47] Sara Horowitz, 'The Paradox of Jewish Studies', 123; on pp. 124–9 there are detailed answers to this question.   [48] Galchinsky, 'Scattered Seeds', 187.

[49] Eisen, 'Jews, Jewish Studies, and the American Humanities', 29.

[50] Pinto, 'The New Jewish Europe', 9, 12, 13. Pinto also called for European Jewry 'to contribute positively and meaningfully to world Judaism, and to Israel's own tormented crisis of identity' (ibid. 3). Despite her protestations, Pinto's position is reminiscent of various universalist Jewish political and social programmes that have been proposed since the late 18th century; by her lights any particularist content to Judaism is, by implication, negotiable—at most. I should emphasize again (see n. 36 above) that in line with her vision of a pan-European identity, and unlike the authors of the other quotations adduced here, Pinto saw the Jewish contribution in a pluralist (i.e. subculture) context and not a multicultural one.

by the dean of Jewish historians in their lifetime, Jacob Katz. Yerushalmi spoke of 'its contribution as pure scholarship to the sum of man's historical knowledge and understanding'. Katz declared: 'Any true historical insight with regard to the development of Jewish society has the right to be considered a contribution to general historical research.'[51]

Yerushalmi's talk of 'pure scholarship' and 'man's understanding', and Katz's belief in 'general historical research', and perhaps even 'Jewish society', might raise hackles in a postmodern classroom. However, political incorrectness aside, Yerushalmi's and Katz's 'contributions', conceived in an era when pluralism was the reigning ideal, reflected—in addition to whatever other motivations there may have been—a conviction that Jewish studies had nothing to prove; that including Jewish studies added to the legitimacy of the academy. They displayed a confidence in the worthiness of the subject that is missing in their heirs. The Jewish studies scholars of today leave us with the impression that their circumstances are more akin to those of Jacobs and Roth, or even much earlier contribution explicators, than they might care to acknowledge.[52]

If multiculturalism is the contemporary analogue to nineteenth-century 'civilization', then the two approaches of Jew-as-trope and Jew-as-model might be roughly analogous to the Alliance Israélite Universelle declaring that it could spread civilization better than anyone, while Abraham Geiger asserted that Judaism contains the essence of civilization and the Christians would do well to stop perverting the former and to try to learn from it. The 'trope' school offers the Jews and Judaism as a felicitous vehicle for conducting multicultural discourse. The 'model' school contends that multicultural discourse has much to learn from the Jewish model. Both seek acceptance, legitimacy, and validation.

---

[51] Yerushalmi, *Zakhor*, 87; Katz, 'Marriage and Sexual Life Among the Jews' (Heb.), 54. For further discussion of this point, see Chapter 7 at n. 13.

[52] A different challenge to the 'contribution mentality' was posed from a partisan perspective by Gerson D. Cohen, speaking, in 1971, shortly before assuming the chancellorship of the Jewish Theological Seminary of America, the leading institution of the Movement for Conservative Judaism: 'Fifty years ago, the great concern of Jewish spokesmen was to document the Jewish contribution to civilization. Today, as a result of the hard lessons of history, of our defeats as well as our epoch-making victories, we know that the challenge is not to demonstrate what we have contributed to others, but to consider profoundly what we shall make of ourselves' ('Changing Perspectives of Jewish Historiography', 181–2).

The question of a Jewish contribution to civilization is, then, once again relevant. As before, some unease prompts Jewish intellectuals to try to prove Jewish bona fides to the world. Make no mistake, however. Whatever its genesis, like its predecessors, this discourse will most assuredly produce some works of lasting scholarly value. There is already in formation a master narrative of Jewish history in the multicultural key that will take its place alongside the nationalist and acculturationalist metahistories that have developed over the past century and a half. Only when the multicultural challenge to Jews' position in society and culture is somehow resolved is a still newer perspective likely to emerge.[53]

---

[53] The alienation of Muslim minorities in European countries and the consequent serious problems this arouses has prompted the observation that 'The European vision of multiculturalism, in all its simultaneous good will and self-congratulation, is no longer sustainable' (Rieff, 'The Dream of Multiculturalism Is Over'). Academia has, in fact, been busily preparing a new paradigm to replace multiculturalism—'cosmopolitanism'. See e.g. Appiah, *Cosmopolitanism*; Beck, *Cosmopolitan Vision*; Kwok-bun, *Chinese Identities*; Rajan and Sharma (eds), *New Cosmopolitanisms*. For critiques of multiculturalism, see Beck, *Cosmopolitan Vision*, 66–71; Kwok-bun, *Chinese Identities*, 128–39 (although he seems to be targeting what I would call pluralism). Jewish intellectuals might find that, as formerly with regard to pluralism, it is once again necessary to change their view of how the Jews can fit in. On the other hand, cosmopolitanism, with its espousal of cultural practices like 'alternation' and 'code-switching', might prove more forgiving than multiculturalism towards Jews and more appropriate than its conceptual forebear, hybridity, to historical analysis of Jewish cultural behaviour in the past.

FIVE

Prolegomenon to the Study of Jewish Cultural History

୧

Cultural History

THE NOTION OF cultural history and cultural studies in general, as usually employed in contemporary academic discourse, is derived from social anthropology. The historian reads texts and other historical sources and artefacts not so much as discursive expositions, but rather like an anthropologist studying live behaviour. By doing so, the historian seeks both to discover the ways in which people in the society in question construed meaning, and to develop a catalogue of the fundamental concepts that mediated interpretation of reality and ordered experience for them. Cultural history might be summed up as 'a history of meaning and feelings broadly defined, as embedded in expressive practices widely observed'.[1]

In this way cultural history differs from social history, which emphasizes institutions: their structure, their social functions, and their effects.[2] Contemporary cultural history is also distinct from a different type of 'cultural history': namely, the history of creative production, whether elite, popular, or material—literature, art, tools, architecture, scholarship,

---

[1] Almost all of the examples here are drawn from the case of the history of the Jews in the Polish–Lithuanian Commonwealth of the early modern period. While I am attracted to this case because it is my own research interest, I believe that the issues raised here are generally applicable, at least through early modern times. The quotation is from Agnew, *Worlds Apart*, p. xii. For a survey of approaches to cultural history, see Hunt (ed.), *The New Cultural History*. For examples of essays in cultural history, see Chartier, *Cultural History*. For models of contemporary Jewish cultural historiography, see the many studies by Elliott Horowitz, for example, 'The Early Eighteenth Century Confronts the Beard' and 'The Rite To Be Reckless'.

[2] An example of social historiography is Jacob Katz's *Tradition and Crisis*, originally published in Hebrew in Jerusalem in 1958, translated without the notes and with many inaccuracies in 1961, and then re-translated in a more accurate and complete edition in 1993.

philosophy, food, and so on.[3] The new cultural history does study the products of creativity, but not to trace the process of their creation or to summarize their contents per se. The current goal is to determine the meaning that these products express. The description must therefore be 'thick' and the interpretation 'deep': terms, now more than a generation old, that connote the need to place individual cultural phenomena within a fully articulated cultural-social context and to understand the meanings that adhere to them.[4] A thick description consciously interprets as it describes. A deep interpretation takes into account the cultural infrastructure that underlies a cultural phenomenon.

Cultural history can also include a psychological perspective. Jerome Bruner[5] has attempted to define a new branch of psychology called 'cultural psychology'.

The program of cultural psychology is . . . to show how human minds and lives are reflections of culture and history as well as of biology and physical resources. [In the study of Self cultural psychology mandates] . . . focus upon the *meanings* in terms of which Self is defined *both* by the individual *and* by the culture in which he or she participates . . . By a *culture's* definition of Selfhood . . . I mean more than what contemporary Others, as it were, take as their working definition of Selves in general and of a particular Self.

For there is a historical dimension as well. If Gergen's Self is 'Self from the outside in,' the historical Self is 'Self from the past to the present'. In our own culture, for example, views of Self are shaped and buttressed by our Judeo-Christian theology and by the new Humanism that emerged in the Renaissance.[6]

For Bruner the 'dialogue dependence' of Self formation implied a dialogue, or a 'transactional relationship', not only with a contemporary Generalized Other but with an individual's historical legacy as well.[7] As he noted in discussing the Goodhertz family, a subject of his cultural psychological analysis:

The lives and Selves we have been exploring are, to be sure, shaped by intrapsychic forces operating in the here and now . . . But to let the matter rest at that is to rob the Goodhertzes of history and to impoverish our own understanding of

---

[3] For an example of this approach in Polish Jewish history, see Shulvass, *Jewish Culture in Eastern Europe*.

[4] See Ryle, *Collected Studies*; Geertz, *The Interpretation of Cultures*. Cf. my characterization of 'thick description' in the Introduction at n. 3.

[5] Bruner, *Acts of Meaning*.   [6] Ibid. 116–17, 138, emphases in the original.

[7] Ibid. 101.

their lives and their plight. For individually and as a family they are, always have been, and never can escape being expressions of social and historical forces. Whatever constituted those 'forces', whatever view one may take of historical forces, they were converted into human meanings, into language, into narratives, and found their way into the minds of men and women.[8]

With this in mind, it would be appropriate to approach the cultural history of a traditional society, as Jewish society was everywhere until the onset of modernity, by examining the history of the interaction of a society and its members with their collective history. Research can focus on how historical traditions are 'converted into human meanings' and 'find their way into the minds of men and women' on the collective/societal—as opposed to the individual/psychological—level. The objective is to clarify how society in the present mediates the heritage of the past to facilitate meaningful life into the future.

The advantage to this approach is that it begins where the people under study assumed they were beginning: with received tradition. It privileges, as they did, the legacy of the past. The researcher sees, however, that tradition was in dialectic with the conditions of the present; neither automatically dominant nor dominated, but always a factor with which to contend; sometimes victorious, but sometimes altered or even subtly rejected. This kind of cultural history examines how traditional categories for ordering experience and investing life with meaning were transformed in reaction with other elements.

A text from one of the leading Ashkenazi rabbinic authorities in history, Moses Isserles of Cracow (the Rama or Remu), who lived in the sixteenth century, can lend brief insight into this type of cultural history:

Some have written that a menstruating woman may not enter the synagogue or pray or speak God's name or touch a [holy] book; while some say that such a woman is permitted to do all of these things—and this opinion is primary. However, the custom in these lands [Poland and Ashkenaz] follows the first position; but during the 'white' days [i.e. the seven days between the cessation of the menses and the resumption of sexual contact between wife and husband] they would permit [these things]. And even where they are strict [in the application of the restrictive custom], on the high holidays and other such occasions, when many gather to go to the synagogue, it is permitted for [menstruating women] to go to the synagogue like other women, because it causes them great distress when everyone assembles and they stand outside.[9]

---

[8] Ibid. 136–7.

[9] This passage appears in the *Mapah*, Isserles' glosses on the *Shulḥan arukh*, 'Oraḥ ḥayim' 88: 1.

The genesis of the opinion expressed here by Rabbi Isserles is the biblical-talmudic precept that a menstruating woman (in Hebrew, *nidah*) is ritually impure. During the time of the Temple, she would be considered impure for the purposes of the ritual there. In addition, up to and including the present day, a menstruant is barred by halakhah from any physical contact with her husband. In traditional Jewish society, the complex rules governing menstruating women's behaviour were a foundation stone of ritual life, akin to *kashrut* and sabbath observance.[10]

In late antiquity in Erets Yisrael, and especially in medieval Ashkenaz, popular customs developed that went beyond the proscriptions mandated by talmudic law, to forbidding menstruating women from any 'holy activity' such as the examples Isserles mentioned. By the fifteenth century, however, the distress that the customary exclusion caused was taken into account by the important German rabbi Israel Isserlein (1390–1460), who set a precedent for part of Isserles' ruling by permitting menstruating women to attend the synagogue on the High Holidays and such 'because it brought them distress and melancholy when everyone gathered to be together and they stood outside'.[11]

Although Isserles explicitly recognized the legally non-binding nature of the extra restrictions, he was evidently both resigned to their entrenchment among significant sectors of the populace and well aware of the dissension that they aroused from others. Apparently, the trend implied by Rabbi Isserlein in the fifteenth century had continued, and there were more and more women (and their husbands?) who were not prepared to refrain from public ritual participation because of the expanded strictures. For them, the significance of public religious expression, as well as the social experience it entailed, overrode the meaning of the exclusionary practices. Isserles' response, in addition to denying the legal validity of the supernumerary prohibitions, was to reiterate Isserlein's indulgent ruling with regard to major holidays, and to affirm another way of mitigating the popular cus-

[10] For discussion of the category of *nidah*, see the article by I. Ta-Shma in the *Encyclopaedia Judaica*, xii. 1141–8; Fonrobert, *Menstrual Purity*; Wasserfall (ed.), *Women and Water*.

[11] On the history, development, and halakhic status of these customs, see Grossman, *Pious and Rebellious* (Heb.), 47–51, 318–19, and esp. the literature cited on p. 48 n. 106; Woolf, 'Medieval Models of Purity and Sanctity'. The quotation from Rabbi Isserlein appears in his miscellaneous rulings and writings compiled and edited by S. Avitan in *Terumat hadeshen*, pt II, no. 132, p. 377. For further studies of women and the synagogue, see Grossman and Haut (eds), *Daughters of the King*.

tom, which was probably an existing popular expedient in any case, namely, leniency with regard to the 'white' days.

Thus a traditional category—menstrual impurity—retained basic meaningfulness over the ages, but came to be interpreted and applied differentially by Jewish societies in different eras. In this case the prohibition was variably elaborated and relaxed. Jews did not disconnect from a cardinal practice and what it represented; but a particular mandate of tradition might be either intensified or attenuated in dialectic with other values that gained or lost their own meaning for society in various ages.

Issues of Culture

The objective of writing the cultural history of the Jews (at least up until the twentieth century) can be construed, then, as the elucidation of the ways in which traditional categories of meaning have been transmitted and transmuted in order to shape and express meaning for the generation under study. To do so, however, it is important to take into account a number of issues that are perennially associated with research in Jewish cultural history.

The Elusiveness of Historicist Analysis

Historians are trained to contextualize. Much of historical explanation is, in essence, supplying the historical context of a particular phenomenon. Sources are usually approached with the goal of uncovering what they indicate about the particular circumstances of the people and society that produced them. For example, in analysing a source, typically we seek to explicate what we can learn from it about the time and place of its composition which will identify it with its era and locale, and help to distinguish these from other places and periods. However, when dealing with traditional Jewish sources, whose authors regarded themselves as transmitting tradition and tended to blur the signs of their own time and place, historicizing can be problematic.

A good example of this is Isserles' *Mapah*,[12] glosses on the *Shulḥan arukh* law code of Joseph Karo, from which the above example regarding female

---

[12] This composition does not exist in manuscript versions and was never published as an independent book. It was intended to be read in tandem with the *Shulḥan arukh* of Joseph Karo, and indeed represents a new redaction of that work which effectively converted it into a halakhic textbook; see Reiner, 'Ashkenazi Elite at the Beginning of the Modern Era', 97; id., 'Urban Jewish Community', 13–24. The *Mapah*'s publishing history began when one part of a combined edition of the two works was printed in Cracow in 1571. This imprint quickly sold out and the entire double work was published,

synagogue attendance is taken. Isserles cited the gamut of medieval Ashkenazi halakhic sources and claimed that the very *raison d'être* of his work was to give them their expression and their due. Is there anything in his citation of halakhic sources that is particularly sixteenth-century or particularly Polish? With the exception of sporadic, explicit, salient examples (such as the one adduced above), how different are his halakhic decisions on sabbath observance or business ethics from those of his predecessors in thirteenth-century Ashkenaz? When he emphasized a particular subject, was there anything more to it than a loyal continuation of the hermeneutic and homiletic traditions he inherited? When he took sides in a halakhic dispute, was there necessarily something of his own society's problems influencing him, or was he engaged in a closed-circuit intellectual endeavour, insulated from the pressures of everyday life?

Some scholars have successfully contended with the daunting task of identifying differences between treatments of similar halakhic problems in sources from different environments. They have then explained how those differences allude to the specific conditions in which their authors lived.[13] This is a necessary and important historiographical approach. There is, however, an additional and perhaps tougher problem: not the exegesis of differences, but their frequent absence. Practically speaking, historians who have tried to use halakhic and other rabbinic works as indices of the issues,

---

again in Cracow, in 1578–80 (this edition was republished in facsimile in two volumes in 1974). Subsequently, every standard edition of the *Shulḥan arukh* has incorporated the *Mapah*. Perhaps more than any other factor it was this joining of the rulings of two prominent halakhic authorities—one Sephardi, one Ashkenazi—that enabled the *Shulḥan arukh* to attain canonical halakhic status throughout most of the Jewish world. Their mode of juxtaposition in one work indicated agreement on the fundamental questions of the need for codification and the possibility of arriving at a halakhic consensus—albeit filled with demurs, fine-tuning remarks, and agreements to disagree. See Twersky, 'The Shulhan 'Aruk'.

[13] The process of separating halakhic precedent and standard practice from contingencies and extra-legal concerns that 16th-century Polish circumstances gave rise to is a complex and arduous one that is not guaranteed to produce results. For examples of successful analysis of important differences between Polish and other Ashkenazi practice (and, by implication, how difficult and exceptional such analysis appears to be), and what these differences say about Polish Jewish life, see Fram, *Ideals Face Reality*, index, s.v. Isserles, Moses; id., 'Two Cases of Adultery'; cf. Elbaum, *Openness and Insularity*, 15, 27–8, 222, 376; Ben-Sasson, 'Statutes for the Enforcement of the Observance of the Sabbath' (Heb.); Soloveitchik, 'Religious Law and Change'; Katz, *Shabbes Goy*; Zohar, *Tradition and Change* (Heb.).

attitudes, and *mentalité* of the societies of their authors have repeatedly come up against the fact that these same issues, attitudes, and *mentalités*—and the modes of expressing them—are present in earlier works with negligible differences. The later authors can be seen to be repeating themes and motifs that are part of their received tradition rather than representing their own time and place.

As summarized by Mendel Piekarz, who criticized the efforts of scholars of hasidism to define its characteristic theological and spiritual features by studying the words of the early *tsadikim*:

The more deeply I probed the literary substance of the homiletical and moralistic literature, including the writings of Jacob Joseph of Polonnoye, I came to realize that various ideas and literary motifs which appear to be emblematic of their generation were actually the product of long ago ages and their literary source was the classic moralistic books . . . as well as works written a generation or two before hasidism.[14]

The conclusion of Piekarz's study was that the theological innovations usually credited to hasidism were not new at all, and that the movement's essence must be found in other of its features.

The difficulty is not only a practical one of developing the hermeneutic tools that allow for identifying the historical contingency of source material. One very influential school of scholarship insists that even in theory rabbinic texts are essentially ahistorical intellectual exercises 'for the sake of Heaven'. Their authors were dedicated to the distillation of halakhic, theological, or some other truth, and were not making subtle references to, or justifications for, circumstances in their own times. As Jacob Elbaum asserted:

It is conventional in our age to scrutinize every dispute of the past for political and quasi-political conflicts of interest; this may be no more than projection onto the past. It should be remembered that the feeling of mutual responsibility beats in the hearts of the sages of every generation and the concept that 'all Israel are responsible for each other' was the axiom which dictated the nature of their responses.[15]

According to Elbaum, when dealing with traditional texts written to further the comprehension of Torah, the attempt at historicization is dubious.

---

[14] Piekarz, *The Beginning of Hasidism*, 7–8 (Heb.); cf. Hisdai, *The Emergence of the Hasidim and Mitnagedim* (Heb.).

[15] Elbaum, *Openness and Insularity*, 15, and cf. 27–8, 222, 376; Rosman, 'Culture in the Book' (Heb.).

The approach of cultural history can diminish the need for the frequently frustrating search for what distinguishes one source from its intellectual and spiritual predecessors by focusing on the continuity present across sources. To be sure, much of sixteenth-century Polish Jewish culture is virtually identical with earlier German Jewish, or even talmudic, culture. Not everything is subject to historicist analysis, but that which is traditional and beyond contextualization is also part of the cultural—even if not the social, economic, or political—milieu. The *Mapah* anthologized tradition, picking and choosing the authorities and views to be juxtaposed to the *Shulḥan arukh*, in order to establish a standardized practice appropriate to the needs of the large urban Polish Jewish communities that were also organized into supracommunal co-operative councils.[16] Although much that is in Isserles' citations and decisions may not be original, the act of anthologizing implies that from the panoply of Jewish tradition there was a particular cultural canon that was relevant to his society. The components of the past that he repeated had cultural meaning in his present. We are right to analyse as part of Polish Jewish culture, not only material that obviously originated in Poland, but also earlier material that was repeated in the Polish context.

Another gender-related passage in the *Mapah* can illustrate this point. With respect to women and slaves wearing a *talit* (prayer shawl) with attached *tsitsit* (fringes), Isserles said:

In any case, if they want to wear [a *talit*] and make the blessing over it, [they] may as with all other time-bound positive commandments; however, it appears

---

[16] Reiner, 'Ashkenazi Elite at the Beginning of the Modern Era', 97; id., 'Urban Jewish Community' (Heb.). Joseph Davis, 'The Reception of the *Shulhan 'Arukh*', 262–5, has averred, based on his interpretation of criticism of Isserles' work by R. Hayim ben Bezalel of Prague and his own understanding of Isserles' use of the term 'these lands' (*medinot eilu*), that Isserles intended his code specifically for the Polish Jewish community, a position that accords with Reiner's thesis as to the purpose of Isserles' codificatory work. However, Davis also was persuaded that 'the "customs of these lands" that Isserles codified in his notes to the *Shulhan 'Arukh* were the customs of the Polish Jews' (p. 265). Even if this is the case, it is still incontrovertible that most of what Isserles wrote in the *Mapah*, and most of the halakhic practice of Polish Jewry, had earlier Ashkenazi precedents, making it difficult to prove a Polish *origin*—as opposed to *audience* and *practitioners*—for the contents of the *Mapah*. Also, Ashkenaz is not a monolith. As Zimmer, *Society and its Customs* (Heb.), 296–8, has pointed out, there are various streams—French, Rhenish, 'Ostreikh', and Byzantine—within Ashkenazi tradition. Both Zimmer and Edward Fram have suggested to me in personal communications that the 'Polish' customs Isserles was advocating (and that R. Hayim ben Bezalel was objecting to) probably derived mainly from 'Ostreikh' and did not originate in Poland.

to be arrogance [*yoharah*] and therefore they should not wear *tsitsit*, since [in any case] it is not a personal obligation [*ḥovat gavrah*]; that is, a person is not required to purchase a *talit* in order to be obligated to wear *tsitsit*.[17]

Isserles' ruling here is certainly not original. He was echoing a decision voiced circa 1400 by Rabbi Jacob Moellin of Mainz, repeated by Rabbi Jacob Landau in his late fifteenth-century code *Ha'agur*, published in Italy, and stated again by the Sephardi Joseph Karo in his sixteenth-century code *Beit yosef*, which preceded the *Shulḥan arukh*.[18] Yet this was not merely a ritual formulaic repetition of a halakhic cliché. It was, rather, a sixteenth-century Polish affirmation of a fundamental Jewish cultural conviction—that conventional gender roles were sacrosanct.

'Arrogance', as employed here, can be understood as behaviour that the practitioner engaged in so as to pretend to a status that does not properly adhere to her; similarly, it applies to a student who put himself on the same level as his teacher or a religious commoner who assumed certain pietistic affectations without being a fully fledged pietist (medieval-style ascetic, mystic hasid)—both of whom are also accused by rabbinic authorities of 'arrogance'.[19] Women who put on a *talit* were attempting to arrogate unto themselves male status (and slaves, freeman status) in contravention of their proper gender role. The technical permissibility, in halakhic terms, of women wearing a *talit* was not sanction for violation of one of Jewish culture's basic premises; that properly, men and women filled separate, complementary roles in all spheres, particularly in the area that symbolically represented the others—ritual.

The fact that Isserles asserted the prohibition against trespass of gender roles by repeating the view of an earlier authority rather than by making a fresh argument did not mean that the construction of gender roles was not a genuine issue for him and his readership. Citing an earlier source made the prohibition more compelling; it did not imply contemporary irrelevance.[20] Despite technical permissibility, Jewish culture as transmitted in Ashkenaz had other, perhaps less halakhically well defined but cogent,

[17] *Shulḥan arukh*, 'Oraḥ ḥayim' 17: 2.

[18] Moellin, *She'elot uteshuvot maharil*, no. 7; *Ha'agur hashalem* (Heb.), no. 27; *Beit yosef*, 'Oraḥ ḥayim' 17: 1.

[19] See e.g. *Beit yosef*, 'Oraḥ ḥayim' 3: 1, 24: 2, 34: 3, 90: 24–5, quoting earlier sources.

[20] Isserles' belief in the importance of maintaining gender boundaries is also implied in his comment concerning women wearing *tefilin*: *Shulḥan arukh*, 'Oraḥ ḥayim' 38: 3: 'and if women want to be stricter [and put on *tefilin* even though they are exempt] we prevent them'.

reasons for outlawing this practice that posed a threat to one of the foundation pillars of Jewish society. By treating it as Jacob Moellin had, Isserles could drive this point home. The lack of original views in no way signifies a lack of cultural urgency.

The Influence Model Versus the Polysystem[21] Model of Jewish–non-Jewish Relations

Given that Jewish culture is continuous with past tradition, a dichotomy is often drawn between 'authentic' Jewish culture that grew out of the Jewish past, and alien 'influences' which impinged on it from other cultures. In the Polish context, discussions of Jewish culture in Poland have to some extent even emphasized its genuine Jewishness by noting how little it was influenced by Polish culture. Certainly in contemporary discourse about assimilation, Polish Jewry in all ages is usually held up as one of the most 'Jewish' of Jewries, the least 'affected' by its surroundings.

Such a view might derive support from Chone Shmeruk's study implying that direct contact between Polish and Jewish creativity in the cultural sphere is hard to find even on the popular level. Both Jews and Poles have legendary traditions about a woman named Esterke, who was the queen (in the Jewish version) or mistress (in the Polish version) of King Casimir the Great (fourteenth century). Shmeruk's analysis showed, however, that the two traditions were, perhaps surprisingly, independent of each other.[22] The implication is that Jews had no interest in Polish culture, made no effort to become familiar with it, and even disdained it as inferior. Conversely, in literary form, Jewish culture was inaccessible to Poles.

More subtly, however, the Jewish Esterke tradition, as well as the Jewish foundation myth about Abraham Prochownik, who was supposedly instrumental in choosing the first king of Poland, and the famous story about the putative Jewish king of Poland for a day, Saul Wahl,[23] all denote a profound identification with Poland on the level of meanings and feelings. For a Jew to feel empowered, empowerment had to be legitimate and recognized in the Polish context. For Jews, people who were influential in Polish politics and society—and many more examples could be added to the three

[21] For definition and discussion of polysystems, see Even-Zohar, *Polysystem Studies*, esp. pp. 9–26.

[22] Shmeruk, *Esterke Story* (Heb.). See also Chapter 3 above for discussion of the significance of this story.

[23] Weinryb, *The Jews of Poland*, 17–18, 336; Karpeles, 'A Jewish King in Poland'. For analysis of this story and more sources, see Chapter 6 at nn. 8–12.

already adduced—were cultural heroes. Is such identification to be classified as an 'alien' influence on Jewish society, discretely separable from 'genuine' Jewish culture? Certainly, as a matter of policy, the Poles made no attempt to polonize the Jews as they did with other ethnic and religious groups. Jewish adoption of Polish categories of meaning with regard to power seems to be a measure of the extent to which Jewish culture processed the realities of life in Poland and responded to them. Is this response not a legitimate part of Jewish culture? Does it not also demonstrate that Jews were an integral, even if distinctive, element of the Polish polysystem?[24]

Jewish culture in Poland did not only incorporate features resembling specifically Polish culture, and there are numerous parallels between Jewish culture and more general European culture. For example, regnant pre-Enlightenment political theory held that government was not the representative of the public but its custodian. The oligarchic Jewish communal governing institutions, largely similar in structure and function to municipal bodies that functioned throughout Europe, certainly reflected this principle. In pre-modern times most people believed that the misfortunes of life were facilitated by demons who were invisible and everywhere. A huge amount of energy was devoted to preventing their machinations. Jewish books on practical kabbalah, in Poland as elsewhere, make it abundantly clear that Jews were parties to this belief and concomitant behaviour. In European economic life there was a basic prejudice against competition, and highly developed local protectionist practices were calculated to stymie it. Whereas Jews tended to circumvent such protectionism in their dealings with non-Jews, within Jewish communities protectionism was the rule. Similarly, the Jewish belief in the absolute necessity of maintaining complementary gender roles so that society could function properly was virtually the same as that which obtained in all other contemporary communities.[25]

Once elements like these, whatever their origin, were embedded in Jewish culture, is it appropriate to call them 'influences'? Having been long assimilated into Jewish culture, were not these characteristics also part of Polish Jews' 'Jewish heritage' that pre-dated their settlement in Poland? If authorities such as Isserles made halakhic rulings against gender trespass; if elaborate rituals were developed to ward off demons; if communal by-laws vested oligarchy and legislated economic protectionism for generations, does not

---

[24] Cf. Chapter 3 at nn. 29–32; Rosman, 'Innovative Tradition', 526–7.
[25] Ibid. 528–30.

this imply that these subtle cultural features that happen to parallel European or Polish culture were regarded as just as authentically Jewish by those who identified with them as any other part of Jewish culture? After the conservative forces in Jewish culture brought these elements into co-ordination with halakhic requirements, they were rendered tolerable and lent legitimacy. These things came to be taken for granted as part of the way Jews did things and, in practice, were as much part of Jewish cultural identity in the early modern period as biblically mandated commandments.[26]

Moreover, the usual impossibility of tracing modes of transmission renders the question of who influenced whom moot. Some of these common cultural components may indeed have originated from Jewish sources ('Judaeo-Christian heritage'). By the same token, the Jews did not inherit traditions only defined as Jewish, but also broader medieval European and even earlier traditions, which they adapted, made their own, and put into practice just as their non-Jewish neighbours did. Sometimes the Jewish version of a cultural practice shared with others has a distinctly Jewish flavour to it.[27] So cultural parallels should not be seen through the prism of influence, but rather that of comparison, as two variations of a common tradition whose roots are obscure. Jewish variations on the common culture can provide a useful tool for historical reflection on the nature of that culture and serve as a test case.[28]

Even ostensibly traceable practices related to dress, music, diet, and popular literature might be better characterized as cultural accretions by default—as the most viable alternatives—rather than isolated influences which by virtue of the power of the hegemonic culture displaced some pre-existing 'authentic' Jewish custom. These putatively alien accretions could be rapidly incorporated and deeply rooted in the array of Jewish symbols. Non-Jewish melodies were easily (too easily, according to some rabbis) adopted by cantors as music for Jewish liturgy and subsequently acquired

[26] Cf. Idel, 'Subversive Catalysts', 64; Satlow, 'Beyond Influence'.

[27] Brann and Sutcliffe (eds), *Renewing the Past, Reconfiguring Jewish Culture*, 9; cf. Chapter 3.

[28] Cf. Chapter 1 at n. 75; Elliott Horowitz's review of Mark R. Cohen (trans. and ed.), *The Autobiography of a Seventeenth-Century Venetian Rabbi: Leon Modena's Life of Judah*, 460–1. For reflections on the appropriateness of the notion of 'influence' to describe the relations between Jewish and non-Jewish culture see Satlow, 'Beyond Influence'; id., 'Defining Judaism'; the introduction to Myers and Ruderman (eds), *The Jewish Past Revisited*, 11, and chapters in that volume by Martha Himmelfarb, Elliott Horowitz, Moshe Idel, Gideon Libson, David Myers, David Ruderman, and Yisra'el Yuval.

their own venerability.[29] Festive-style, central European braided white bread became the definition of *ḥalah* for Jews in Europe and then, interestingly, was polonized as *chałka* by Poles.

Jews are a multi-coloured strand within the European cultural polysystem. In Chapter 3 I suggested that the metaphor for Jewish–non-Jewish cultural interaction should not be that of two magnetic fields coming into contact with each other and influencing or distorting each other, but rather a metaphor of recombinant DNA that originates from a widely available repertoire of building blocks, but achieves a unique character by virtue of the combining process. Put differently, it is a kind of intertextuality that defines Jewish culture, not the degree of purity of the origins of the 'texts' themselves. Authenticity is dependent not on pedigree, but on practice.[30]

The Place of Non-Jews in Jewish Culture

An important aspect of Jewish culture everywhere is attitudes towards non-Jews. Yet, while non-Jewish attitudes towards Jews have been a frequent subject of study, the corresponding Jewish feelings have not received much scholarly attention. Obviously, in Poland, as elsewhere, people who weren't Jewish were everywhere. Moreover, for Jews they were not an invisible Other. Judging from the attention paid to them in Jewish sources they were not only physically but culturally omnipresent. Communal record books and rabbinic sources have myriad references to non-Jews as adversaries, allies, and as falling somewhere between these categories: litigation with non-Jews; debts to non-Jews; business transactions and partnerships with non-Jews; the need to maintain felicitous relations with them and not arouse their ire; lobbying and co-operating with non-Jewish authorities; non-Jewish courts; non-Jewish testimony; episodes of anti-Jewish actions and persecution; the proper response to non-Jewish religion; casual relations with non-Jewish neighbours, acquaintances, and even friends; and much more. It has been observed that in Polish culture there was a range of attitudes towards the Jews across sectors of society and often a duality when comparing theory with practice.[31] Examination of Jewish sources shows a similarly complex situation in Jewish culture relative to Christians in the Polish–Lithuanian Commonwealth.

---

[29] Shulman, *Authority and Community*, 80–1.

[30] See Bruner, *Acts of Meaning*, 116, 118, on the importance of practices as opposed to contemplation in negotiating the formation of Self.

[31] Jacob Goldberg, 'Poles and Jews in the Seventeenth and Eighteenth Centuries'.

While the theoretical non-Jew was typically a monolithic, threatening character, real non-Jewish people came from a variety of social categories and were encountered in numerous contexts. In some they were feared and hated, in others they were dealt with matter-of-factly, learned from, even liked and trusted. The Jewish establishment in Poland believed that the safest policy was to limit Jewish–non-Jewish intercourse to an instrumentally necessary minimum. In contrast, many ambitious individuals aspired to close relations with powerful people who were not Jewish, which could be an important source of pride, power, and accomplishment. In the eighteenth century, some Polish Jews who had left Poland expressed scorn for the country and its people, and there are signs that some early hasidic leaders contemplated moderating the demonic image assigned to non-Jews by Jewish folklore and mandating relations with them based on ethical considerations.[32]

Such determinations as these, however, merely scratch the surface of this subject. Systematic research can expand the catalogue of Jewish attitudes towards non-Jews and show their development and nuances. It would raise and treat many new questions, such as: What were the typologies and stereotypes that Jews used to simplify thinking about non-Jews? To what extent were Jewish attitudes towards non-Jews typical of minority attitudes concerning the hegemonic group? What were the sources of the attitudes? What canonical Jewish texts were enlisted as expressions of Jewish attitudes and how were they reinterpreted to do this? How did different attitudes dovetail or conflict? How were attitudes concretized in both ritual and unprescribed behaviour? What role did attitudes towards non-Jews play in the formulation of rabbinic law and communal policies? What role did such attitudes play in the inner dynamics of the Jewish community?[33]

The Transition from Oral to Written Culture

In an influential article on the development of (post)modern fundamentalist Orthodoxy in Judaism, Haym Soloveitchik has posited that traditional Ashkenazi Judaism was perpetuated in large part via an oral culture. This was lost, however, due to assimilation in America and then replaced by a book culture that enshrines unprecedented legalism and ritual punctiliousness. Classically, Jewish culture, anchored in texts, was transmitted in a

---

[32] Weinryb, *The Jews of Poland*, 165–76; Fram, *Ideals Face Reality*, 28–37; Hundert, *The Jews in a Polish Private Town*, 40–5; Rosman, 'A Minority Views the Majority'.

[33] An important study that does consider many of these questions is Yuval, *Two Nations in Your Womb* (Heb.).

fashion that was 'mimetic, imbibed from parents and friends, and patterned on conduct regularly observed in home and street, synagogue and school . . . the classic Ashkenazic position for centuries . . . saw the practice of the people as an expression of halakhic truth . . . on frequent occasions the written word was reread in light of traditional behavior'.[34] As implied here, the dialectic between orality and literacy is very old. The early modern period represents a major stage in its development. The foundational nature of oral components in early Polish Jewish culture can be traced in many sources.

For example, one of the most common genres of Jewish text in Poland was the *pinkas* (minute book). Every community maintained a *pinkas* which was the official record of communal life, noting such items as by-laws, *kahal* decisions, court rulings, real-estate transactions, election results, budgets, expenses, revenues, taxation, credit transactions, and other communal business and events. *Pinkasim* offer direct evidence of how life was lived, of the problems and issues facing people in these communities, and of the perceptions and opinions of at least the leadership of the community. They also lend insight into the processes by which decisions were made and solutions were adopted.[35] The *pinkas* was under the control of the political elite, the elders of the *kahal*. Kept under lock and key, it was actually seen only by the scribe, the *kahal* official who told him what to write, and a few other authorized persons. Its contents were communicated through reading aloud at *kahal* meetings and selected public announcements (occasionally posted in written form) in the synagogue. Most people knew what the *pinkas* mandated by hearing it read or being told about it, not by reading it. It engendered a local tradition known orally and through intermediaries, not by ready reference to the authoritative text.

A manuscript entitled *Sefer haheshek* is a book of *segulot* (magical practices), a guide for *ba'alei shem* (shamans or faith healers) instructing them in the praxis of practical kabbalah, specifying what medical and mystical measures to apply to various human problems of the body, heart, and soul. Written by Hillel Ba'al Shem circa 1741, it indicates what was on people's minds and how they tried to make sense of life or how to deal with it when

---

[34] Soloveitchik published this article in two versions: 'Migration, Acculturation and the New Role of Texts in the Haredi World', and 'Rupture and Reconstruction: The Transformation of Contemporary Orthodoxy'; the quotation is from the first version, pp. 197–8.

[35] There are extensive excerpts from Polish *pinkasim* and some analysis of them in Weinryb, *Texts and Studies in the Communal History of Polish Jewry*.

they couldn't. It is a classic example of the role of kabbalah in everyday life.[36] Hillel Ba'al Shem asserted that he wrote his manuscript as a protest against a series of four *segulah* books that were published in the first half of the eighteenth century in Żółkiew, and against the general popularization of practical kabbalah which those four books both symbolized and promoted. Hillel insisted that the popularization of mystical practices through printing bastardized them by making them available to people who did not really understand what they were doing. Inexpert kabbalistic manipulation based on 'half-baked' learning gained from popular guides was at best ineffectual and at worst dangerous. It gave all kabbalistic practice a bad name.[37] Kabbalah should remain the domain of learned experts who would communicate with the masses—orally—on a need-to-know basis. His book was not to be printed; that would have made it widely available. It was to serve as a handbook for an expert, professional *ba'al shem* who would only get to see it if the manuscript's possessor deemed him fit and worthy.

Sefer haḥeshek offers a glimpse of the process of transition from orality to literacy. Hillel was fighting a rearguard action against a trend ascendant in Jewish culture since the appearance of printing: the popularization of knowledge through books. Traditionally, formal study was accomplished by oral instruction from a teacher based on a manuscript that students might copy, adding their teacher's glosses (*hagahot*). The educational text was the manuscript plus the teacher's oral interpretation. Without access to this 'text', represented by a teacher, students would find it difficult to learn.[38] Informal study was also oral, with parents and others instructing children at home by reciting quotations, citing various halakhic rules relevant to the daily tasks of life, telling stories, and demonstrating proper behaviour. Haym Soloveitchik called this method of transmission of culture 'mimetic'.

Printing changed this paradigm. Books, both holy and secular, now came into every home offering a much broader range of material that could be drawn upon for the edification of family members. In the formal educational setting, printed books gave students a degree of independence from their teachers. The study text was no longer the teacher's oral interpretation of the manuscript, but a printed, immutable book. The study curriculum

---

[36] The manuscript was discovered by Dr Yohanan Petrovsky-Shtern in the Jewish collection of the Vernadsky Library in Kiev. He has analysed it in his article 'Master of an Evil Name'.   [37] *Sefer haḥeshek*, 119*b* and *passim*.

[38] Reiner, 'Ashkenazi Elite at the Beginning of the Modern Era', 85–93.

could also be broadened to include the works of scholars whose focus was other than that of the teachers of a given area. Thus in Poland, for example, students could learn not only Ashkenazi texts, but Sephardi ones as well; not only halakhah, but philosophy, homiletics, biblical exegesis, and the full complement of subjects covered in Jewish books.[39]

Paradoxically, Isserles' *Mapah*—which exists in printed form only—was also a confirmation of the weakening of the oral tradition as printed books took hold. In his introduction Isserles noted that his primary reason for writing this work was to counter the power of the printed *Shulḥan arukh* which was such that students would be likely to accept its pronouncements 'without controversy and thereby contravene the customs of the[se] lands'. Rabbi Isserles was moved to anthologize and reduce to writing Ashkenazi oral tradition, largely based on oral teaching, in order to save it from oblivion in the face of Karo's code, as well as to shape it into a standardized halakhic practice for Poland's large urban Jewish communities. Being in an accessible, printed form would add to its presumption of authority.[40]

Sefer haḥeshek and the *Mapah* demonstrate that the old oral culture and its promulgators were on the defensive. The advent of printing and the consequent change in attitudes towards knowledge and its 'rightful' possession exercised their influence among Polish Jews. Each of these works, in its own way, is an indicator of the demand for printed books that could serve as the sources for Jewish culture. Book culture could empower broad sectors of the population, who now might come to know the halakhah as well as practical mystical rites by themselves without dependence on elitist experts (consider, for example, the spate of halakhic and prayer books for women that began to be printed in this period).[41] Because it was written

---

[39] Baruchson, *Books and Readers* (Heb.), 105, demonstrated that in Mantua in 1595 the average number of books to be found in Jewish households was approximately fifty. As to the exposure to a broad variety of Jewish intellectual trends and schools that printing facilitated, see Elbaum, *Openness and Insularity* (Heb.), 24, 63–4, 179–80, and *passim*; Reiner, 'The Attitude of Ashkenazi Society'; and Rosman, 'Innovative Tradition', 530–2.

[40] Isserles' introduction is included in the Cracow 1578–80 edn and the 1974 facsimile; see n. 13 above. On the objective of Isserles' work, see Reiner, 'Urban Jewish Community' (Heb.).

[41] Roskies, 'Yiddish Popular Literature and the Female Reader'; Segal, 'Yiddish Works on Women's Commandments in the Sixteenth Century'; Shmeruk, *Yiddish Literature in Poland* (Heb.), 11–74, 147–64; Turniansky, 'Old Yiddish Biblical Epics'; Zinberg, *A History of Jewish Literature*, vol. vii; Fram's edition of Slonik, *Seder mitsvot nashim*. On women's prayers, see Weissler, *Voices of the Matriarchs*.

and permanent, this culture would be more precise but also less flexible and adaptable. Once the rules were printed in an easily accessible form, life could be more readily measured against them. Mitigation of their rigidity through personal rabbinic intervention required a courageous assumption of responsibility, a towering authoritativeness, or both. Over time there was a tendency to enforce strictly the written demands and to articulate them ever more pedantically. It appears, then, that Soloveitchik was actually describing the culmination of a process that had begun centuries earlier.

Norms versus Praxis

The difficulties involved in using laws and other decretive works as historical sources are well rehearsed. There is no guarantee that behaviour mandated by authorities was actually implemented. Prohibitions are typically more indicative of the existence of the forbidden behaviour than of its prevention. Historians who base themselves on normative books are likely to be describing what elites wanted life to be like rather than what it was like in reality. For pre-nineteenth-century Jewish history in general, however, there is a particular dependence on prescriptive sources. The relative lack of Jewish archival documents as a result of the vicissitudes of the history we are studying forces Jewish historians to consider over and over again the books of rabbinic instruction.

Most Hebrew sources pre-dating the Haskalah are prescriptive works. There are no easy means for determining the extent to which the strictures of the rabbinic codes, the decisions of *kehalim* registered in *pinkasim*, or the directives of *ba'alei shem* preserved in *segulah* books were actually observed. Virtually every case requires careful textual analysis of the way in which the source presents its demands, and diligent search after collateral or comparative material that can shed light on the lives the authors of these texts intended to shape. In this process of analysing and searching we can be guided by the example Jacob Katz set in the 1950s in writing his classic study *Tradition and Crisis*. As he explained in the preface:

My description is derived from the various primary sources of the period: communal and provincial *pinkasim*, ethical and polemical works, and the like. I have drawn on the halakhic literature of the period—responsa, codes and commentaries—more than is common among historians. Moreover, I have not restricted myself to noting historical realia incidentally recorded in these works. I have focused on the laws themselves, which, after all, formed an obligatory religious norm for the Jews of that era. For me these laws stand out as evidence of the life and spirit of the time, and bear witness to the many theoretical and practical conflicts that affected both the individual and the community. I have drawn upon the religious training of my youth in order not to treat as dead letters that which was, for our subjects, a philosophy of life.[42]

What in the 1950s Katz called evidence of 'the spirit of the time', 'theoretical conflicts', and 'a philosophy of life' is today considered to be the stuff of cultural history. Normative sources do not represent sets of arbitrary demands originating with the authors of these books. They do present a considered exposition of how members of society should express that which all hold to be meaningful. They contain guidelines for responding to life in a way consistent with the cultural meanings held in consensus. They are not only codes of law or codes of conduct, but codes of meaning. As such they offer profound insights into culture, even if they do not necessarily reflect how people always behaved.

Recalling, for example, the use of the category of 'arrogance' (*yoharah*) to forbid various practices (as Isserles did with regard to women wearing a *talit*), we can surmise that the society that was expected to respect such rulings—regardless of whether or not every individual always did so—placed a premium on people knowing their place. Conformity was valued and promoted; it was important that people played the roles that tradition and society had delineated for them.

The Genderization of Society

The highly genderized nature of traditional Jewish society and culture is a commonplace. Yet as perusal of any standard survey discloses, Jewish men's lives have been explicated in rich detail while Jewish women are mostly described in brief, stereotypical fashion. It has taken work such as Chava Weissler's on the *tekhines* prayers, Renee Levine-Melammed's on Converso women and Converso religion, and Elisheva Baumgarten's on medieval Jewish mothers and children to demonstrate that Jewish women had a complex cultural identity, and a contoured religious role which paralleled and contrasted with those of men.[43]

The new slant on Jewish history we have gained from these and other feminist scholars is added to the basic lesson provided by Joan W. Scott in

---

[42] See Katz, *Tradition and Crisis*, p. xiii; for further discussion of this point, see Chapter 7 at n. 27.

[43] Weissler, *Voices of the Matriarchs*; Melammed, *Heretics or Daughters of Israel*; Baumgarten, *Mothers and Children*.

how to use gender as a tool of historical analysis.[44] We are now equipped to inspect sources with a view towards analysing how they depict differential gender roles. For example, from prayer collections we see that men's prayer was rigidly standardized, while women's prayer was more occasional and topical. From halakhic codes it is evident that men's ritual life was paced almost entirely by the calendar, women's more by biology and contingency. Educational texts show men's religious education to be designed to train them for public ritual participation; the purpose of that for women was for theological fundamentals, and personal and home practices.

We can also understand how these roles interlocked to undergird the structure of meaning and practice that supported Jewish culture. The elaborate sabbath and holiday rituals were well served by the combination of women's 'freedom' to serve as facilitators and men's 'obligation' to serve as performers, which in turn reinforced the facilitator/performer dichotomy in the family, social, and political realms. Children's initiation into the culture was premised on the mother having a flexible ritual schedule and the father a more regularized one.[45] When Isserles protested against women's acceptance of the daily obligations to put on *tsitsit* and *tefilin*, he was demarcating gender roles in a way that fostered the facilitator/performer dichotomy. However, increased female presence in the synagogue and Isserles' leniency in this connection, as noted earlier, indicate that gender roles could evolve. There were also spheres where the facilitator/performer dichotomy was undermined. In the marketplace there were women who were on their own or were real partners with their husbands. Their 'performance' was essential to ensuring the economic health of their families and of society as a whole.[46] *Sefer haheshek*'s numerous rituals connected to fertility, pregnancy, and birth indicate a domain of culture where women were the main performers and men the observers.

There was no more pervasive factor than gender in determining the structure of Jewish culture. Defining its parameters will go a long way towards clarifying the nature and dynamics of that culture.

[44] See Scott, *Gender and the Politics of History*, esp. pp. 28–50. Jewish analogues are Hyman, 'Feminist Studies and Modern Jewish History'; Magnus, 'Out of the Ghetto'; Shoub, 'Jewish Women's History'. On the development of Jewish gender roles, see the controversial study by Daniel Boyarin, *Unheroic Conduct*.

[45] Cf. Rosman, 'History of Jewish Women', 35 n. 29.

[46] On the economic role of women in Polish Jewish society in the early modern period, see Rosman, 'To Be a Jewish Woman' (Heb.); for medieval Ashkenaz, see Grossman, *Pious and Rebellious* (Heb.), 256–65.

The Place of Kabbalah

Since Gershom Scholem, one of the important directions in research on Jewish culture in the early modern period has been the elucidation of the significance of kabbalah in forging the normative Jewish ethos. In the nineteenth century, *maskilim* and reformers had charged that one of the main problems with Judaism as it emerged from the Middle Ages was the ascendancy in it of magical, superstition-inducing, practical kabbalah which occluded much of the rational religious substance of Jewish culture. Traditionalist practitioners of Judaism and apologist scholars of Wissenschaft des Judentums (the first incarnation, in the nineteenth century, of the academic study of Judaism) reacted to this charge by suppressing the contributions of kabbalah to Jewish life throughout history. Scholem burst upon the scene in the 1920s asserting that it is impossible to understand Judaism without kabbalah. With regard to the early modern period he was sure that the kabbalistically inspired reactions to the Spanish Expulsion reverberated throughout the Jewish world, and were somehow involved in all of the important developments of Jewish history from 1492 until at least the rise of Reform.[47]

Scholem's thesis, that the popularization of Lurianic kabbalah laid the groundwork for the spread of Shabateanism, has been stood on its head in recent years. Scholars have demonstrated convincingly that Lurianic kabbalah was not widely known before Shabetai Tsevi, and that it is likely that the impetus for its spread among the masses was supplied by the Shabateans. Moreover, Scholem's general view of the power of kabbalah to affect history has been criticized as reductionist.[48]

Be that as it may, the prevalence of kabbalistic practices and beliefs in everyday Judaism, in part thanks to the availability of popular kabbalah books as alluded to earlier, from at least the late seventeenth century on, is now conventionally recognized. Why—as opposed to how—this occurred awaits full explanation and the systematic exposition of the popular religion

[47] Biale, *Kabbalah and Counter-History*, esp. the chapters 'Mysticism' and 'Messianism'; Dan, *Gershom Scholem and the Mystical Dimension of Jewish History*, esp. the first chapter; Scholem, 'What Others Rejected: Kabbalah and Historical Criticism', 78–79.

[48] Scholem's thesis was stated concisely in the first chapter of his *Sabbatai Sevi*; for critiques, see Idel, 'One from a Town, Two from a Clan'; Gries, *Conduct Literature* (Heb.), introduction; Barnai, *Shabateanism* (Heb.), 10, 15–20. See also Elbaum, *Openness and Insularity* (Heb.), 356–76; Hubka, 'The "Zohar" and the Polish Synagogue'; Zimmer, *Society and its Customs* (Heb.), according to the index, s.v. kabbalah.

of the period has just begun.[49] Perhaps most importantly, the implications of kabbalah's entry into the lives of normal people have barely been explored. With the exception of researching the roots of hasidism, which drew much from popularized kabbalah, no one has asked which basic concepts, relations, and institutions changed. For example, was genderization affected? Was the educational process transformed? Did people sin less?

The contrast between the 'rational' and kabbalistic sides of Jewish culture is evident in comparing the *Mapah* and *Sefer haheshek*. Isserles, writing in the second half of the sixteenth century, rarely cited kabbalistic sources in his halakhic work. His hints at the Zohar serve only to reinforce the impression that this was a closed book to his readership and that he had no intention of basing his rulings on it. Compare this to the eighteenth-century *Sefer haheshek*, which is overflowing with demons, incantations, inscriptions, magical pictures and formulas, and prescriptions for behaviour intended to lead to beneficial contact with the supernatural sphere.

The *Mapah* reflects a view of life where God is in Heaven and all is right with the world. What the Jew is called upon to do is simply to follow the tradition of previous generations in the service of the Lord in order to qualify for an assured ultimate reward. *Sefer haheshek* assumes a world fraught with danger and excitement. One can never anticipate, nor be sure how to respond to the obstacles that life (or demons) erects. The Jew—and particularly the Jewish woman—must live with psychological tension with regard to the overriding question of whether she has sufficiently provided for the supernatural security of the members of her family.

From this differential approach to the basic human condition follow two different goals for religious life. Isserles' rules were the means to fulfil God's will and thus the individual and collective Jewish destinies. By following his halakhic decisions a person could hope to attain personal redemption and contribute the maximum to the ultimate Redemption. The goal of *Sefer haheshek* is something else: protection from harm at the hands of agents that are human or supernatural. The reward was simple survival. This certainly might explain part of kabbalah's popular appeal. Whether the objectives of the *Mapah* and *Sefer haheshek* were complementary and whether one took precedence are questions that deserve study.

---

[49] Chajes, *Between Worlds*; Nigal, *Magic, Mysticism and Hasidism*.

Conclusion

Wissenschaft des Judentums concentrated on the products of the Jewish spirit. Nationalist-inspired scholarship produced a Jewish political history. The Jewish historiography created in the decades after the Shoah and the establishment of Israel has turned in significant measure to social history. The postmodern age that has been so occupied with the deconstruction of symbols and meanings that were previously self-evident would seem to have prepared the ground for a new synthesis of cultural meaning. We can return to the study of the spirit; not what it produced, but what it was.

SIX

Methodological Hybridity: The Art of Jewish Historiography and the Methods of Folklore

❧

IN HIS ARTICLE 'Legends and History: Historians Read Hebrew Legends of the Middle Ages', the folklorist Eli Yassif takes a conciliatory approach to historians. He states his hope for 'cooperation between the two disciplines', shows his willingness 'to bring about mutual enrichment by learning from each other',[1] and employs more expressions in this spirit. However, from reading his article it is difficult to see what Yassif thinks folklorists can learn from historians. The article is primarily a critique of the work of three historians (Reuven (Robert) Bonfil, Ivan Marcus, and Elchanan Reiner) who based their studies on folkloristic sources, as well as being an admonition to historians in general.[2] Yassif maintains that their methodological amateurishness in approaching folklore research prevented these historians from realizing the full potential of their sources and led to misguided historical interpretations. The conclusion: only someone who is a professionally trained folklorist can treat legendary material. As Yassif put it: 'When he comes to deal with historical legends . . . a [historian] cannot give himself an exemption; he must be a "part-time folklorist".'[3] The tone of the article makes it clear that few historians have attained the requisite knowledge that would qualify them to analyse this kind of source.

Yassif's criticism should put historians on notice. He not only teaches an important lesson in how to utilize historical legends, but also raises a fundamental question about the historiographical enterprise: what is the methodology of history?

Kernels of Truth?

Yassif opens his article by making a bid to settle a perennial argument among researchers concerning the historical value of legends. In its latest

---

[1] Yassif, 'Legends and History' (Heb.), 192, 218.

[2] Cf. Yassif's previous article on this topic: 'Folklore Research and Jewish Studies' (Heb.).   [3] Yassif, 'Legends and History' (Heb.), 220.

incarnation this controversy finds, on one side, those who believe that legends contain 'historical kernels'—whether in the form of realistic details or as 'collective memory'—which 'reflect' the character and meaning of a hero, event, movement, or period. On the other side are those who claim 'The folk legend does not preserve any past, it expresses a present. It does not describe its hero, but rather its teller. It tells nothing about the time in which it is set; it tells about the time in which it is told.'[4]

With respect to the 'historical kernel' school, Yassif makes a pyrrhic concession: 'There is no doubt', he states, that historical facts were preserved in many legends. However, their existence is meaningless, because the effort required to sift the facts from the rest of the story material far outweighs the yield in useful knowledge. As he says:

But the attempt to reconstruct [the facts] is difficult and its results are dubious. Moreover, the effort required usually does not validate the results. No historian will base the conclusions of his research solely on facts that were discovered in legends of this type. They must be grounded and proven by additional sources. If the objective is to uncover historical 'facts' preserved in the legends, what is the point of discovering them if they will not be relied on in any case?[5]

What's more, the historical significance of a legend lies not in 'its matching known historical facts', but in 'the causes that led to its creation and in the way that it contributes to the historical understanding and knowledge of the society that tells it'.[6] In the rest of his article Yassif surveys what it is possible to learn about the tellers of the legends from the legends themselves, and how to go about learning it. Yassif praises some historians, for example Gerson Cohen and Aryeh Grabois, who abandoned the historical kernel approach and realized the true potential of legends: that is, to teach about their creators, their society, and their culture. In my study on the Ba'al Shem Tov (the Besht), I likewise contended that legendary material, like hagiography, can be used to prove things about the tellers.[7] It is not

---

[4] Zfatman, *The Jewish Tale in the Middle Ages* (Heb.), 103–4. For bibliography on this controversy, see Yassif, 'Legend and History—Second Thoughts' (Heb.), 188–9, nn. 3–4; Rosman, *Founder of Hasidism*, 264–6, nn. 15, 41, 42, 45, 46. For more discussion of legends in the Jewish context and bibliography on legends in general, see Teter, 'Legend of Ger Żedek of Wilno', 249–51.

[5] Yassif, 'Legends and History' (Heb.), 190.　　　　　　　　　[6] Ibid.

[7] Rosman, *Founder of Hasidism*, 153–5; cf. Heffernan, *Saints and their Biographies in the Middle Ages*.

clear, however, if adopting this stance necessarily precludes the historical kernel approach. As already noted, in contrast to some of his colleagues, in principle Yassif recognizes the potential of legends to teach both about their tellers and about facts from the past. He hesitates only because he is convinced that the effort required to analyse the story in order to clarify the historical reality that it reflects is not worth it.

In my opinion Yassif neglects one possible research use of legends. In a situation where other sources are lacking, legends can be helpful in setting the research agenda and the methods to be used in seeking historical information. The legend's details and general portrayal of famous figures, such as the Besht or the Ari (Rabbi Isaac Luria), and of central events, such as the Crusades or the establishment of a major Jewish community, suggest to the researcher directions worth pursuing. Names of places and people, periodization, events that supposedly occurred—all of these are heuristics that can lead the historian to accurate, reliable, and useful information in various non-legendary sources. Even if in the final analysis it is proven that the legend has no historical foundation, the legend can set the course of the research.

Take, for example, a source I have touched on briefly in other contexts: the legend about Saul Wahl. According to the story, after the death of the Polish king Stefan Batory, the Polish noblemen could not agree on a candidate to be crowned as the new king by the legal deadline for the election.[8] On the last day they chose a Jew, Saul Wahl, a counsellor and courtier to the aristocratic magnate Radziwill, as regent or acting king pending election of the permanent king. That night 'King' Saul declared laws that granted many rights to the Jews of Poland. On the morrow he conducted the negotiations that resulted in the election of King Zygmunt III to the Polish throne.[9]

It is easy to demonstrate the fictitiousness of this story. In those days it was well established that the interrex serving until the new king was elected would be the head of the Polish Church, the archbishop of Gniezno. There was no deadline by which the king had to be chosen: the voters gathered at an appointed time and did not disperse until they had elected a new king. It is difficult to imagine a situation in which there would have been the

[8] The Polish king was elected by the nobility.
[9] Edelman, *The Greatness of Saul* (Heb.); Karpeles, 'A Jewish King in Poland'; Bałaban, *Jews in Poland* (Yid.), 21–4; Bloch, 'Die Sage von Saul Wahl'; cf. Yassif, 'Folklore Research and Jewish Studies' (Heb.), 9; Bar-Itzhak, *Legends of Origins*.

need to choose an emergency, temporary, special ruler, other than the archbishop, so as not to leave the country leaderless. In addition, the appointment of the archbishop as interrex was institutionalized and routinized with no pre-set limit on the length of time he could rule. Similarly, examination of the protocols of the Sejm (Polish parliament) deliberations demonstrates that at the time of this interregnum there was no crisis such as the one alleged in the legend. The option of making the Jew Saul Wahl temporary king of Poland was never considered.[10]

On the other hand, the significance of this legend for Polish Jewry is plain. Like other weak and vulnerable minority groups, the Jews wished to affirm to themselves that they were placed at the centre of the affairs of state; that they played an important political role; that their rights in Poland were not the result of either undependable Polish kindness or Jewish manipulations. Also, as they had gained honour in the past, so might they be honoured once again.[11] Thus the legend attests, first, that the Poles needed a Jew to arrange their political affairs, and that Jews do have a political role to play; second, that the absence of Jews from high office is not a law of nature, for Jews can even reach the throne itself; and third, that the rights Polish Jews enjoyed were legitimate, granted legally according to lawful procedure by a licit ruler.

This legend does contain historical kernels. It names the hero, mentions the precise date, and holds Saul to be an associate of kings and noblemen. The research question it raises, then, is: was there a Jew in Poland at the end of the sixteenth century named Saul Wahl who was politically active? If there was, what was the nature of his political labours? What made him the candidate to be the hero of the legend that confirms the political legitimacy of the Jews in Poland? Both Bershadskii and Bałaban explored these questions and rendered a detailed description of Saul Wahl, who lived in Brest-Litovsk, served two kings, was close to the Radziwiłł family, and attained an important position in the Polish economy and polity, as well as in the Polish Jewish community, in the late sixteenth century.[12] It is probable that, were it not for the legend, the scholars would not have searched for the

---

[10] Bardach (ed.), *Historia państwa i prawa*, vol. ii: *Volumina Legum*, 221; cf. Karpeles, 'A Jewish King in Poland', 278–84; Bałaban, *Jews in Poland*, 26–35; Bershadskii, 'A Polish Jewish King'.

[11] Davis, *Minority-Dominant Relations*, 131–45; Rosman, 'A Minority Views the Majority'; Karpeles, 'A Jewish King in Poland', 288–92.

[12] Bershadskii, 'A Polish Jewish King' (Rus.); Bałaban, *Jews in Poland* (Yid.).

material on Saul Wahl and would have not have discovered this interesting and important figure. Despite their historical inaccuracy, the details of the legend guided Bershadskii and Bałaban, leading them to significant historical discoveries.

An additional historiographical role that legends play is parallel to that of the historical novel or historical play in our own day. This type of work is a dramatization of situations or events that happened in the past, although it is clear that the author's primary concern is with the problems of her or his own period, and not with history. However, the dramatization, in its attempt to revive historical circumstances in order to convey its 'message', has the potential to suggest new insight into the past that is not obvious from historical sources.

Both Jewish and Polish sources have given us rich information on the institution of leasing (arenda) in the sixteenth to eighteenth centuries.[13] However, few sources parallel the stories in the collection of legends *Shivḥei habesht* ('In Praise of the Ba'al Shem Tov', published in Kopys in 1814), which purport to represent the living, social, and emotional circumstances that obtained within the legal and economic framework that circumscribed the leasing institution. What was the impact of the competition for arenda leases on the competitors? How did the Jewish arrendator (lessee) and noble lessor relate to each other? What Jewish–non-Jewish social relations were formed in connection with leasing? In my opinion *Shivḥei habesht* reflects *living* (that is, within three or four generations of the events) 'collective memory' of the general atmosphere that the regulations, statistics, and reports can only allude to. This memory of mood is not connected to the historicity or lack thereof of the details of the story (names, places, dates, specific events, and quotations of dialogue). As Wilson (cited by Yassif) put it: 'Sketches and graphs teach us what people did; folklore tells us what they thought and felt while doing it.'[14] The stories of *Shivḥei habesht* offer an interpretation of the human and social consequences of the murderous competition for leases among the Jews, point to the possible variations in the tenor of relations between nobles and Jews, confirm that Jewish women and non-Jewish men could become romantically involved, and so

[13] See Jacob Goldberg, 'The Jewish Estate Lessees and their Rule Over the Peasants' (Heb.), 'The Jew and the Country Inn' (Heb.), and 'The Jew and the City Inn in Podlasie' (Heb.); Rosman, *The Lords' Jews*, ch. 5; Hundert, *Jews in a Polish Private Town*, 64–8; Teller, *Money, Power and Influence* (Heb.), chs 4 and 5.

[14] Yassif, 'Legends and History' (Heb.), 219 n. 71.

on.[15] The dramatization of the events reflected by the living folk memory suggests types of psychological and emotional reaction of people in situations, the historical context and details of which we can discover from other sources. In essence, the legends are an interpretation that can be compared with more conventional types of sources, providing possible ways to understand them. Although it is only a single interpretation, the legend has the advantage of reflecting the understanding of generations close to the events and characters it evokes.

Here we must heed one of the lessons of Yassif. The legends are above all folklore. They must be examined in the literary and historical contexts of the time of their crystallization as well as in terms of what they meant to the original tellers and their listeners, who may have preceded final redaction of the legendary narrative by generations. The legend was not told in order to transmit history, but rather for the purpose of dealing with a problem vexing the teller's society. Only in subordination to this assumption is the historian allowed to attempt to identify the historical elements of the legend. Failure to execute the folkloristic analysis will probably result in failure of the historical analysis.

In *Shivḥei habesht*, for example, the stories play up opposition to the Besht. I have demonstrated elsewhere that these stories about opposition were shaped to show that the Besht had to contend with organized and determined opposition on the part of the Jewish communal elite. This theme served the hasidic leadership at the time of the book's appearance in 1814 in two ways. First, it lent them legitimacy. If the Besht faced organized opposition, this was a sign that the hasidic movement was already institutionalized in his time and it was he who initiated the forms that typified nineteenth-century hasidism: *tsadik*, court, hereditary leadership, and so on. Second, it set an inspiring precedent. If the Besht could succeed in overcoming his establishment opposition, then it is likely that they would also ultimately gain acceptance as leaders of a bona fide Jewish religious movement.

However, comparison of the legends with other sources shows that only individuals opposed the Besht, not the communal establishment. Moreover, these individuals were disturbed by what they regarded as his arrogant and spurious claims of possessing supernatural powers to heal and perform miracles. They did not express any dismay at some supposed

---

[15] Dov Ber ben Samuel, *In Praise of the Baal Shem Tov*, see index, s.v. arrendators, arrendeh.

doctrinal or institutional innovations that might have signalled the founding of a new movement.[16] This is an example of how the interpretation of events offered by the legends cannot be properly evaluated until after the legends themselves are analysed in the context of the time of their appearance and in comparison with other sources.

A further historical use of legends is connected to Yassif's assertion that 'No historian will base the conclusions of his research solely on facts that were discovered in legends of this type. They must be grounded and proven by additional sources.'[17] This assumption bears qualification. It is true that legends cannot stand on their own as historical sources. Identification of historical material in legends requires comparison with other types of material. However, once the requisite analyses and comparisons are done, it can happen that a legend or series of legends are shown to contain historical elements. In such a situation there are historians who are prepared to use the legend as a secondary support or illustration in the service of a thesis resting primarily on other material. The call for grounding the legend in more historically minded material does not mean that every single detail of the legend must also appear elsewhere. On the contrary, legend can enrich interpretation derived mainly from more conventional historical sources.

The case of the Besht can illustrate this. Various sources attest to his being a hasid of the mystical-ascetic type in the tradition of the medieval German pietists, Hasidei Ashkenaz.[18] This seems to agree with the legendary descriptions of the Besht performing kabbalistic rituals, such as self-sequestration (*hitbodedut*) or having twelve loaves of sabbath bread. Similarly, it can be demonstrated that, when he was young, the Besht's economic circumstances were typical of those of a lower-class Jew of his time and place. This should incline us to believe the legendary portrayal of him as a typical multi-occupational Jew who was at various times a ritual slaughterer (*shohet*), circumciser (*mohel*), elementary school teacher's aide and teacher (*behelfer*, *melamed*), and secondary arrendator. A further example is that, from the Besht's letters, we know that he sometimes experienced ascents of his soul in the synagogue during prayer services on the High Holidays. This would

---

[16] Rosman, *Founder of Hasidism*, 118–19, 126, 152–3; cf. Bartal, 'Emigration of R. Elazar' (Heb.).   [17] Yassif, 'Legends and History' (Heb.), 190.

[18] On the Besht as an 'old-style' hasid, see Rosman, *Founder of Hasidism*, ch. 2, and Etkes, *The Besht*, ch. 2. On Hasidei Ashkenaz, see Marcus, *Piety and Society*, and Soloveitchik, 'Piety, Pietism and German Pietism'.

incline us to credit the description in *Shivḥei habesht* of his outward appearance during such an ascent on Yom Kippur 5518 (1757).[19]

In light of this, while it seems incontrovertible that legends teach primarily about the time in which they are created, this does not mean that they can never have anything to report about the past. True, we should reverse the order set by previous Jewish scholarship and analyse legends *after* mastering other types of sources (except when using legends for their heuristic value), and then mainly as expressions of the generation that told them. However, while the historical kernel method has been demoted, it has not been completely confuted. It must be utilized more systematically and with greater discernment; and it must be applied more sparingly than in the past.

Typical Sources?

In summing up his criticism of the historians, Yassif declares:

> The legend is transmitted orally and thus undergoes a process of transformation and adjustment to the changing social reality, the historical events and the psychological situation of the tellers among their audiences. From this perspective the historical legend is fundamentally different from the historical document . . .
>
> It is fundamentally important to recognize that the legend is not a typical historical document.[20]

Yassif's contrasting of the 'historical legend' with the 'historical document' introduces a category that doesn't exist: the 'typical historical document'. There are many types of written historical sources: letters, memoirs, protocols of organizations and law courts, communal record books, account books, laws, population registers, to name a few. As with folklore, each source genre requires preparation and methodological treatment appropriate to its character. A business balance sheet cannot serve as a historical source until it has been analysed as an accounting tool, with its business and economic significance understood. Autobiography, a literary genre, must undergo literary analysis on its way to historical interpretation. Without understanding why it was written, for whom, what thesis it seeks to prove, what rhetorical strategy it takes and what rhetorical devices it utilizes, it cannot be evaluated as a historical source. This is true of all source genres; they each have their own methodological peculiarity.

---

[19] Dov Ber ben Samuel, *In Praise of the Baal Shem Tov*, 55.
[20] Yassif, 'Legends and History' (Heb.), 218–19.

Folklore has no special standing in this regard. Yassif's criticism of historians for how they misunderstand his type of material might be repeated by jurists, economists, literary scholars, anthropologists, sociologists, and demographers. As Yassif seems to feel that historians in their methodological amateurishness cannot make proper use of folklore material, experts in other fields might feel exactly the same. There are, then, no 'typical documents' which can be approached with general knowledge and informed rational judgement alone. Every source type requires some particular disciplinary background. The ramifications of this for historians are far-reaching, and I will discuss them in the next section.

There is, however, one thing that most written source genres—whether a dry chronicle or a long, complex legend—have in common. They are all narrative and all present history from the viewpoint of the narrator who produced the source. As I have already emphasized in this book, no account—primary or secondary—can report on a historical event transparently or objectively. Description always entails interpretation. Selection and rhetoric shape the report in accord with the needs and interests of the writer and the intended audience. These must be considered when studying folklore just as they are when studying any kind of narrative. This means that the analysis of all types of narrative—including folklore—has a common basis and must utilize literary theory.

At this point Yassif might point out that folklore differs significantly from other types of narrative because of its oral and folk origins: 'Here, then, there is no writing, no author and no copying'; 'The use of terms like "author" or "copy", and the like, in relation to legend means missing its social character and social functions.'[21] Yassif is convinced that putting the story down on paper 'happens merely by chance—as when a traveler might visit [and request or make a written version so as to remember the tale]'.[22] Yassif seems to assume that the person who actually wrote the legend down was not involved in the process of redacting it and did not influence the content; that he was only a neutral vessel for transmitting the traditional folk narrative in its entirety.[23]

---

[21] Yassif, 'Legends and History' (Heb.), 213, 218.   [22] Ibid. 213.

[23] In his response to the original version of this essay, Yassif, 'Legend and History—Second Thoughts' (Heb.), insisted that I misunderstood him on this point: 'Every recorder of folk texts—myths, legends, parables, etc.—changes and adapts them in line with religious, class, artistic or ideological interests . . . However, it is wrong to relate to all recorders as if they are cut from the same cloth . . . from the missionaries who consciously and grossly changed the Native American myths so that they might serve as

The historian will certainly agree that the origin and essence of the legend is in folk oral tradition. He will not, however, accept the assumption that in every case the recorder of the story performed a purely mechanical task. The historiographical question that arises is: why was the legend first written down precisely when it was, by the certain person who did it, in the particular language and specific form in which it appeared? The answer to this question will often lead to the conclusion that the writer of the legend added a layer of his own to the story, and shaped the legend in accordance with his own approach and the situation of his audience. Even if there are no significant written variants of a story and all the versions point to an original canonic account which was repeatedly copied—as Yassif showed for the legend of Rabbi Amnon and the prayer 'Unetaneh tokef'[24]—still the influence of the recorder of the canonic account on the final text must be clarified.[25] The writing is an additional, late stage in the development of the 'chronikat' (the narrative testimony of the event[26]).

In other words, there is no reason to assume that legends are different from any other type of source that is subject to the influence of the person who actually did the writing down. A scholar who skips over this layer of the text narrative is likely to misstep. It may very well be that legends do not have an 'author', but there is always an editor, and editors add and delete, create a context, insert rhetorical devices, write transitions, and interfere in the text in numerous other ways, modifying the legend to fit the

---

supporting "proof" for Christian dogma, to reliable recorders who change a few words or several sentences so that they might be better understood by a broad, modern audience, there is a wide and significant gap' (p. 220). In this context, I think Yassif still must explain what he meant by the sentences I quote in the text.

[24] Yassif, 'Legends and History' (Heb.), 195–200.

[25] Even before it was written down the legend could have been changed by each teller according to his needs and the nature of his audience: see Ong, *Orality and Literacy*, 78–80, 96, 132–3, 145–7. On *Shivḥei habesht* as an example of the shaping of folklore by its writers, see Rosman, 'On the History of a Historical Source' (Heb.), 194–210. In this connection we should note Yassif's observation that the descriptive and dialogic expansions that appear in the Yiddish version of the Rabbi Amnon legend in the *Ma'aseh bukh* 'did not add or change anything' (ibid. p. 199). Any historian influenced by deconstructionism will assume that, unless proven otherwise, the recorder of the legend also shaped it and Yassif's assertion cannot be accepted without close analysis of the Yiddish version. On the face of it, expansions and the change in language would be expected to be a means to adapt the story to a new audience and this requires investigation; cf. n. 23.   [26] Yassif, 'Legends and History' (Heb.), 189.

editor's intentions, without changing the basic plot. So folklore is not as unique as Yassif would have us believe. As narrative it resembles other literary sources. It is also typical of many types of historical sources in that it 'belongs' to a non-history discipline, yet serves as a historical source and requires customized methodological treatment.

A Methodology for History?

Yassif criticizes historians for not defining their source genre properly. They fail to clarify the literary structure of the legends and the social role of the story. They also do not understand the nature of orally transmitted literature. Typically historians do not compare the internal structure of the legend to other legends and narratives. They describe the historical situation at the time of the formation of the legend without noting the literary context in the past or the present. These delinquencies are not, however, the primary problem. The heart of the matter is that historians do not check adequately the parallel versions of the stories that they analyse. Yassif maintains that it is imperative to check all of the parallels, both those that antedate the version that interests us and those that came later. He shows how such comparison can teach us the social function and the social status of each story.

We could thank Yassif for his valuable instruction in methodology, learn our lesson, and move on.[27] However, as noted at the outset, Yassif's critique raises a fundamental issue. If historians must borrow their methods from other disciplines such as folklore, and learn to apply them from specialists such as Yassif, what is the methodology of history?

In the past the methodology of history was close, critical reading of archival documents, analysing them with the tools of philology. Eventually this approach began to seem narrow, limiting, and, above all, subjective. With only general theoretical guidelines and hermeneutic principles, there

[27] This does not mean that Yassif's interpretations of the legends are always to be preferred to those of the historians he criticizes. Some of his points strike me as forced or speculative. For example, with regard to the story about R. Aaron the lion-tamer, Yassif determines that the true subject of the story is the efficaciousness of the use of holy names and magic in general. Only in a note (p. 208 n. 51) does he mention that in the story itself there is no reference to R. Aaron's use of names. Considering Yassif's great efforts to interpret each and every detail of the legends and all of the parallel versions, the absence from the story of a detail central to his interpretation of it piques one's curiosity. To my mind, he does not offer a satisfying explanation of this anomaly.

was no way to test or measure the relative accuracy or quality of different interpretations of a given source. There was no systematic, sophisticated methodology that would enable a researcher to transcend bias. Furthermore, archival documents tended to reflect only certain groups in society and but a fraction of the human behaviour worthy of historical description. Finally, when all was said and done, how many times could the same documents be interpreted on the basis of rational judgement? The range of possible logical interpretations was limited.[28]

After the Second World War historians began in earnest to adopt social science methods, especially quantitative ones. These methods promised precision and a lack of tendentiousness while opening up new avenues of historical research. Their application to historical material led to some stimulating and impressive new presentations of the past. Social science concepts, such as class, race, and gender, gave historians new perspectives on old material and lent analytical tools that yielded original interpretations. The social science approach also enlarged the reservoir of available sources and fostered analysis of additional sections of society. No more white male elites only. Now historians could find women and minorities too. No more limitations on studying political, intellectual, and economic activists. Now common people in all their variety and all their manifold activities could be included.[29] As noted in the Introduction, this new conception of the methodologies and subjects of history helped turn Jewish history into a legitimate, perhaps even mainstream, subject for historical research.

This rose does have its thorn. The process of adopting new tools of analysis, borrowing methodologies from other fields, expanding the source base, changing perspective, and broadening the subjects of research led to a crisis of disciplinary identity. In assessing the impact of scholarly innovations, the methodological type is highest on the list because it has the potential to lay the foundation for new directions in research in many fields and not just the one in which it first developed. We have seen in our generation how a single or small group of pioneering historians can develop a new methodology which turns into a fashion and is applied across the discipline: quantitative history following Lee Benson, demographic history in the wake of E. A. Wrigley, cultural history after Natalie Davis, Carlo

---

[28] Nichols, 'Postwar Reorientation of Historical Thinking', 78–89; cf. Novick, *That Noble Dream*, 379–80.

[29] Lipset and Hofstadter, *Sociology and History*; Hughes, 'The Historian and the Social Scientist'; Landes and Tilly, *History as Social Science*; Burke, *History and Social Theory*; cf. Iggers, *Historiography in the Twentieth Century*, chs 5–7; cf. Introduction at nn. 34–5.

Ginzburg, and Robert Darnton, book history emulating Lucien Febvre, Henri-Jean Martin, Elizabeth Eisenstein, and Roger Chartier, social history modelled on Marc Bloch and Charles Tilly, feminist history such as that of Gerda Lerner and Joan W. Scott.

These innovations, however, evolved from other disciplines and have been applied to history.[30] Historians have borrowed their working tools from others. As Yassif claimed in his area, sometimes historians' control of these tools is less than complete or up to date. Can a discipline based on eclectic, and not always expert, application of 'alien' methodologies be autonomous? If a historian is always dependent on the methods of other disciplines (such as demography, economics, sociology, anthropology, bibliometrics, literature, folklore), what defines her or his professional expertise? If an expert in a discipline such as folklore can apply the method better than the historian, or if the historian is an amateur in every field, who needs historians? The experts in the methodologies can just apply them to historical material. If there is historical economics, historical demographics, historical sociology and anthropology, is there still a call for economic history, demographic history, social or cultural history?

A historian will, of course, answer 'Yes'. These disciplinary experts specialize in methods; the historian specializes in knowledge. He or she must master myriad details that come together to form a context that makes it possible to apply the methods and formulate an interpretation with respect to a given phenomenon. This mastery qualifies the historian to understand which methodological tool is appropriate for analysing this set of knowledge. The autonomy of historiography lies in its historicist assumptions and the questions they beget. Yassif also recognizes differences between the questions of folklorists and the questions of historians. Historiography doesn't have a particular methodology; it has particular ways of thinking and particular objectives.[31]

Perhaps a historian can be compared to a clinical physician who does not need to be a researcher in order to utilize the results of various research projects to heal her or his patients. The clinician must know the scientific studies that indicate which procedures or medications are effective and can be applied to patients' problems. He or she then must master this knowledge to the extent necessary to apply it practically and effectively in order

---

[30] The classic and conventional historiographical use of philology was also borrowed, from classical studies and linguistics.

[31] For a summary of these, see Weinryb, *Historical Thinking* (Heb.), vol. i.

to achieve a peculiarly medical objective. Historiography is not a social science. It is a humanistic occupation, an art of interpretation which uses among other things the tools offered by the social sciences and other disciplines.

If historians did not properly utilize the variant versions of the legends they analysed, then they must try harder. This does not mean that they should not turn to folklore as a historical source, asking of it the questions that characterize historiography. The sting is in the questions and not in the borrowed methodology. On the contrary, it is incumbent upon folklorists and other specialists to formulate the methods of their discipline in a way that will facilitate its application to other fields and ease the transition from the 'scientist' to the 'clinician'. There is a wide range of methods that can assist humanities researchers—including historians—in their work. More and more disciplines—and not only in the humanities—borrow methods from other fields. It is becoming progressively more difficult to define fields methodologically (for example political science, geography, anthropology, sociology, psychology, biology) and the trend is towards more method-ological hybridism.

The historian's work begins before methodology enters the picture: identifying sources, gathering data or information, formulating questions, and then choosing the appropriate methodology. It continues after methodology has done its work with interpretation in light of the assumptions, questions, knowledge, and methodological analysis that have been proffered. Eli Yassif demands that historians become better folklorists; that does not mean that they need to stop being historians.

SEVEN

Jewish Women's History: First Steps and a False Start— the Case of Jacob Katz

❦

Katz as Functionalist

IN DISCUSSIONS ABOUT Jacob Katz's contribution to the study of the history of the early modern Jewish community it is standard to emphasize his methodological innovation. In his earlier works Katz applied the methods of 'social history' to his research and writing about Jewish history. It is customary to observe that he had been trained in sociological method by important interwar German sociologists, especially his mentor, Karl Mannheim. Through Mannheim, Katz was exposed to the theories of the founding giants of modern sociology, Max Weber and Emile Durkheim. By applying what he learned to Jewish history, Katz's work took on ground-breaking significance.[1]

This perspective bears clarification. Given the slipperiness of the definition of 'social history' and the undisciplined way in which the expression is used, it is important to be precise as to Katz's own understanding of the meaning of this term.[2] It is also imperative to remember that Katz did not work in a vacuum or against the tide. He did not inhabit a new theoretical bubble of his own making, detached from the mainstream. In his methodological approach, Katz may have appeared unusual on the Jewish history scene, but by virtue of his methods and their theoretical grounding he was a member in good standing of the dominant school of sociology in his generation. The scholarly and human focus on the often prickly relations between Katz and his rivals in the community of Jewish historians has

The original Hebrew version of this chapter, in *Jacob Katz Reconsidered* [Iyun meḥadash bemishnato hahistorit shel ya'akov kats] (Jerusalem, 2007), contains cross-references to other articles in that volume that touch on some of the points raised here.

[1] Myers, 'Rebel in Frankfurt', 12–20.
[2] Hyman, 'Jacob Katz as Social Historian', 86–7.

obscured the fact that Katz most certainly did fit into the international and Israeli sociology research communities of the 1940s and 1950s.

Katz can be classed in what Dennis Smith called 'the second long wave' of historical sociology. (According to Smith the first wave began with seventeenth-century philosophers such as Montesquieu and Hume, and reached its climax with the activities of Weber, Durkheim, and their students.) This second wave began to take shape in the 1930s and continued through to the 1970s. Its pioneers were sociologists such as Talcott Parsons and Robert K. Merton in the United States, T. H. Marshall in England, and the historian Marc Bloch in France.[3] This wave had two vectors: sociological and historical. Katz clearly distinguished between them when he defined his concept of social history in his programmatic article in *Scripta Hierosolymitana* in 1956.[4]

In that article Katz posited that 'social history' meant giving history a sociological interpretation of a certain type. As a rule, historical sociology utilizes sociological procedures and tools in order to analyse societies of the past with the aim of formulating universal axioms of human behaviour. This is identical with the objective of sociologists who analyse contemporary societies. According to Katz, however, 'social history' had a different aim. It used the tools of sociology, but did so in order to understand the development of a particular historical society over time—that is, through history. Katz was not interested in extrapolating universal laws.[5]

Methodologically speaking (especially in view of his attachment to the principle of functionalism), Katz belonged to the school of sociology associated with Talcott Parsons.[6] As such, he was a faithful representative of the first generation of Israeli sociologists who were functionalists par excellence.[7]

---

[3] Dennis Smith, *The Rise of Historical Sociology*, 1–14.

[4] Katz, 'The Concept of Social History'.   [5] Ibid. 302–3.

[6] For discussion of Parsons' methods, see e.g. Adriaansens, 'Talcott Parsons and Beyond'; Barber, 'Talcott Parsons and the Sociology of Science'; Buxton, *Talcott Parsons and the Capitalist Nation-State*; Foss, 'The World of Talcott Parsons'; Hamilton, *Talcott Parsons*; Munch, *Theory of Action*; Robertson and Turner, 'Talcott Parsons and Modern Social Theory'. On the relationship between the work of Parsons and that of Shmuel Eisenstadt, who was the leading Israeli sociologist during Katz's tenure in the Hebrew University's sociology department, see Dennis Smith, *The Rise of Historical Sociology*, x. 17–21.

[7] For a description of Israeli sociology at its beginning as founded on functionalism (and acid criticism of it), see Ram, *The Changing Agenda of Israeli Sociology*. Cf. Lissak, ' "Critical" Sociology and "Establishment" Sociology'.

However, in his descriptive aim and his style Katz—whose desire was to analyse historical phenomena objectively, and to formulate a historical description that was not primarily a narrative of events, but a description of institutions and relationships organized by theme—drew close to the spirit of the historians who, inspired by Marc Bloch, came together under the rubric of the journal *Annales*.[8] It would be fair to say that, with his particular mix of motivation and methodology, the early Katz was more of a sociologist than the *Annalistes*, and more of a historian than the Parsonians.

Parenthetically, we might point out that, in contrast to the typical circumstance in Jewish historiography whereby Jewish historians usually adopt a methodological approach only after others have made it conventional, Katz can be seen as one of the developers of the second wave of the historical branch of historical sociology.[9] There is a need for research that would clarify the relationship of Katz's work to that of his contemporary historical sociologists, and his place among them.[10] Another point usually forgotten in discussions of Katz's work is that he was not only a pioneer in applying sociological method to Jewish history (seen in a broader context, that does not seem so iconoclastic), but he also made some revolutionary determinations and came to some pathbreaking conclusions. Here are just a few examples of his courageous statements:

the traditional early modern Jewish community practiced a double standard of morality vis-à-vis Gentiles[11]

---

[8] This is the commonly used shorthand name of the famous journal which has gone through four incarnations and various name changes since 1929. Katz did have some criticism of this school: see 'On Jewish Social History', 92–3. Katz's affinity to the themes, approaches, methods, and style of both the historians and sociologists of the sociological history school can be readily detected by comparing *Tradition and Crisis* with the works of Bloch, Parsons, Merton, and Homans.

[9] Retrospectively, Katz hinted at his membership in this historiographical trend in his article 'On Jewish Social History'.

[10] It is interesting, for example, to compare Katz's approach in *Tradition and Crisis* with that of his colleague Shmuel Eisenstadt in his famous book, *Israeli Society*, where he declared that he intended to explore 'the development of a social system capable of generating and absorbing continuous change. It must be capable of absorbing changes beyond its own initial premises' (p. 2). This is a functionalist goal and similar to what Katz tried to do for traditional early modern Jewish society. Unlike Eisenstadt, however, Katz was never tempted to try to quantify his theories about society. See Eisenstadt, *The Political Systems of Empires*, and the critique in Dennis Smith, *The Rise of Historical Sociology*, 18–21.   [11] Katz, *Tradition and Crisis*, 32–4.

in the traditional Jewish community there were sexual perversion, Jewish prostitution, and illegitimate children[12]

not only was the *halakhah* routinely reinterpreted in response to new social and economic circumstances, but . . . sometimes it was simply ignored[13]

Werner Sombart was partially correct in his analysis of the Jewish relationship to commerce[14]

there is no significance to invidious comparisons of the moral levels of Jewish and Gentile societies to the detriment of the latter[15]

Perhaps most important was Katz's declaration at the end of his first scholarly article, on marriage and sexual life: 'Any true historical insight with regard to the development of Jewish society has the right to be considered a contribution to general historical research.'[16] Jewish historiography is not only for Jews and it should not be in an academic ghetto. It has something to teach of general interest and deserves as much respect as any other type of history.

As original, innovative, courageous, and profound as his research and writing were, Katz's social historiography[17] did lack a certain type of critique. While analysing his sources critically, he never questioned the structure, function, or effect of the institutions they described. Traditional communal arrangements were never subject to searching criticism. In contrast to the surveys of Ben-Zion Dinur, Rafael Mahler, and others,[18] in his depiction of traditional society Katz never presented systematic corruption that went unchecked; tyranny was always effectively opposed. Katz left his readers with the impression that this was a well-organized, well-tempered society that easily manoeuvred between the ideal and the real, actualized its

---

[12] Katz, *Exclusiveness and Tolerance*, 55–63.

[13] Katz, 'Marriage and Sexual Life' (Heb.), 31

[14] Ibid. 37–8. Sombart, *The Jews and Modern Capitalism*, has frequently been dismissed by Jewish historians as little more than an antisemitic tract.

[15] Katz, 'Marriage and Sexual Life' (Heb.), 44–7.

[16] Ibid. 54. Katz's opinion on the 'contribution' of Jewish history was compared to that of some contemporary scholars in Chapter 4 at n. 51. On the relationship between Jewish and other historiography, see Chapter 1.

[17] 'Marriage and Sexual Life' (Heb.); *Tradition and Crisis*; *Exclusiveness and Tolerance*; *Out of the Ghetto*. Below I will claim that in his later work Katz ceased writing social history.

[18] e.g. Dinur, 'The Beginning of Hasidism' (Heb.); Mahler, *History of the Jews in Poland* (Heb.), 357–415; Bałaban, *History of the Jews in Cracow and Kazimierz*, ii. 608–18, 755–65.

basic values, and succeeded in doing whatever was necessary to facilitate and secure Jewish existence in what was, at bottom, a hostile world.

I think Katz's functionalist analysis was the key to this perception. The basic functionalist question is: is this phenomenon functional or dysfunctional? If the object of study passes this test, that means that it succeeded in its context and should not be criticized on the basis of today's values. Accordingly, Katz described the early modern Jewish community as a machine dedicated to supplying the social needs of its members. All of its parts were essential and worked in tandem in order to ensure that the machine functioned properly and performed its appointed task.[19] If this machine functioned and succeeded in preserving the Jews, it fulfilled its mission and there is no place for judging it beyond this fact.

Since functionalist analysis was standard in social science research in Katz's era, he had a right to feel that his research conformed to the strictest requirements of the field. With time, however, it became clear that functionalism tends to defend the status quo, the conventional. After all, existing arrangements have usually demonstrated their ability to work to some degree. Functionalism also has difficulty explaining variations and internally generated change in the models it is studying. (If all of the elements of the machine mesh, there is no internal factor to disturb the equilibrium and cause change.)[20]

Katz's functionalism was not different.[21] The upshot of his description of the traditional Jewish community was that the daring assertions mentioned earlier were embedded in a portrayal of a community that was ideal, not only in the sense that a sociological model is ideal, but also in reality. Jews who wanted to could take pride that scholarship had confirmed the traditional community as a sterling example of a properly working social institution and, not least, in consonance with halakhah.[22]

Katz the Social Historian on Women

All of the foregoing can help us understand Katz's relationship to the subject of women. For approximately the first half of the period that marked Katz's academic career, from the mid-1940s until the early 1970s, women

---

[19] Katz, 'Marriage and Sexual Life' (Heb.), 21, and *Tradition and Crisis*, 49–50.

[20] For critiques of functionalism, see Stocking, *Functionalism Historicized*; Alexander, *Neofunctionalism and After*. See also the works cited in nn. 6–7 above.

[21] Hyman, 'Jacob Katz as Social Historian', 88.

[22] Twersky, review of Katz, *Tradition and Crisis*.

were virtually absent from historiography, and certainly from its Jewish subset. When historians wrote about 'the Jew' or 'Jews', they almost always referred to the men of the group. The man was the primary maker of history and therefore its prime subject. In historiography he was the default choice. When women were mentioned, it was often in the context of exceptional women, such as Berurya, wife of Rabbi Meir, who figured in the Mishnah, or the powerful Spanish financier, merchant, and political activist Dona Gracia Mendes, or the Polish-Russian industrialist Haya Luria. Sometimes women entered the narrative when the issues in question entailed obvious female participation and were of a highly ideological nature, such as martyrdom and 'the status of the woman in Judaism'. Usually such presentations manifested an overtly apologetic tone.[23]

When the grand themes of Jewish historiography were the subject—Jewish intellectual and spiritual production, autonomous institutions, the relationship to non-Jewish culture and society, attitudes of non-Jews towards Jews and antisemitism, Jewish legal status, education, religious movements, the rabbinate, nationalism—women did not command more than cursory attention. As with historiography in general, this was justified by the claim that women were not normally active in the public sphere and thus did not 'make' history. Moreover, they were virtually absent from the historical sources.[24] What was not understood was that there was circularity at work here. So long as the historiographic focus was on topics that derived from sources created by the economic and rabbinic male elites, the members of those elites would be seen as the main historical actors, and their deeds, thoughts, problems, and attainments would be the ones studied. Even most men would be excluded.

Katz, setting as his aim the study of Jewish *society*, changed the map. He specified that he desired 'to present all aspects, institutions and functions of [traditional Jewish] society'.[25] In line with his sociological approach, he

---

[23] See e.g. Roth, *The Jews in the Renaissance*, 44–58; Baron, *Social and Religious History of the Jews*, index vols, s.v. women.

[24] Ironically, in view of his early contribution to the subject of Jewish women in history, late in his career Katz echoed these excuses in his debate with Chava Weissler: 'On Law, Spirituality, and Society in Judaism': 'This "brush-off" is not the work of the historians but of history itself' (p. 107).

[25] Katz, *Tradition and Crisis*, p. xii. Of course, Katz was not the first historian of the Jews to touch on social topics, but he was the first to attempt to do so according to a defined and systematic methodology and to formulate far-reaching conclusions with theoretical implications.

expanded the definition of 'institution' to include not only defined, structured institutions such as the organized community (*kehilah*), but also systems of relationships such as the family, kinship, and links to non-Jews.[26] He also exploited a very old and traditional source—halakhic literature—in a new way. The conventional mode was to mine halakhah for bits of historical realia that appeared in it secondarily and sporadically. Katz related to the laws as social norms and used them to learn about the values of the society, the structure of its relationships, and the nature of its institutions.[27] This change shed new light on traditional subjects, but also created new questions and new subjects.

One of these subjects was the family. Before Katz, discussion of the Jewish family belonged more to the orbit of the rabbis than to that of the historians, with stress being placed on the ideal of the Jewish family. Katz, however, asked how the family, a non-coercive institution, satisfied the needs of the individuals who belonged to it. What was 'the matrix of elements that determined the forms of connubial life and the modes of experience that accompanied it'?[28]

One result of Katz's questions was the insight (original in its time) that to really understand the Jews' historical situation it is necessary to explore the circumstances and activities of Jewish women. When Katz began examining the institution of the family, he did not limit himself to the thoughts, feelings, and actions of the men in it, but also turned to its women.[29] His dedication to researching 'social history', according to his conception of the term, led him to broach the subject of women and history. To be sure, he was not so far ahead of his time not to still think of the man as the 'default choice',[30] but he did introduce women into his field of discourse. When he referred to children he discussed both sons and daughters. He spoke much of the 'couple', and distinguished between the motives and reactions to family life of men and women, as well as noting its differential effects on them.[31]

---

[26] Katz, *Tradition and Crisis*, table of contents and pp. 4–6; cf. Hyman, 'Jacob Katz as Social Historian', 89.

[27] Cf. Chapter 5 at n. 42.

[28] Katz, *Tradition and Crisis*, 113–14, and 'Marriage and Sexual Life' (Heb.), 22.

[29] 'Marriage and Sexual Life' (Heb.), 34–5, 41–3, and *Tradition and Crisis*, 113–14, 121–2.

[30] e.g. 'Marriage and Sexual Life' (Heb.), 23–5, 28, 33, 40.

[31] Ibid. 28, 30, 33, 34, 38, 41, 44, 45; *Tradition and Crisis*, 113–14, 121–2; id., *Out of the Ghetto*, 84–6.

Katz made women's lives a subject for historiography. He recognized that sexual life fulfilled important functions for women no less than for men. He discerned how important women's economic activities were to the viability of both family and communal economies, maintaining that the typical woman was a partner in the economic endeavours of her husband. He also commented on the contradiction between women's activist role in real life and the more quiescent halakhic ideal that they were supposed to realize.[32]

Writing in the 1940s and 1950s, Katz did not employ the term 'gender' (which had not yet assumed the sense that it eventually acquired when used in historiography), but he anticipated it by describing basic differences between the behaviour and roles of the sexes as being the outcome of social organization, not biology. Matchmaking customs, family responsibilities, sex life, economic tasks, and divorce calculations—all of these were different for women and men, not because of the laws of nature but because of social arrangements in *this* particular society. In another society the differences might take on other forms.[33]

As with his work in other subject areas, Katz arrived at a number of audacious conclusions in his research on women. One was that the normative male perspective regarded women's social role to be primarily facilitative, to make it possible for men to live in sexual purity, to provide an economic foundation for their families with the dowries they brought into their marriages, and to have children.[34] Here Katz contributed a key concept to understanding women's historic role: that is, women as facilitators of the realization of men's cultural, religious, and economic goals.[35] He also made a further significant observation: *Eshet ḥayil* (literally, a valiant woman), a woman who was the main breadwinner for her family, with a full-time scholar for a husband, was not a common institution in the early modern period.[36] In further anticipation of later feminist scholarship, Katz hinted in *Tradition and Crisis* that hasidism impinged on family life and placed an extra burden on women. Similarly, in *Out of the Ghetto* he stated that, because of a lack of formal Jewish education, women in general—not just

[32] 'Marriage and Sexual Life' (Heb.); *Tradition and Crisis*, 113–14, 121–2.

[33] 'Marriage and Sexual Life' (Heb.), 23–45; *Tradition and Crisis*, 113–24.

[34] 'Marriage and Sexual Life' (Heb.), 22–8, 34; *Tradition and Crisis*, 113–24.

[35] See Rosman, 'History of Jewish Women', 46–50.

[36] 'Marriage and Sexual Life' (Heb.), 43; *Tradition and Crisis*, 313. This important observation has been missed by many later researchers, who have assumed that 'Eshet ḥayil' was normative; see Rosman, 'History of Jewish Women', 39–40.

the so-called 'salon women'—were the avant-garde of Jewish acculturation from the eighteenth century on.[37]

By packaging his analysis in a functionalist envelope Katz implied that the justification for women's inferior cultural and social position was its necessity for the proper functioning of Jewish society. In this respect his writing on women joins the long list of targets of Joan W. Scott's famous critique, written in the late 1980s, in which she contended that a functionalist analysis of gender, even if based on a social and not a biological approach, always construes the gender matrix it is describing as natural, even inevitable, under the given circumstances.[38]

Considering the social and scholarly context in which he functioned, what is remarkable about Katz is not what he missed, but that he understood enough in order to raise the issue of women as a historical subject. He opened a window by setting a research framework, identifying relevant sources, and reaching challenging conclusions. Alas, he was ahead of his time. There was almost no response to his pronouncements about women in Jewish history (except for Hayim Hillel Ben-Sasson's call to return to the more idyllic conventional image of traditional Jewish women as invariably—and ahistorically—pious, chaste, and noble).[39] As for family life in general, for decades scholars used Katz's trailblazing article 'Marriage and Sexual Life Among the Jews at the Close of the Middle Ages' not as a point of departure for further exploration of this subject, but as a vehicle to excuse themselves from dealing with the subject of the family, often writing something to the effect: 'On Jewish family life, see Katz, *Zion*, 1945. We can now return to the matter at hand.'

Something else worth thinking about is that Katz pioneered the subject of women in history *before* the feminist wave broke on the shore of Western societies. More interesting still, once feminism gathered momentum and began to have an influence on historiography, women virtually disappeared from his work. After *Out of the Ghetto* (1973), he rarely mentioned women again in his writings. This reinforces the thesis that Katz engaged the subject of women, not out of a feminist consciousness, but from a commit-

---

[37] *Tradition and Crisis*, 212; *Out of the Ghetto*, 85–6; cf. Rapoport-Albert, 'On Women in Hasidism'; Parush, *Reading Jewish Women*.

[38] Scott, *Gender and the Politics of History*, 32–3; cf. Chapter 5 at nn. 44–5, and Rosman, 'History of Jewish Women', 35 n. 29.

[39] Ben-Sasson reviewed *Tradition and Crisis*, negatively, in *Tarbiz*, 29 (1960), 297–312. Katz responded in *Tarbiz*, 30 (1961), 62–8, and Ben-Sasson answered him on pp. 69–72 of the same issue.

ment to social history. The turn of the academic world to feminist-informed scholarship during the last part of his life was not a factor in his relationship to the subject he had raised so long before. Taking this a step further, I would claim that since Katz's occupation with women was a function of his interest in social history in general, the absence of women from his later studies, just as feminism was becoming a formidable force, reflects a more general change in his historical approach.

Katz Changes Direction

Here I think we can identify a feature of Katz's oeuvre that has not been accentuated enough. From the 1970s he essentially abandoned social history/historical sociology as an interpretative framework and rhetorical strategy, as he had laid out in his 1956 essay.[40] His later books, and the great majority of his articles from the 1970s, tended towards the representational style of continuous narrative conventionally used in describing past people and events. His work still was studded with sociological insights and innovative and important conclusions. However, from his book on the Masons and the Jews[41] (which preceded *Out of the Ghetto*) until *A House Divided: Orthodoxy and Schism in Nineteenth-Century Central European Jewry*—with the exception of *The Shabbes Goy*—Katz stopped presenting reality in an abstracted, generalized form. He stopped social science-style modelling, and reverted to describing figures, events, and processes instead of themes, institutions, and relationships.

This shift was a move in the direction of a long-standing interest. From the beginning of his scholarly activity, Katz demonstrated that he was curious about how ideas affected reality, and, especially, he desired to plumb the history of halakhah. Therefore, in the second half of his career he invested many resources in explicating the history of ideas and of halakhah.[42] He actually announced his change of direction, if only in retrospect. In an article that appeared in both German and English (but, interestingly, not in Hebrew),[43] Katz criticized his own approach to social history, citing various shortcomings of his erstwhile methodology, and especially 'The picture

---

[40] See n. 4 above.   [41] Katz, *Jews and Freemasons in Europe, 1723–1939* (Heb.).

[42] See Katz, *From Prejudice to Destruction* and *The Shabbes Goy*, and almost all of the collections of his articles. On Katz as a historian of ideas, see Twersky, review of *Tradition and Crisis*, and Hyman, 'Jacob Katz as Social Historian', 91–4. For a full bibliography of Katz's writings, see *The Writings of Jacob Katz, 1933–1998*.

[43] Jacob Katz, 'On Jewish Social History'.

delineated portrays society in a quasi-static state, tending to neglect that essential element characteristic of all historiographic description, namely, the tracing of temporal change.'[44]

It is almost startling to recall how, in his 1956 programmatic article, Katz emphasized that the difference between historical sociology and social history was to be found precisely in the task of the latter to describe development over time. Apparently at some point between 1956 and 1991, probably in the 1970s, he understood that the sociological method cannot, in fact, track temporal change. He was forced to choose between presenting the essential features of a phenomenon by means of sociological method, and describing change and what caused it. He decided in favour of the second option, changing direction and style accordingly. As he characterized it: 'The social-historical approach cannot do justice to the entire array of questions raised in historiographical research. Alongside this perspective there is ample justification for tracing events and processes within a longer time frame.'[45]

The absence of women from Katz's later work is one indicator of his fundamental change of historiographic approach. It is not necessarily a statement about his attitude towards feminist history—but such a statement does exist.

Katz the Intellectual Historian on Women

In 1994 Katz gave the keynote lecture 'Law, Spirituality and Society' at the annual conference of the Center for Advanced Judaic Studies of the University of Pennsylvania. Chava Weissler attacked his lecture from a feminist perspective. Katz, who truly believed in the value of intellectual debate and the power of criticism when attempting to attain clarity and new knowledge, suggested that he and Weissler develop and preserve their exchange in print, and in 1996 it was published in *Jewish Social Studies*.[46]

In his half of the article Katz explored the relationship between halakhah, Jewish spirituality in its various forms, and Jewish society. He stressed the role of halakhah and kabbalah in shaping society and its life. The essay was

[44] Jacob Katz, 'On Jewish Social History', 92; cf. Hyman, 'Jacob Katz as Social Historian', 95–6.   [45] Katz, 'On Jewish Social History', 96.
[46] It appeared as 'On Law, Spirituality, and Society in Judaism: An Exchange Between Jacob Katz and Chava Weissler'.

an exercise in essentialism, that is, an attempt to understand the basic elements that characterized traditional Jewish society from the days of the Talmud until Emancipation. Katz assumed that these basic elements were primarily intellectual, lending outsize significance to the activities and intellectual production of the Torah elite. With such an essentialist approach and the highlighting of intellectual-elitist activity, this essay seemed like a return to the Jewish historiography of the pre-1960 period, certainly disconnected from the postmodern climate of the 1990s.

Weissler did not, however, criticize him on these grounds. Her main complaint was that, for Katz, it was axiomatic that women had no place in this discussion. Katz, who long before had had so much new to say about women's lives in Jewish society, now seemed to have joined those who believed that women were uninvolved in Jewish spiritual life, being neither producers nor consumers. As Weissler put it: 'Once we leave the world of kinship and family institutions behind and enter the "serious" intellectual world, women are not merely brushed aside but made to disappear entirely. Their absence is not even raised as a question; it engenders no curiosity. It is so much a part of "the order of things" as to be invisible in itself.'[47] She then proceeded to develop two theses: the first, that women did indeed have a spiritual life, and the second, that this female spirituality had a significant impact on society, and was itself affected by the phenomena Katz had described.

In his response Katz put forward two claims of his own. He began by insisting that 'the historian remains sovereign in the choice of his research subject'. Having defined the parameters of the subject, he (or she) has no obligation to relate to every question that the sources might imply. Therefore he had the right to consider male spiritual life only.[48] In my opinion, in the context of the exchange with Weissler, this was an evasion. Once a historian has defined the subject, he or she may not have to pursue all of the lines of enquiry that the *sources* suggest, but is obligated to at least demonstrate awareness of all of the questions that the *subject* entails. Critics are within their rights to criticize a failure on this score.

In the 1990s, after some twenty years of feminist scholarship, any thinking person might have been expected to recognize the appropriateness of Weissler's question within the parameters of the subject defined by Katz.

---

[47] Katz and Weissler, 'On Law, Spirituality, and Society', 99.

[48] Ibid. 106. This was a basic principle of Katz's; see 'Marriage and Sexual Life' (Heb.), 21, and 'On Jewish Social History', 91.

In fact, Katz admitted as much. He expressed an opinion on the subject of women's spiritual lives—in the original essay by implication, and in his response to Weissler explicitly: 'Women in this society were not creative or even active in these fields . . . The fact is that in traditional Jewish society women had no active role in the sphere of law and spirituality.'[49]

This declaration led to Katz's second claim against Weissler and feminist historians as a group: namely, that in their enthusiasm to create a history with which they could identify,[50] and to turn women into historical agents (as opposed to passive objects), they distorted history. They presented exceptions as typical and imagined that women in general filled social and cultural roles that only a very few attained. They refused to see how in reality women were 'enmeshed in' or 'absorbed into' their culture, but not active in its creation.[51]

This is the voice of a conventional intellectual historian that Katz, the social historian, had challenged fifty years earlier. In his early work Katz shifted the general perspective on traditional society. He prompted new questions and focused attention on phenomena that had been invisible. He also suggested new interpretations of the meaning of the various elements of society in the past. Among other things, he identified women as a significant social element. But in this debate Katz faced the feminist revolution wearing the hat of the historian of ideas, after having doffed the cloak of the historical sociologist. If I may be permitted some speculation, I believe that the Katz of 1960, imbued with the feminist consciousness of 1990, could have been expected to carve out new paths in this area, asking new questions of old sources, and finding new sources and new types of sources, defining new categories of social action, and constructing novel theories inclusive of women. Instead, Katz of 1990, no longer a social historian—as he himself had defined the term[52]—responded to the feminist challenge offhandedly and defensively.

---

[49] Katz and Weissler, 'On Law, Spirituality, and Society', 107.

[50] Weissler, for example, in her article, 'The Religion of Traditional Ashkenazic Women', 94, and in her book, *Voices of the Matriarchs*, 50, pronounced that it is possible to 'reclaim' alternative models of gender construction that Ashkenazi Judaism offered throughout history.

[51] Katz and Weissler, 'On Law, Spirituality, and Society', 108.

[52] If one accepts some other definitions of social history, based more on subjects than methodology, then Katz might still qualify as a social historian; see Hyman, 'Jacob Katz as Social Historian', 86–7.

Katz, the social historian of the mid-twentieth century, originated some principles, methods, and concepts that have become critical in pursuing the history of Jewish women and in writing gender-conscious historiography. It remained to others to develop the potential inherent in these, and to try to write a fully articulated history in which women are an integral part of the story.

CONCLUSION

Jewish History and Postmodernity: Challenge and Rapprochement

꧁

IT IS POSSIBLE to incorporate postmodern sensibilities and methods into researching and writing Jewish history while preserving—and even enhancing—the fundamental coherence of the subject and the basic integrity of traditional historiographical methodology. Research, evidence, close reading, rational enquiry, and the positivist assumptions that historical description really does have a referent, and that logic or empirical proof can confirm new knowledge, still are the touchstones of the historical endeavour.

This positivism, however, is a reformed one. It is both critical, deconstructing sources and reading them 'against the grain' (that is, exposing alternative views of reality to those their authors intended to convey), and self-critical, being candid about perspectives and presumptions. It is self-conscious about its epistemological assumptions, its interpretative principles, its rhetorical strategies and devices, and its practitioner's metahistorical biases. It accepts its own constructed, contingent, and tentative nature: that it is but one of many probative narratives and is therefore more open and more responsive to criticism. However, this approach to historiography still insists that the narrative it creates is not arbitrary. While my construction of the past may be only one of many true stories, it is demonstrably not a false one. It can and should be judged by intersubjective—and modifiable—standards of evaluation shared by the community of historians.

The historical description-cum-interpretation proffered accounts for a range of perspectives, both from the past and in the present, and refers to the broad scope of human experience (from political to social to cultural to economic) and experiencers (the voiceless as well as the voiced, the dominating and the dominated, the female and the male, the elite alongside the plebeian).

The relationship between Jewish and other cultures is an example of how a problem can be analysed usefully from multiple perspectives, although not every conceivable perspective might be appropriate. In the case of this relationship, juxtaposing and comparing Jewish and non-Jewish culture, considering autonomous origins and mutual influences, seeing Jewish culture as embedded in the non-Jewish, and positing a shared band of cultural axioms—all can contribute to comprehension of the basic issue. However, despite historiographical fashion, standard postcolonial cultural hybridity theory cannot be applied mechanically to the Jewish case. If it is to be used profitably in Jewish history, the notion of cultural hybridity must be significantly modified and then employed with due diligence.

As for self-consciousness and self-criticism, there are tacit and explicit assumptions that underlie Jewish historical writing, and writers and readers should be sensitive as to how these may affect research, analysis, and presentation. For example, presentism—the reading of the past through the concerns of the present—colours the past, but it also has the potential for focusing attention on aspects of past experience that those with other agendas have missed. The friction between seeing the past as leading to the present and using it to justify—or vilify—the present is inherent in the historiographical enterprise, and constantly strains Jewish historians' telling of the story of an at once prominent and fragile minority group.

Postmodern inclinations against metanarratives and essentialism induce experimentation with a different method for arriving at periodization. Rather than attempting to define a historical period on the basis of some essential event or process that might define, epitomize, or dominate it (e.g. Shabateanism, emancipation, Haskalah), it can be a constellation of phenomena in interaction that earn the 'period' epithet. What lends the construct 'period' meaning is the interaction among factors and not the interaction's outcome. The Jewish 'modern period' didn't end when modernization of the Jews was 'completed'; it ended when the constellation of factors that for a long time formed the matrix of Jewish experience ceased to be relevant to most Jews' lives. At that point a historian can search for a new constellation that composed the environment within which people thought, decided, and behaved. What were the constituents of the macro that set the parameters for the micro?

For Jews, since about 1950 the parameters have been very different from those that had been in place since around 1700. This means we are in the postmodern period of Jewish history and lends a consciousness that the modern past really is past for us. We are in a different historical period, with a new perspective on what happened before 1950. When we talk about 'the Jewish modern period' we are no longer talking about 'us'. There is a new critical distance priming reconsideration of the phenomena of modernity outside the metahistorical paradigms conceived by the moderns who were at the same time modernists. Jewish history will once again be rewritten.

The most fundamental question that postmodernism has raised is how to define our subject, Jewish history: the problem of constructivism versus essentialism. If postmodern theory is correct that Jewishness is always being reconstituted according to the historical circumstances, and if its meaning is always contested, how might it be possible to define a subject as 'Jewish'? Must there not be something continuous, something essential, which denotes a historical phenomenon as belonging to the Jewish genus? As with periodization, my approach here is polythetic: to say that Jewishness is defined by a constellation of factors, all of which are never present simultaneously, but a significant number of which, in various permutations, are always in evidence.

The rationale for the inclusion of the subject of Jewish history, and indeed all of Jewish studies, in the academic curriculum can be non-instrumentalist. Whatever implications it may have for other sub-disciplines and disciplines, the study of Jewish history has intrinsic value. This is not the way many Jewish academics have faced the difficulty of fitting Jews, Jewish history, and Jewish studies into the postmodern new academy that espouses a multicultural ethos in place of the modernist pluralist one. Their strategy has been a postmodern version of an old Jewish pattern: invoking the Jewish contribution to civilization as a means for ensuring—or at least justifying—Jews' fully fledged membership in society and culture. Such an effort, implying that it is not enough for Jewish history to be Jewish, leads to apologetics and the demeaning of our subject. Perhaps it also implies that, in a multicultural world, Jews are compelled to subordinate their Jewishness to something else.

Postmodernism can be hospitable to Jewish historiography by offering a broader view of what should properly be included in historical study, providing new categories of analysis, and allowing the traditionally marginal to attract the spotlight. Jewish cultural history exemplifies this. Postmodern cultural history, which looks at people's behaviour in order to understand how they made sense of the world and their experience of it, is a congenial way to approach Jewish history. Jewish history raises many questions pertinent to the new cultural history and offers a relative abundance of historical sources lending themselves to cultural analysis. Culturally speaking, Jewish history is at least as fecund and intricate as any other, and the variety and intellectual challenge of the issues adhering to Jewish cultural history indicate the rich potential in this research direction. Moreover, in the wake of the postmodern deconstruction of so much in Jewish historiography that was once taken for granted—for example, the nature of Jewish religion, the role of the rabbis, the place of Erets Yisrael, the significance of Diaspora, the Jews' stance towards non-Jews—postmodern-style cultural history, recasting as it does symbols and meanings, offers the tools for a new construction.

Whereas cultural history offers Jewish historiography an *approach* (a direction, a definition, a set of axioms, and a range of questions) through which it can examine Jewish history in a postmodern key, the question of the *methodology* (procedures of discovery and analysis) appropriate to history—and to Jewish history—is something else again. The historical turn taken by the social sciences (historical sociology, historical economics, historical anthropology, historical demography, and so on) has called into question whether history has its own methodology, indeed whether it might be considered a discrete discipline. Based on the example of the methodology of folklore, it is apparent that (Jewish) history's identity as a discipline indeed lies mainly in its approach, the types of knowledge it mandates its researchers to command, the historicist assumptions they make, and the questions they bring to their sources. Jewish history can and should take advantage of the methodologies of other disciplines to help it find the answers to its particular brand of questions.

Nothing has done more to transform postmodern historiography than feminist theory and the use of gender as a category of analysis, analogous to class and race. Whole swaths of an invisible past became apparent once research questions were formulated in terms of women's experience and the division of social and cultural labour between the sexes. It was Jacob Katz who authored the first attempt to apply this perspective in Jewish history, and who then abandoned the effort. Only in our time have Jewish historians begun to renew it.

In the service of the goal of creating accommodation and even synergy between Jewish history and postmodern consciousness, this book has explored the challenges that postmodernism poses to Jewish historiography, and has suggested some responses which those concerned with Jewish history might consider. By presenting some exercises in applied postmodern Jewish historiography, it has also demonstrated how a Jewish historiography that is sensitive to postmodern concerns might begin to take shape.

To reiterate: a postmodern Jewish historiography is possible. It probably must give up on the classic metahistories, although it will not be able to avoid replacing them. It will have to work hard to gain the confidence of its audience in its critical judgement, its interpretative probity, and its awareness of the multiplicity of historical experiences and historical perspectives. It cannot, however, allow its subject to be contextualized to the point of dissolution, and can demand for itself a seat at the multicultural table as a matter of right and not reward. It can combine new consciousness and new, powerful conceptual and methodological tools with traditional-style research, analysis, and presentation, eschewing the most extreme postmodern epistemological and methodological strictures.

How Jewish is Jewish history? As Jewish as the Jews have been, and as Jewish as historians have the courage to present it.

Bibliography

❦

ABRAHAMS, ISRAEL, *Jewish Life in the Middle Ages* (New York, 1896).

ADLER, CYRUS, ISIDORE SINGER, et al. (eds), *The Jewish Encyclopedia: A Descriptive Record of the History, Religion, Literature, and Customs of the Jewish People from the Earliest Times to the Present Day*, 12 vols (New York, 1901–6).

ADLER, MICHAEL (ed.), *British Jewry Book of Honour* (London, 1922).

ADRIAANSENS, H. M., 'Talcott Parsons and Beyond: Recollections of an Outsider', *Theory, Culture and Society*, 6 (1989), 613–21.

AGNEW, J. C., *Worlds Apart: The Market and the Theatre in Anglo-American Thought 1550–1750* (Cambridge, 1986).

ALEXANDER, EDWARD, 'Multiculturalism's Jewish Problem', *American Jewish Congress Monthly* (Nov./Dec. 1991), 7–10.

ALEXANDER, J. C., *Neofunctionalism and After* (Malden, Mass., 1998).

American Historical Society, 'AHR Forum: Peter Novick's *That Noble Dream*, the Objectivity Question and the Future of the Historical Profession', *American Historical Review*, 96 (1991), 675–708.

ANDERSON, B. S., *Imagined Communities* (London, 1983).

ANKERSMIT, FRANK, *History and Tropology* (Berkeley, Calif., 1994).

—— and HANS KELLNER (eds), *The New Philosophy of History* (Chicago, Ill., 1995).

APPIAH, KWAME ANTHONY, *Cosmopolitanism: Ethics in a World of Strangers* (New York, 2006).

APPLEBY, JOYCE, LYNN HUNT, and MARGARET JACOB, *Telling the Truth About History* (New York, 1994).

ARAD, GULIE NE'EMAN (ed.), *Israeli Historiography Revisited* [=*History and Memory*, 7/1] (Bloomington, Indiana, 1995).

ASHCROFT, BILL, GARETH GRIFFITHS, and HELEN TIFFIN (eds), *The Post-Colonial Studies Reader* (London, 1995).

ASSAF, DAVID, *The World of Torah in Poland* [Olam hatorah bepolin], Units 5–6 of I. Etkes, D. Assaf, and I. Bartal (eds), *Polin: The Jews of Eastern Europe: History and Culture* [Polin: perakim betoledot yehudei mizraḥ eiropah vetarbutam] (Tel Aviv, 1990).

AVINERI, SHLOMO, *Varieties of Zionist Thought* [Hara'ayon hatsiyoni ligevanav] (Tel Aviv, 1980).

BACON, GERSHON, 'Polish–Jewish Relations in Modern Times: The Search for a Metaphor and a Historical Framework', in Eli Lederhendler and Jack Wertheimer (eds), *Text and Context: Essays in Modern Jewish History and Historiography in Honor of Ismar Schorsch* (New York, 2005).

BAER, YITZHAK FRITZ, *Studies in the History of the Jewish People* [Meḥkarim umasot], 2 vols (Jerusalem, 1985).

—— and BEN-ZION DINABURG (Dinur), 'Our Purpose' (Heb.), *Zion*, 1 (1936), 1–5.

BAŁABAN, MAJER, *Historja i literatura żydowska ze szczególnem uwzględniem historji Żydów w Polsce: dla klas wyższych szkół średnich*, 3 vols (1925; Warsaw, 1982). An abridged Hebrew version is available in Halperin (ed.), *The Jewish People*, i. 1–109.

—— *History of the Jews in Cracow and Kazimierz 1304–1868* [Historja Żydów w Krakowie i na Kazimierzu 1304–1868], 2 vols (Cracow, 1931–6); Hebrew edition, ed. Jacob Goldberg and Elchanan Reiner, trans. David Weinfeld et al., 2 vols (Jerusalem, 2002).

—— *Jews in Poland* [Yidn in poiln] (Vilna, 1930).

BAND, ARNOLD J., 'The New Diasporism and the Old Diaspora', *Israel Studies*, 1 (1996), 323–31.

BARBER, BERNARD, 'Talcott Parsons and the Sociology of Science: An Essay in Appreciation and Remembrance', *Theory, Culture and Society*, 6 (1989), 623–35.

BARDACH, JULIUSZ (ed.), *Historia państwa i prawa Polskiego*, 4 vols (Warsaw, 1979).

BAR-ITZHAK, HAYA, *Jewish Poland: Legends of Origins* (Detroit, Mich., 2001).

BARNAI, JACOB, *Historiography and Nationalism: Trends in the Study of Eretz Israel and its Jewish Settlement, 434–1881* [Historiyografiyah ule'umiyut: megamot beḥeker erets yisra'el veyishuvah hayehudi, 634–1881] (Jerusalem, 1995).

—— 'The Jews in the Ottoman Empire' [Hayehudim ba'imperiyah ha'otmanit], in Shmuel Ettinger (ed.), *History of the Jews in Islamic Lands* [Toledot hayehudim be'aretsot ha'islam] (Jerusalem, 1981).

—— *Shabateanism: Social Aspects* [Shabeta'ut: hebetim ḥevratiyim] (Jerusalem, 2000).

BARON, SALO WITTMAYER, 'Aspects of the Jewish Communal Crisis in 1848', *Jewish Social Studies*, 14 (1952), 199–244.

—— 'Ghetto and Emancipation', *Menorah Journal*, 14 (1928), 515–26.

—— *History and Jewish Historians: Essays and Addresses*, compiled and edited by Arthur Hertzberg and Leon A. Feldman (Philadelphia, 1964).

—— 'The Impact of the Revolution of 1848 on Jewish Emancipation', *Jewish Social Studies*, 11 (1949), 195–248.

—— 'The Jewish Factor in Medieval Civilization', *Proceedings of the American Academy for Jewish Research*, 12 (1942), 1–48; repr. in Robert Chazan (ed.), *Medieval Jewish Life* (New York, 1976).

—— 'Problems of Jewish Identity from an Historical Perspective: A Survey', *Proceedings of the American Academy for Jewish Research*, 46/7 (1979–80), 33–67.

—— *A Social and Religious History of the Jews*, 3 vols (1937); 2nd edn, 18 vols (Philadelphia and New York, 1952–83).

BARTAL, ISRAEL, 'The Emigration of R. Elazar from Amsterdam to the Land of Israel in 1740' [Aliyat r. elazar roke'aḥ le'erets yisra'el bishnat 5501], in id., *Exile in the Homeland* [Galut ba'arets] (Jerusalem, 1994).

—— '"True Knowledge and Wisdom": On Orthodox Historiography', *Studies in Contemporary Jewry*, 10 (1994), 178–92.

—— and SHMUEL FEINER (eds), *Jacob Katz Reconsidered* [Iyun meḥadash bemishnato hahistorit shel ya'akov kats] (Jerusalem, 2007).

BARUCHSON, SHIFRA, *Books and Readers: The Reading Interests of Italian Jews at the Close of the Renaissance* [Sefarim vekore'im: tarbut hakeriah shel yehudei italyah beshilhei harenesans] (Ramat Gan, 1993).

BAUMGARTEN, ELISHEVA, *Mothers and Children: Jewish Family Life in Medieval Europe* (Princeton, 2004).

BEARD, CHARLES A., 'Written History as an Act of Faith', *American Historical Review*, 39 (1934), 219–31.

BECK, ULRICH, *Cosmopolitan Vision*, trans. Ciaran Cronin (Cambridge, 2006).

BECKER, CARL L., 'Everyman His Own Historian', *American Historical Review*, 37 (1932), 221–36.

BECKNER, MORTON, *The Biological Way of Thought* (New York, 1959).

BELLOMO, MANLIO, *The Common Legal Past of Europe, 1000–1800*, trans. Lydia G. Cochrane (Washington, DC, 1995).

BENAYAHU, MEIR, 'The "Holy Brotherhood" of Rabbi Judah Hasid and their Settlement in Jerusalem' (Heb.), *Sefunot*, 3–4 (1960), 135–82.

BEN-RAFAEL, ELIEZER, *Jewish Identities: Fifty Intellectuals Answer Ben-Gurion* (Leiden, 2002).

—— YOSEF GORNY, and YA'ACOV RO'I (eds), *Contemporary Jewries: Convergence and Divergence* (Leiden, 2003).

BEN-SASSON, HAYIM HILLEL, *History of the Jewish People* (Cambridge, Mass., 1976).

—— Review of *Tradition and Crisis* (Heb.), *Tarbiz*, 29 (1960), 297–312.

—— 'Statutes for the Enforcement of the Observance of the Sabbath in Poland and their Social and Economic Significance' (Heb.), *Zion*, 21 (1956), 183–206.

—— *Theory and Practice* [Hagut vehanhagah] (Jerusalem, 1959).

—— *Trial and Achievement: Currents in Jewish History* (Jerusalem, 1974).

BENTLEY, MICHAEL, *Modern Historiography: An Introduction* (London, 1999).

BERKHOFER JR., ROBERT F., *Beyond the Great Story: History as Text and Discourse* (Cambridge, Mass., 1995).

—— 'The Challenge of Poetics to (Normal) Historical Practice', *Poetics Today*, 9 (1988), 435–52.

BERKOVITZ, JAY R., *Rites and Passages: The Beginnings of Modern Jewish Culture, 1650–1860* (Philadelphia, 2004).

BERLIN, ISAIAH, 'History and Theory: The Concept of Scientific History', *History and Theory*, 1 (1960), 1–31.

BERSHADSKII, SERGEI A., 'Yevrei korol polsky', *Voskhod*, 9 (1889), fascicles i–ii. 3–37, iii. 3–17, iv. 11–23, v. 101–15.

BEST, STEVEN, and DOUGLAS KELLNER, *Postmodern Theory: Critical Interrogations* (New York, 1991).

BEVAN, EDWIN R., and CHARLES J. SINGER (eds), *The Legacy of Israel* (Oxford, 1927).

BHABHA, HOMI K., *The Location of Culture* (London, 1994).

—— (ed.), *Nation and Narration* (London, 1990).

BIALE, DAVID, 'Between Polemics and Apologetics: Jewish Studies in the Age of Multiculturalism', *Jewish Studies Quarterly*, 3 (1996), 174–84.

—— *Kabbalah and Counter-History*, 2nd edn (Cambridge, Mass., 1982).

—— (ed.), *Cultures of the Jews: A New History* (New York, 2002).

—— MICHAEL GALCHINSKY, and SUSANNAH HESCHEL, 'Introduction: The Dialectic of Jewish Enlightenment', in eid. (eds), *Insider/ Outsider*.

—— —— —— (eds), *Insider/Outsider: American Jews and Multiculturalism* (Berkeley, Calif., 1998).

BICKERMAN, ELIAS, *From Ezra to the Last of the Maccabees* (New York, 1962; originally published 1947).

BIRKENTHAL, BER, *The Memoirs of Ber of Bolechow*, ed. M. Vishnitzer (London, 1922; repr. New York, 1973).

BLOCH, PHILIP, 'Die Sage von Saul Wahl, dem Eintags Koenig von Polen', *Zeitschrift der Historischen Gesellschaft für die Provinz Posen*, 4 (1889), 234–58.

BODEMANN, Y. MICHAEL, *In der Wogen der Erinnerung, Jüdische Existenz in Deutschland* (Munich, 2002).

BODIAN, MIRIAM, *Hebrews of the Portuguese Nation: Conversos and Community in Early Modern Amsterdam* (Bloomington, Ind., 1997).

BONFIL, ROBERT, 'The Historian's Perception of the Jews in the Italian Renaissance: Towards a Reappraisal', *Revue des études juives*, 143 (1984), 59–82.

—— *Jewish Life in Renaissance Italy* (Berkeley, Calif., 1999).

BOYARIN, DANIEL, *Unheroic Conduct: The Rise of Heterosexuality and the Invention of the Jewish Man* (Berkeley, Calif., 1997).

—— and JONATHAN BOYARIN, 'Diaspora: Generation and the Ground of Jewish Identity', *Critical Inquiry*, 19 (1993), 693–725.

BOYARIN, JONATHAN, 'The Other Within and the Other Without', in Laurence J. Silberstein (ed.), *The Other in Jewish Thought and History* (New York, 1994).

BRANN, ROSS, and ADAM SUTCLIFFE (eds), *Renewing the Past, Reconfiguring Jewish Culture: From al-Andalus to the Haskalah* (Philadelphia, 2004).

BREARLEY, MARGARET F., 'Possible Implications of the New Age Movement for the Jewish People', in Jonathan Webber (ed.), *Jewish Identities in the New Europe* (London, 1994).

BREUER, MORDECHAI, *The Tents of Torah: The Yeshiva, its Structure and History* [Oholei torah: hayeshivah, tavnitah vetoledoteihah] (Jerusalem, 2003).

BRINKER, MENAHEM, 'Literature and History: Small Notes on a Big Subject' [Sifrut vehistoriyah: he'erot ketanot lenose gadol], in Richard Cohen and Joseph Mali (eds), *Literature and History* [Sifrut vehistoriyah] (Jerusalem, 1999).

BRUNER, JEROME, *Acts of Meaning* (Cambridge, Mass., 1990).

BURKE, PETER, *History and Social Theory* (Ithaca, NY, 1993).

BUXTON, WILLIAM, *Talcott Parsons and the Capitalist Nation-State: Political Sociology as a Strategic Vocation* (Toronto, 1985).

CAHILL, THOMAS, *The Gifts of the Jews: How a Tribe of Desert Nomads Changed the Way Everyone Thinks and Feels* (New York, 1998).

CANTOR, AVIVA, *Jewish Women/Jewish Men: The Legacy of Patriarchy in Jewish Life* (New York, 1995).

CARDOSO, ISAAC, *Las excelencias de los hebreos* (Amsterdam, 1679).

CESARANI, DAVID, 'The Dynamics of Diaspora: The Transformation of British Jewish Identity', *Jewish Culture and History*, 4/1 (2001), 53–64.

CHAJES, J. H., *Between Worlds: Dybbuks, Exorcists, and Early Modern Judaism* (Philadelphia, 2003).

CHARTIER, ROGER, *Cultural History* (Ithaca, NY, 1988).

CHEYETTE, BRYAN, and LAURA MARCUS (eds), *Modernity, Culture, and 'the Jew'* (Oxford, 1998).

CHLENOV, MIKHAIL, 'Jewish Communities and Jewish Identities in the Former Soviet Union', in Jonathan Webber (ed.), *Jewish Identities in the New Europe* (London, 1994).

CLIFFORD, JAMES, and GEORGE E. MARCUS (eds), *Writing Culture: The Poetics and Politics of Ethnography* (Berkeley, Calif., 1986).

COHEN, ASHER, 'From Arranged Democracy to Crisis Democracy: The Struggle over Collective Identity in Israel' (Heb.), *Politika*, 3 (1999), 9–30.

—— 'Israeli Assimilation: On Changes in Identity Definition and the Boundaries of the Jewish Collective' (Heb.), *Gesher*, 145 (2002), 17–27.

COHEN, GERSON D., 'The Blessing of Assimilation in Jewish History', in id., *Jewish History and Jewish Destiny*, ed. Neil Gillman (1966; New York, 1997).

—— 'Changing Perspectives of Jewish Historiography', in id., *Jewish History and Jewish Destiny*, ed. Neil Gillman (New York, 1997).

COHEN, JEREMY, and RICHARD COHEN (eds), *The Jewish Contribution to Civilization* (Oxford, 2007).

COHEN, MARK R., 'Leone de Modena's Riti: A Seventeenth-Century Plea for Social Toleration of Jews', *Jewish Social Studies*, 34 (1972), 287–319.

COHEN, MITCHELL, 'In Defense of Shaatnez: A Politics for Jews in a Multicultural America', in David Biale, Michael Galchinsky, and Susannah Heschel (eds), *Insider/Outsider: American Jews and Multiculturalism* (Berkeley, Calif., 1998).

COHEN, SHAYE J. D., *The Beginnings of Jewishness: Boundaries, Varieties, Uncertainties* (Berkeley, Calif., 1999).

—— '"Those who say they are Jews and are not": How Do You Know a Jew in Antiquity When You See One?', in Shaye J. D. Cohen and Ernest S. Frerichs (eds), *Diasporas in Antiquity* (Atlanta, Ga., 1993).

COHEN, STEVEN M., and GABRIEL HORENCZYK (eds), *National Variations in Jewish Identity* (Albany, NY, 1999).

—— and JACK WERTHEIMER, 'Whatever Happened to the Jewish People?', *Commentary*, 121/6 (June 2006), 33–7.

CONFORTI, YITZHAK, *Past Tense—Zionist Historiography and the Shaping of National Memory* [Zeman avar: hahistoriyografiyah hatsiyonit ve'itsuv hazikaron hale'umi] (Jerusalem, 2006).

COOPER, FREDERICK, 'Conflict and Connection: Rethinking Colonial African History', *American Historical Review*, 99 (1994), 1516–45.

DAN, JOSEPH, *Gershom Scholem and the Mystical Dimension of Jewish History* (New York, 1987).

DANZGER, M. HERBERT, *Returning to Tradition: The Contemporary Revival of Orthodox Judaism* (New Haven, Conn., 1989).

DAVIDMAN, LYNN, *Tradition in a Rootless World: Women Turn to Orthodox Judaism* (Berkeley, Calif., 1991).

DAVIES, NORMAN, *God's Playground: A History of Poland*, 2 vols (Oxford, 1981).

DAVIS, FLOYD JAMES, *Minority-Dominant Relations: A Sociological Analysis* (Arlington Heights, Ill., 1978).

—— (ed.), *Understanding Minority-Dominant Relations: Sociological Contributions* (Arlington Heights, 1979).

DAVIS, JOSEPH, 'The Reception of the *Shulḥan 'Arukh* and the Formation of Ashkenazic Identity', *AJS Review*, 26 (2002), 251–76.

DAWIDOWICZ, LUCY, *What Is the Use of Jewish History?* (New York, 1992).

DELLAPERGOLA, SERGIO, *World Jewry Beyond 2000: The Demographic Prospects* (Oxford, 1999).

—— 'An Overview of the Demographic Trends of European Jewry', in Jonathan Webber (ed.), *Jewish Identities in the New Europe* (London, 1994).

DERRIDA, JACQUES, *Of Grammatology*, trans. Gayatri C. Spivak (Baltimore, Md., 1998).

—— *Positions*, trans. A. Bass (London, 2002).

DERSHOWITZ, ALAN M., *The Vanishing American Jew* (Boston, Mass., 1997).

DEUTSCHER, ISAAC, *The Non-Jewish Jew and Other Essays* (London, 1968).

DINER, DAN, 'Geschichte der Juden—Paradigma einer europaischen Geschichtsschreibung', *Gedachtniszeiten* (2003), 246–62.

DINUR, BEN-ZION, 'The Beginning of Hasidism and its Social and Messianic Foundations' [Reishitah shel haḥasidut viyesodoteihah hasotsialiyim vehameshiḥiyim], in id., *Historical Writings* vol. i [Bemifneh hadorot].

—— *Historical Writings*, vol. i [Bemifneh hadorot] (Jerusalem, 1954).

—— *Israel and the Diaspora* (Philadelphia, 1969).

DOV BER BEN SAMUEL, *In Praise of the Baal Shem Tov* [Shivḥei habesht]: *The Earliest Collection of Legends About the Founder of Hasidism*, trans. and ed. Dan Ben-Amos and Jerome Mintz (Bloomington, Ind., 1970).

DUBIN, LOIS C., *The Port Jews of Trieste: Absolutist Politics and Enlightenment Culture* (Stanford, Calif., 1999).

DUBNOW, SIMON, 'The Sociological View of Jewish History', in Koppel S. Pinson (ed.), *Nationalism and History* (Philadelphia, 1958), 336–53.

DUBNOW, SIMON, *History of the Jews*, trans. Moshe Spiegel (New York, 1967); 1st published in Russian as *Vsemirnay istoriya yevreiskovo naroda* (Berlin, 1924); German edn: *Weltgeschichte des judischen Volkes* (Berlin, 1925–9); Hebrew edn: *Divrei yemei am olam*, trans. B. Karu (Tel Aviv, 1958).

EDELMAN, TSEVI, *The Greatness of Saul* [Gedulat sha'ul] (London, 1854).

EISEN, ARNOLD, *Galut: Modern Jewish Reflection on Homelessness and Homecoming* (Bloomington, Ind., 1986).

—— 'Jews, Jewish Studies, and the American Humanities', *Tikkun,* 45 (1989), 23–9.

—— 'The Problem Is Still Very Much with Us', *Conservative Judaism* (special supplement), 56 (2004), 21–4.

EISENSTADT, SHMUEL, *Israeli Society* (London, 1967).

—— *The Political Systems of Empires* (New York, 1970).

ELBAUM, JACOB, *Openness and Insularity* (Jerusalem, 1990).

Encyclopaedia Judaica (Jerusalem, 1972; CD-ROM edn, 1997).

ENDELMAN, TODD M., 'Anglo-Jewish Scientists and the Science of Race', *Jewish Social Studies,* 11 (2004), 52–92.

—— *The Jews of Georgian England, 1714–1830: Tradition and Change in a Liberal Society*, 2nd edn (Ann Arbor, Mich., 1999).

ENGEL, DAVID, 'Crisis and Lachrymosity: On Salo Baron, Neobaronism, and the Study of Modern European Jewish History', *Jewish History*, 20 (2006), 243–64.

ERMARTH, ELIZABETH D., *Sequel to History: Postmodernism and the Crisis of Representational Time* (Princeton, 1992).

ETKES, IMMANUEL, *The Besht: Magician, Mystic and Leader* (Waltham, Mass., 2005).

ETTINGER, SHMUEL, 'The Beginning of Change in the Attitude of European Society Towards the Jews', *Scripta Hierosolymitana*, 7 (1961), 193–219.

—— *Modern Antisemitism: Studies and Essays* [Ha'antishemiyut be'et haḥadashah: pirkei meḥkar ve'iyun] (Tel Aviv, 1978).

—— 'The Position of the Deists on Judaism and its Influence on the Jews' [Emdat hade'istim kelapei hayahadut vehashpa'atah al hayehudim], in id., *Studies in Modern Jewish History* [Iyunim betoledot hayehudim be'et haḥadashah], vol. i: *History and Historians* [Historiyah vehistoriyonim] (Jerusalem, 1992), 215–24.

EVANS, RICHARD J., *In Defense of History* (New York, 1999).

EVEN-ZOHAR, ITAMAR, *Polysystem Studies* [=*Poetics Today,* 11] (Tel Aviv, 1990).

FEINER, SHMUEL, *The Jewish Enlightenment* (Philadelphia, 2003).

FELDMAN, ABRAHAM J., *Contributions of Judaism to Modern Society* (Cincinnati, Ohio, 1930).

FERZIGER, ADAM, *Exclusion and Hierarchy: Orthodoxy, Non-Observance and the Emergence of Modern Jewish Identity* (Philadelphia, 2005).

FINKELSTEIN, LOUIS (ed.), *The Jews*, 3 vols; vol. ii: *Their Religion and Culture*, 4th edn (New York, 1971).

FINKIELKRAUT, ALAIN, 'In the Name of the Other: Reflections on the Coming Antisemitism', *Azure*, 18 (Autumn 2004), 21–33.

FISCHER, DAVID HACKETT, *Historians' Fallacies: Toward a Logic of Historical Thought* (New York, 1970).

FISHMAN, SYLVIA BARACK, *Double or Nothing: Jewish Families and Mixed Marriage* (Waltham, Mass., 2004).

FOA, ANNA, *The Jews of Europe after the Black Death*, trans. Andrea Grover (Berkeley, Calif., 2000).

FONROBERT, CHARLOTTE E., *Menstrual Purity: Rabbinic and Christian Reconstructions of Biblical Gender* (Stanford, Calif., 2000).

FOSS, DANIEL A., 'The World of Talcott Parsons', in M. Stein and A. Vidich (eds), *Sociology on Trial* (Englewood Cliffs, NJ, 1963).

FOUCAULT, MICHEL, *The Archaeology of Knowledge,* trans. A. M. Sheridan Smith (New York, 1972).

—— *Discipline and Punish: The Birth of the Prison*, trans. A. M. Sheridan (New York, 1995).

—— *The Foucault Reader*, ed. Paul Rabinow (New York, 1984).

—— *The History of Sexuality,* trans. R. Hurley (New York, 1990).

—— 'What Is an Author?', in Josue V. Harari (ed.), *Textual Strategies: Perspectives in Post-Structuralist Criticism* (Ithaca, NY, 1979).

FOXMAN, ABRAHAM, *Never Again? The Threat of the New Antisemitism* (San Francisco, 2003).

FRAM, EDWARD, *Ideals Face Reality: Jewish Law and Life in Poland 1550–1655* (Cincinnati, Ohio, 1997).

—— 'Two Cases of Adultery and the Halakhic Decision-Making Process', *AJS Review*, 26 (2002), 277–300.

FRANKEL, JONATHAN, 'Assimilation and the Jews in Nineteenth-Century Europe: Towards a New Historiography?', in Jonathan Frankel and Steven J. Zipperstein (eds), *Assimilation and Community: The Jews in Nineteenth-Century Europe* (Cambridge, 1992).

—— and S. J. ZIPPERSTEIN (eds), *Assimilation and Community: The Jews in Nineteenth-Century Europe* (Cambridge, 1992).

FRIEDLANDER, SAUL (ed.), *Probing the Limits of Representation: Nazism and the 'Final Solution'* (Cambridge, Mass., 1992).

FRIESEL, EVYATAR (ed.), *Carta's Atlas of the Jewish People in Modern Times* [Atlas karta letoledot am yisra'el bazeman heḥadash] (Jerusalem, 1983).

FUNKENSTEIN, AMOS, *Perceptions of Jewish History* (Berkeley, Calif., 1993).

GALCHINSKY, MICHAEL, 'Scattered Seeds: A Dialogue of Diasporas', in David Biale, Michael Galchinsky, and Susannah Heschel (eds), *Insider/Outsider: American Jews and Multiculturalism* (Berkeley, Calif., 1998).

GARTNER, LLOYD P., *History of the Jews in Modern Times* (Oxford, 2001).

GEERTZ, CLIFFORD, *The Interpretation of Cultures* (New York, 1973).

GELLNER, ERNEST, *Nations and Nationalism* (Ithaca, NY, 1983).

GERHOLM, TOMAS, and YNGVE G. LITHMAN (eds), *The New Islamic Presence in Western Europe* (London, 1988).

GILMAN, SANDER, *Jews in Today's German Culture* (Bloomington, Ind., 1995).

GINZBERG, LOUIS, *On Jewish Law and Lore* (Philadelphia, 1955).

GINZBURG, CARLO, *The Cheese and the Worms: The Cosmos of a Sixteenth-Century Miller*, trans. John and Anne Tedeschi (Baltimore, Md., 1980).

—— *History, Rhetoric and Proof* (Hanover, NH, 1999).

GITELMAN, ZVI, 'The Decline of the Diaspora Jewish Nation: Boundaries, Content and Jewish Identity', *Jewish Social Studies*, 4/2 (1998), 112–32.

—— 'Jews and Judaism in the USSR: Ethnicity and Religion', *Nationalities Papers*, 20 (1992), 75–85.

—— 'The Meanings of Jewishness in Post-Soviet Russia and Ukraine', in Eliezer Ben-Rafael, Yosef Gorny, and Yaacov Ro'i (eds), *Contemporary Jewries: Convergence and Divergence* (Leiden, 2003).

GOLDBERG, DAVID T., 'Introduction: Multicultural Conditions', in id. (ed.), *Multiculturalism: A Critical Reader*.

—— (ed.), *Multiculturalism: A Critical Reader* (Cambridge, Mass., 1994).

GOLDBERG, JACOB, 'The Jew and the Country Inn' [Hayehudi vehapundak hakafri], in id., *The Jewish Society in the Polish Commonwealth* [Haḥevrah hayehudit bemamlekhet polin-lita] (Jerusalem, 1999).

—— 'The Jewish Estate Lessees (Arendarze) and their Rule Over the Peasants' [Ḥokherei ha'aḥuzot hayehudim umarutam al ha'ikarim], in id., *The Jewish Society in the Polish Commonwealth* [Haḥevrah hayehudit bemamlekhet polin-lita] (Jerusalem, 1999).

—— *The Jewish Society in the Polish Commonwealth* [Haḥevrah hayehudit bemamlekhet polin-lita] (Jerusalem, 1999).

—— 'The Jew and the City Inn in the Podlasie Region' [Hayehudim vehapundak ha'ironi be'ezor podlasheh], in id., *The Jewish Society in the Polish Commonwealth* [Haḥevrah hayehudit bemamlekhet polin-lita] (Jerusalem, 1999).

—— 'Poles and Jews in the Seventeenth and Eighteenth Centuries: Rejection or Acceptance', *Jahrbücher für Geschichte Osteuropas*, 22 (1974), 248–82.

GOLDBERG-NAIMARK, NATALIE, 'Jewish Women in Berlin and Enlightenment Culture at the End of the Eighteenth and the Beginning of the Nineteenth Century—a Gender Analysis' [Nashim yehudiyot beberlin vetarbut hane'orut besof hame'ah hashemoneh esreh uvereishit hame'ah hateshah esreh—nituaḥ migdari] (doctoral dissertation, Bar-Ilan University (Ramat-Gan), 2005).

GORDON, MILTON M., *Assimilation in American Life* (New York, 1964).

GOREN, ARTHUR A., *New York Jews and the Quest for Community: The Kehillah Experiment, 1908–1922* (New York, 1970).

GRAETZ, HEINRICH, *The Structure of Jewish History*, trans., ed., and introd. I. Schorsch (New York, 1975).

GRAFTON, ANTHONY, 'History's Postmodern Fates', *Daedalus* (Spring 2006), 54–69.

GREENBERG, CHERYL, 'Pluralism and its Discontents: The Case of Blacks and Jews', in David Biale, Michael Galchinsky, and Susannah Heschel (eds), *Insider/Outsider: American Jews and Multiculturalism* (Berkeley, Calif., 1998).

GRIES, ZEEV, *Conduct Literature* [Sifrut hahanhagot] (Jerusalem, 1989).

GROSSMAN, AVRAHAM, *Pious and Rebellious: Jewish Women in Europe in the Middle Ages* [Ḥasidot umoredot: nashim yehudiyot be'eiropah bimei habeinayim] (Jerusalem, 2001).

GROSSMAN SUSAN, and RIVKA HAUT (eds), *Daughters of the King. Women and the Synagogue: A Survey of History, Halakhah, and Contemporary Realities* (Philadelphia, 1992).

GUTWEIN, DANIEL, 'The New Europe and the Zionist Dilemma', in Jonathan Webber (ed.), *Jewish Identities in the New Europe* (London, 1994).

Ha'aretz, English edn, 14 Nov. 2005.

HAAS, JACOB DE (ed.), *The Encyclopedia of Jewish Knowledge* (New York, 1934).

HABERMAS, JÜRGEN, *Eine Art Schadensabwicklung* (Frankfurt am Main, 1987).

—— *Lectures on the Philosophical Discourse of Modernity* (Cambridge, Mass., 1987).

HALBERTAL, MOSHE, 'Commentary, the Last Judgment—A Talmudic Account', in Michael Walzer, Menachem Lorberbaum, Noam J. Zohar, et al. (eds), *The Jewish Political Tradition*, vol. ii: *Membership* (New Haven, Conn., 2000).

HALPERIN, ISRAEL (ed.), *The Jewish People in Poland* [Beit yisra'el bepolin], 2 vols (Jerusalem, 1948–53).

HAMILTON, PETER, *Talcott Parsons* (London, 1983).

HAMMER, M. F., K. SKORECKI, S. SELIG, et al., 'Y Chromosomes of Jewish Priests', *Nature*, 385/6611 (2 Jan. 1997), 32.

HASKELL, THOMAS L., 'The Curious Persistence of Rights Talk in an "Age of Interpretation" ', *Journal of American History*, 74 (1987), 984–1012.

—— 'Objectivity Is Not Neutrality: Rhetoric vs. Practice in Peter Novick's *That Noble Dream*', *History and Theory*, 29 (1990), 129–57.

HARVEY, VAN A., *The Historian and the Believer: The Morality of Historical Knowledge and Christian Belief* (1966; Urbana, Ill., 1996).

HAZAZ, HAYIM, 'The Sermon' [Haderashah], in *Boiling Stones* [Avanim rotehot] (Tel Aviv, 1946), 227–44.

HEFFERNAN, THOMAS, *Saints and their Biographies in the Middle Ages* (Oxford, 1988).

HERTZBERG, ARTHUR, *The Zionist Idea: A Historical Analysis and Reader* (New York, 1959).

HESCHEL, SUSANNAH, *Abraham Geiger and the Jewish Jesus* (Chicago, Ill., 1998).

—— 'Anti-Judaism in Christian Feminist Theology', *Tikkun*, 5/3 (1990), 25–8, 95–7.

—— 'Configurations of Patriarchy, Judaism and Nazism in German Feminist Thought', in Tamar Rudavsky (ed.), *Gender and Judaism* (New York, 1995).

—— 'Jewish Studies as Counterhistory', in David Biale, Michael Galchinsky, and Susannah Heschel (eds), *Insider/Outsider: American Jews and Multiculturalism* (Berkeley, Calif., 1998).

HILLEL BAAL SHEM, *Sefer haheshek*, MS Or 178, Vernadsky Library, Kiev.

HISDAI, YAAKOV, 'The Emergence of the Hasidim and Mitnagedim in Light of the Homiletic Literature' [Reishit darkham shel hahasidim vehamit-nagedim le'or sifrut haderush], doctoral disseration, Hebrew University of Jerusalem, 1984.

HOBSBAWM, ERIC, and TERENCE RANGER (eds), *Invented Traditions* (Cambridge, 1992).

HOLLINGER, DAVID A., *In the American Province: Studies in the History and Historiography of Ideas* (Bloomington, Ind., 1985).

HOROWITZ, ELLIOTT, 'The Early Eighteenth Century Confronts the Beard: Kabbalah and Jewish Self-Fashioning', *Jewish History*, 8 (1994), 95–115.

—— '*Jewish Life in the Middle Ages* and the Jewish Life of Israel Abrahams', in David N. Myers and David B. Ruderman (eds), *The Jewish Past Revisited: Reflections on Modern Jewish Historians* (New Haven, Conn., 1998).

—— Review of Mark R. Cohen (trans. and ed.), *The Autobiography of a Seventeenth-Century Venetian Rabbi: Leon Modena's* Life of Judah, *Jewish Quarterly Review*, 81 (1991), 453–61.

—— 'The Rite To Be Reckless: On the Perpetration and Interpretation of Purim Violence', *Poetics Today*, 15 (1994), 9–54.

HOROWITZ, SARA R., 'The Paradox of Jewish Studies in the New Academy', in David Biale, Michael Galchinsky, and Susannah Heschel (eds), *Insider/Outsider: American Jews and Multiculturalism* (Berkeley, Calif., 1998).

HUBKA, THOMAS C., 'The "Zohar" and the Polish Synagogue: The Practical Influence of a Sacred Text', *Journal of Jewish Thought and Philosophy*, 9 (2000), 173–250.

HUGHES, H. S., 'The Historian and the Social Scientist', *American Historical Review*, 66 (1960), 20–46.

HUNDERT, GERSHON D., *The Jews in a Polish Private Town* (Baltimore, Md., 1992).

—— *Jews in Poland–Lithuania in the Eighteenth Century: A Genealogy of Modernity* (Berkeley, Calif., 2004).

—— 'On the Problem of Agency in Eighteenth-Century Jewish Society', in Adam Teller (ed.), *Studies in the History of the Jews in Old Poland in Honor of Jacob Goldberg* [= *Scripta Hierosolymitana*, 38] (Jerusalem, 1998).

HUNT, LYNN (ed.), *The New Cultural History* (Berkeley, Calif., 1989).

HUYSSEN, ANDREAS, *After the Great Divide* (Bloomington, Ind., 1986).

HYMAN, PAULA E., *The Emancipation of the Jews of Alsace: Acculturation and Tradition in the Nineteenth Century* (New Haven, Conn., 1991).

—— 'Feminist Studies and Modern Jewish History', in Lynn Davidman and Shelly Tenenbaum (eds), *Feminist Perspectives on Jewish Studies* (New Haven, Conn., 1994).

—— 'Jacob Katz as Social Historian', in Jay M. Harris (ed.), *Pride of Jacob* (Cambridge, Mass., 2002).

IDEL, MOSHE, 'One from a Town, Two from a Clan: The Diffusion of Lurianic Kabbalah and Sabbatianism, a Re-examination', *Jewish History*, 7 (1993), 79–104.

—— 'Subversive Catalysts: Gnosticism and Messianism in Gershom Scholem's View of Jewish Mysticism', in David N. Myers and David B. Ruderman (eds), *The Jewish Past Revisited: Reflections on Modern Jewish Historians* (New Haven, Conn., 1998).

IGANSKI, PAUL, and BARRY KOSMIN (eds), *A New Antisemitism: Debating Judeophobia in 21st Century Britain* (London, 2003).

IGGERS, GEORG G., *Historiography in the Twentieth Century: From Scientific Objectivity to the Postmodern Challenge* (Hanover, NH, 1997).

ISRAEL, JONATHAN I., *European Jewry in the Age of Mercantilism, 1550–1750* (Oxford, 1985).

—— *Diasporas Within a Diaspora: Jews, Crypto-Jews and the World Maritime Empires (1540–1740)* (Leiden, 2002).

ISSERLEIN, ISRAEL, *Terumat hadeshen*, part II, ed. S. Avitan (Jerusalem, 1991).

JACOBS, JOSEPH, *Jewish Contributions to Civilization: An Estimate* (Philadelphia, 1919).

JENKINS, KEITH (ed.), *The Postmodern History Reader* (London, 1997).

JOLY, DANIELLE, *Britannia's Crescent* (Aldershot, 1995).

JPPPI (Jewish People Policy Planning Institute), *Annual Assessment 2005: Facing a Rapidly Changing World, Executive Report* (Jerusalem, 2005).

KAHN, SUSAN M., *Are Genes Jewish? Conceptual Ambiguities in the New Genetic Age*, the twelfth David W. Beilin Lecture in American Jewish Affairs, Frankel Center for Jewish Studies, University of Michigan (Ann Arbor, Mich., 2005).

—— *Reproducing Jews: A Cultural Account of Assisted Conception in Israel* (Durham, NC, 2000).

KAMINSKI, ANDRZEJ, *Historia Rzeczypospolitej wielu narodów* (Lublin, 2000).

KAPLAN, MORDECAI, *Judaism as a Civilization: Toward a Reconstruction of American-Jewish Life* (New York, 1934).

KAPLAN, YOSEF, *An Alternative Path to Modernity: The Sephardi Diaspora in Western Europe* (Leiden, 2000).

KARO, JOSEPH, *Beit yosef*, in Jacob ben Asher, *Tur oraḥ ḥayim* (Venice, 1550).

—— *Shulḥan arukh*, with *Mapah* by Moses Isserles (Cracow, 1578–80; facsimile edn, Jerusalem, 1974).

KARPELES, GUSTAV, 'A Jewish King in Poland', in id., *Jewish Literature and Other Essays* (Philadelphia, 1895), 272–92.

KATZ, JACOB, 'The Concept of Social History and its Possible Use in Jewish Historical Research', *Scripta Hierosolymitana*, 3 (1956), 292–312.

—— *Exclusiveness and Tolerance: Studies in Jewish–Gentile Relations in Medieval and Modern Times* (Oxford, 1961).

—— *From Prejudice to Destruction: Anti-Semitism, 1733–1933* (Cambridge, Mass., 1980).

—— *A House Divided: Orthodoxy and Schism in Nineteenth-Century Central European Jewry* (Hanover, NH, 1998).

—— *Jews and Freemasons in Europe, 1723–1939* [Bonim ḥofshim viyehudim], trans. Leonard Oschry (Jerusalem 1968; Cambridge, Mass., 1970)

—— 'Marriage and Sexual Life Among the Jews at the Close of the Middle Ages' (Heb.), *Zion*, 10 (1945), 21–54.

—— 'On Jewish Social History: Epochal and Supra-Epochal Historiography', *Jewish History*, 7 (1993), 89–97.

—— *Out of the Ghetto: The Social Background of Jewish Emancipation, 1770–1870* (New York, 1978).

—— *The Shabbes Goy*, trans. Y. Lerner (Philadelphia, 1989).

—— *A Time for Inquiry, a Time for Reflection: A Historical Essay on Israel Through the Ages* [Et laḥkor ve'et lehitbonen: masah historit al darko shel beit yisra'el me'az tseito me'aretso ve'ad shuvo eleihah] (Jerusalem, 1998).

—— *Tradition and Crisis: Jewish Society at the End of the Middle Ages*, trans. and Afterword, B. D. Cooperman (New York, 1993).

—— *With My Own Eyes: The Autobiography of a Historian*, trans. A. Brenner and Z. Brody (Hanover, NH, 1995).

—— *The Writings of Jacob Katz, 1933–1998* [Kitvei ya'akov kats, 1933–1998], comp. and ed. G. Katz, Shaul Stampfer, and M. Rigler, *Jewish Studies*, 38 (1998), and as a supplement to *Zion*, 63 (1998).

—— 'Zur juedischen Sozialgeschichte; epochale und ueberepochale Geschichtesschreibung', *Tel Aviver Jahrbuch fuer Deutsche Geschichte*, 20 (1991), 429–36.

—— and CHAVA WEISSLER, 'On Law, Spirituality, and Society in Judaism: An Exchange between Jacob Katz and Chava Weissler', *Jewish Social Studies*, NS 2 (1996), 87–115.

KAZAL, RUSSELL A., 'Revisting Assimilation: The Rise, Fall, and Reappraisal of a Concept in American Ethnic History', *American Historical Review*, 100 (Apr. 1995), 437–71.

KELLY, J. M., *A Short History of Western Legal Theory* (Oxford, 1992).

KEMP, ADRIANA, 'Christian Zionists in the Holy Land: Evangelical Churches, Labor Migrants and the Jewish State', *Identities*, 10 (2003), 295–318.

KEPNES, STEVEN (ed.), *Interpreting Judaism in a Postmodern Age* (New York, 1996).

KIRSCHSTEIN, ARTHUR J., *The Jew: His Contribution to Modern Civilization* (Denver, Colo., 1930).

KOSMIN, BARRY, ANTONY LERMAN, and JACQUELINE GOLDBERG, *The Attachment of British Jews to Israel* (London, 1997).

KROCHMAL, NAHMAN, *The Writings of Nahman Krochmal* [Kitvei naḥman krokhmal], ed. S. Rawidowicz (Berlin, 1924).

Księga jubileuszowa dla uczczenia sieśćdziesięciolecia Profesora Majera Balabana (Warsaw, 1938).

KUHN, THOMAS S., *The Structure of Scientific Revolutions* (Chicago, Ill., 1970).

KUROKAWA, MINAKO (ed.), *Minority Responses* (New York, 1970).

KWOK-BUN, CHAN, *Chinese Identities, Ethnicity and Cosmopolitanism* (London, 2005).

LACAPRA, DOMINIQUE, 'Representing the Holocaust: Reflections on the Historians' Debate', in Saul Friedlander (ed.), *Probing the Limits of Representation: Nazism and the 'Final Solution'* (Cambridge, Mass., 1992).

LAMM, NORMAN, 'The Jewish Jew and Western Culture: Fallible Predictions for the Turn of the Century', in Jonathan Webber (ed.), *Jewish Identities in the New Europe* (London, 1994).

LANDAU, JACOB, *Ha'agur hashalem*, ed. M. Herschler (Jerusalem, 1989).

LANDES, DAVID S., and CHARLES TILLY, *History as Social Science* (Englewood Cliffs, NJ, 1970).

LAQUEUR, WALTER, *A History of Zionism* (New York, 1972).

LASKI, NEVILLE, *The Jewish Contribution to Western Civilization* (Cardiff, 1937).

LEDERHENDLER, ELI, *Jewish Responses to Modernity: New Voices in America and Eastern Europe* (New York, 1994).

—— *The Road to Modern Jewish Politics* (Oxford, 1989).

LEHMANN, ROSA, *Symbiosis and Ambivalence: Poles and Jews in a Small Galician Town* (New York, 2001).

LENIN, VLADIMIR I., *Lenin on the Jewish Question*, ed. Hyman Lumer (New York, 1974).

LEVINE, HILLEL, 'Jews and Judaism in the Age of Mercantilism' (Heb.), *Zion*, 53 (1988), 65–71.

LEVINE, ROBERT A., and DONALD T. CAMPBELL, *Ethnocentrism: Theories of Conflict, Ethnic Attitudes, and Group Behavior* (New York, 1972).

LEVINSON, JULIAN, 'Transmitting *Yiddishkeit*: Irving Howe and Jewish-American Culture', *Jewish Culture and History*, 2/2 (1999), 42–65.

LEWIS, BERNARD and DOMINIQUE SCHNAPPER (eds), *Muslims in Europe: Social Change in Western Europe* (London, 1994).

LIBERLES, ROBERT, *Religious Conflict in Social Context: The Resurgence of Orthodox Judaism in Frankfurt am Main, 1838–1877* (Westport, Conn., 1985).

—— *Salo Wittmayer Baron: Architect of Jewish History* (New York, 1995).

LIBSON, GIDEON, 'Hidden Worlds and Open Shutters: S. D. Goitein between Judaism and Islam', in David N. Myers and David B. Ruderman (eds), *The Jewish Past Revisited: Reflections on Modern Jewish Historians* (New Haven, Conn., 1998).

LIPSET, SEYMOUR M., and RICHARD HOFSTADTER, *Sociology and History: Methods* (New York, 1968).

LISSAK, MOSHE, ' "Critical" Sociology and "Establishment" Sociology in the Israeli Academic Community: Ideological Struggles or Academic Discourse', *Israel Studies*, 1 (1996), 247–94.

LITMAN, JACOB, *The Economic Role of Jews in Medieval Poland: The Contribution of Yitzhak Schipper* (New York, 1984).

LOWMIANSKI, HENRYK (ed.), *Historia Polski*, 1 (Warsaw, 1958).

LUEGAR, KARL, *I Decide Who Is a Jew! The Papers of Dr. Karl Luegar*, trans. and ed. Richard S. Geehr (Washington, DC, 1982).

LUZZATTO, SIMONE DI, *Discorso circa il stato de gl'hebrei: et in particolar dimoranti nell'inclita città di Venetia* (Venice, 1638).

LYOTARD, JEAN-FRANÇOIS, *The Differend: Phrases in Dispute*, trans. Georges Van Den Abbeele (Minneapolis, Minn., 1988).

—— *Heidegger and 'The Jews'*, trans. Andreas Michel and Mark S. Roberts (Minneapolis, Minn., 1990).

—— *Peregrinations: Law, Form, Event* (New York, 1988).

—— *The Post-Modern Condition*, trans. Geoff Bennington and Brian Massumi (Minneapolis, Minn., 1984).

MACIEJKO, PAWEL, 'Gershom Scholem's Dialectic of Jewish History', *Journal of Modern Jewish Studies*, 3 (2004) 207–20.

MAGNUS, SHULAMIT, 'Out of the Ghetto: Integrating the Study of Jewish Women into the Study of "The Jews" ', *Judaism*, 39 (1990), 28–36.

MAHLER, RAPHAEL, *History of the Jews in Poland* [Toledot hayehudim bepolin] (Merhavia, 1946).

MALI, JOSEPH, *Mythistory: The Making of Modern Historiography* (Chicago, Ill., 2003).

MALINO, FRANCIS, and DAVID SORKIN (eds), *Profiles in Diversity: Jews in a Changing Europe* (Detroit, Mich., 1998).

MALINOVICH, NADIA, 'Orientalism and the Construction of Jewish Identity in France, 1900–1932', *Jewish Culture and History*, 2/1 (1999), 1–25.

MALLON, F. E., 'The Promise and Dilemma of Subaltern Studies: Perspectives from Latin America', *American Historical Review*, 99 (1994), 1491–1515.

MANFREDINI, A. D., 'Codes and Jurists: Historical Reflections', in Alfredo M. Rabello (ed.), *European Legal Traditions and Israel* (Jerusalem, 1994).

MANNHEIM, KARL, *Ideology and Utopia* (London, 1936).

MARCUS, IVAN G., 'Judaic Studies in University and Jewish Institutional Settings in America', *Jewish Studies Quarterly*, 3 (1996), 136–45.

—— *Piety and Society: The Jewish Pietists of Medieval Germany* (Leiden, 1981).

—— *Rituals of Childhood: Jewish Acculturation in Medieval Europe* (New Haven, Conn., 1996).

MAYBAUM, IGNAZ, *Synagogue and Society: Jewish Christian Collaboration in Defence of Western Civilisation* (London, 1944).

MAYER, EGON, *Love and Tradition: Marriage between Jews and Christians* (New York, 1987).

MEGILL, ALLAN, *Prophets of Extremity: Nietzsche, Heidegger, Foucault, Derrida* (Berkeley, Calif., 1985).

MEIR, ARYEH, and LISA HOSTEIN, *The High Cost of Jewish Living* (New York, 1992).

MELAMMED, RENÉE LEVINE, *Heretics or Daughters of Israel* (Oxford, 1999).

MENASSEH BEN ISRAEL, *Menasseh ben Israel's Mission to Oliver Cromwell: Being a reprint of the pamphlets published by Menasseh Ben Israel to promote the re-admission of the Jews to England, 1649–1656*, ed. L. Wolf (London, 1901).

MENDELSOHN, EZRA, *On Modern Jewish Politics* (New York, 1993).

MENDES-FLOHR, PAUL, *Divided Passions: Jewish Intellectuals and the Experience of Modernity* (Detroit, Mich., 1991).

—— 'The Jew as Cosmopolitan', in id., *Divided Passions*.

—— 'Jewish Continuity in an Age of Discontinuity: Reflections from the Perspective of Intellectual History', *Journal of Jewish Studies*, 39 (1988), 261–8; repr. in id., *Divided Passions*.

—— and JEHUDA REINHARZ, *The Jew in the Modern World: A Documentary History*, 2nd edn (Oxford, 1995).

MEYER, MICHAEL A. (ed.), *Ideas of Jewish History* (Detroit, Mich., 1987).

—— *Jewish Identity in the Modern World* (Seattle, Wash., 1990).

—— 'Modernity as a Crisis for the Jews', *Modern Judaism*, 9 (1989), 151–64.

—— *The Origins of the Modern Jew: Jewish Identity and European Culture in Germany, 1749–1824* (Detroit, Mich., 1967).

—— 'Where Does the Modern Period of Jewish History Begin?', *Judaism*, 24 (1975), 329–38.

MICHALOWSKA, ANNA, *Między demokracja a oligarchia: władze gmin żydowskich w Poznaniu and Swarzędzu* (Warsaw, 2000).

MICHMAN, DAN, 'A Third Partner of World Jewry? The Role of Memory of the Shoah in the Search for a New Present-Day European Jewish Identity', in Konrad Kwiet and Jürgen Matthäus (eds) *Contemporary Responses to the Holocaust* (Westport, Conn., 2004).

MILLER, AVIS, JANET MARDER, and STEVEN BAYME, *Approaches to Intermarriage: Areas of Consensus* (New York, 1993).

MITTELBERG, DAVID, *The Israel Connection and American Jews* (Westport, Conn., 1999).

MODENA, LEON, *Historia degli riti hebraici* (Paris, 1637).

MOELLIN, JACOB BEN MOSES HALEVI (Maharil), *She'elot uteshuvot maharil* [Responsa of Maharil (Rabbi Jacob Moellin)], ed. Yitzchok Satz (Jerusalem 1991).

MONTEFIORE, CLAUDE, *The Dangers of Zionism* (London, 1918).

MOURANT, A. E., ADA KOPEC and K. D. SOBCZAK, *The Genetics of the Jews* (Oxford, 1978).

MUNCH, RICHARD, *Theory of Action: Towards a New Synthesis Going Beyond Parsons* (London, 1988).

MUNSLOW, ALUN, *Deconstructing History* (London, 1997).

MYERS, DAVID N., 'Between Diaspora and Zion: History, Memory, and the Jerusalem Scholars', in David N. Myers and David B. Ruderman (eds), *The Jewish Past Revisited: Reflections on Modern Jewish Historians* (New Haven, Conn., 1998).

—— 'Rebel in Frankfurt', in Jay M. Harris (ed.), *Pride of Jacob* (Cambridge, Mass., 2002).

—— *Re-Inventing the Jewish Past: European Intellectuals and the Zionist Return to History* (New York, 1995).

—— and DAVID B. RUDERMAN (eds), *The Jewish Past Revisited: Reflections on Modern Jewish Historians* (New Haven, Conn., 1998).

NEUSNER, JACOB, Review of Hayim Hillel Ben-Sasson (ed.), *A History of the Jewish People*, *American Historical Review*, 82 (1977), 1030–1.

—— Review of Michael A. Meyer, *Ideas of Jewish History*, *History and Theory*, 14 (1975), 212–26.

—— *Understanding Seeking Faith: Essays on the Case of Judaism*, vol. i: *Debates on Method, Reports of Results* (Atlanta, 1986).

NEWMAN, AMY, 'The Idea of Judaism in Feminism and Afrocentrism', in David Biale, Michael Galchinsky, and Susannah Heschel (eds), *Insider/Outsider: American Jews and Multiculturalism* (Berkeley, Calif., 1998).

NICHOLS, R. F., 'Postwar Reorientation of Historical Thinking', *American Historical Review*, 54 (1948), 78–89.

NIETZSCHE, FRIEDRICH, 'On the Uses and Disadvantages of History for Life', in id., *Untimely Meditations*, trans. R. J. Hollingdale, ed. Daniel Breazeale (Cambridge, 1997).

NIGAL, GEDALYAH, *Magic, Mysticism, and Hasidism: The Supernatural in Jewish Thought*, trans. Edward Levin (Northvale, NJ, 1994).

NOVICK, PETER, *That Noble Dream: The Objectivity Question and the American Historical Profession* (Cambridge, 1988).

OFER, DALIA, 'Linguistic Conceptualization of the Holocaust in Palestine and Israel, 1942–1953', *Journal of Contemporary History*, 31 (1996), 567–95.

ONG, WALTER J., *Orality and Literacy: The Technologizing of the Word* (London, 1988).

OPHIR, ADI, 'Postmodernism: A Philosophical Position' [Postmoderniyut: emdah filosofit], in Ilan Gur-Ze'ev (ed.), *Education in the Age of Postmodern Discourse* [Ḥinukh be'idan hasiaḥ hapostmoderni] (Jerusalem, 1997), 148–60.

PAPPÉ, ILAN, 'A New Agenda for the "New History"' (Heb.), *Teoryah uvikoret*, 8 (1996), 123–37.

PARUSH, IRIS, *Reading Jewish Women: Marginality and Modernization in Nineteenth-Century Eastern European Jewish Society* (Hanover, NH, 2004).

—— and BRAKHA DALMATZKY-FISCHLER, 'Another Reading of "Haderashah"' (Heb.), *Iyunim bitekumat yisra'el*, 16 (forthcoming).

PATAI, RAPHAEL and JENNIFER PATAI, *The Myth of the Jewish Race* (Detroit, 1989).

PELIKAN, JAROSLAV, 'Judaism and the Humanities', in Shaye J. D. Cohen and Edward L. Greenstein (eds), *The State of Jewish Studies* (Detroit, Mich., 1990).

PENSLAR, DEREK J., 'Narratives of Nation-Building: Major Themes in Zionist Historiography', in David N. Myers and David B. Ruderman (eds), *The Jewish Past Revisited: Reflections on Modern Jewish Historians* (New Haven, Conn., 1998).

PETROVSKY-SHTERN, YOHANAN, 'The Master of an Evil Name: Hillel Ba'al Shem and his "Sefer ha-Heshek"', *AJS Review*, 28 (2004), 217–48.

Pew Forum on Religion and Public Life, 'Views of Muslim-Americans Hold Steady After London Bombings', survey, 26 July 2005 (<http://pewforum.org/publications/surveys/muslims-survey-2005.pdf>).

Pew Global Attitudes Project (<http://pewglobal.org/reports/display.php?PageID=811>).

PHILLIPS, BRUCE A., *Re-examining Intermarriage: Trends, Textures, Strategies, Report of a New Study* (Los Angeles, 1998).

PIEKARZ, MENDEL, *The Beginning of Hasidism* [Bimei tsemiḥat haḥasidut] (Jerusalem, 1978).

PINTO, DIANA, 'The Jewish Challenges in the New Europe', in Daniel Levy and Yfaat Weiss (eds), *Challenging Ethnic Citizenship: German and Israeli Perspectives on Immigration* (New York, 2002).

—— *A New Identity for Post-1989 Europe*, JPR Policy Paper 1 (London, 1996).

—— 'The New Jewish Europe: Challenges and Responsibilities', *European Judaism*, 31/2 (1998), 1–15.

PORTER, BRIAN, 'Is the Pope Catholic? Defining Roman Catholicism', unpublished lecture delivered at the University of West Virginia, November 2002.

PRAKASH, GYAN, 'Subaltern Studies as Postcolonial Criticism', *American Historical Review*, 99 (1994), 1475–1490.

RAJAN, GITA, and SHAILJA SHARMA (eds), *New Cosmopolitans: South Asians in the US* (Stanford, Calif., 2006).

RAM, URI, *The Changing Agenda of Israeli Sociology* (New York, 1995).

—— 'Zionist Historiography and the Invention of Modern Jewish Nationhood: The Case of Ben Zion Dinur', *History and Memory*, 7 (1995), 91–124.

RAPOPORT-ALBERT, ADA, 'On Women in Hasidism: S. A. Horodetzky and the Maid of Ludmir Tradition', in Ada Rapoport-Albert and Steven J. Zipperstein (eds), *Jewish History: Essays in Honour of Chimen Abramsky* (London, 1988).

RAVID, BENJAMIN C. I., *Economics and Toleration in Seventeenth Century Venice: The Background and Context of the Discorso of Simone Luzzatto* (Jerusalem, 1978).

—— ' "How profitable the nation of the Jewes are": The "Humble Addresses" of Menasseh ben Israel and the "Discorso" of Simone Luzzatto', in Jehuda Reinharz and Daniel Swetschinski (eds), *Mystics, Philosophers, and Politicians: Essays in Jewish Intellectual History in Honor of Alexander Altmann* (Durham, NC, 1982).

RAZ-KRAKOTZKIN, AMNON, 'The National Narration of Exile: Zionist Historiography and Medieval Jewry' [Yitsugah hale'umi shel hagalut: hahistoriyografiyah hatsiyonit viyehudei yemei habeinayim], doctoral dissertation, Tel Aviv University, 1996.

REIN, ARIEL, 'The Historian as a Nation Builder, Ben Zion Dinur's Evolution and Enterprise, 1884–1948' [Historiyon bevinui umah: tsemihato shel bentsiyon dinur umifalo bayishuv, 1884–1948], doctoral dissertation, Hebrew University of Jerusalem, 2000.

REINER, ELCHANAN, 'The Ashkenazi Elite at the Beginning of the Modern Era: Manuscript versus the Printed Book', *Polin*, 10 (1997), 85–98.

—— 'The Attitude of Ashkenazi Society to the New Science in the Sixteenth Century', *Science in Context*, 10 (1997), 589–603.

—— 'On the Roots of the Urban Jewish Community in Poland in the Early Modern Period' (Heb.), *Gal-Ed*, 20 (2006), 13–37.

RICHMOND, COLIN, 'Introduction: The Jews in Medieval England', *Jewish Culture and History*, 3/2 (2000), 1–6.

RIEFF, DAVID, 'The Dream of Multiculturalism Is Over', *International Herald Tribune*, 23 Aug. 2005, 6.

ROBACK, ABRAHAM A., *Jewish Influence in Modern Thought* (Cambridge, Mass., 1929).

ROBERTSON, R., and B. S. TURNER, 'Talcott Parsons and Modern Social Theory—An Appreciation', *Theory, Culture and Society*, 6 (1989), 539–58.

ROBINSON, IRA, 'The Foundation Documents of the Jewish Community Council of Montreal', *Jewish Political Studies Review*, 8 (1996), 69–86.

ROBINSON, O. F., T. D. FERGUS, and W. M. GORDON, *European Legal History* (London, 1994).

ROSKIES, DAVID, 'Border Crossings', *Commentary*, 115 (Feb. 2003), 62–6.

—— 'Yiddish Popular Literature and the Female Reader', *Journal of Popular Culture*, 13 (1979), 852–8.

ROSMAN, MOSHE, 'Culture in the Book' (Heb.), *Zion*, 56 (1991), 321–44.

—— 'For Critical Scholarship on the Historical Besht' (Heb.), *Zion*, 70 (2005), 537–45.

—— *Founder of Hasidism: A Quest for the Historical Ba'al Shem Tov* (Berkeley, Calif., 1996).

—— 'Historiography of Polish Jewry, 1945–1995' [Historiyografiyah shel yahadut polin, 1945–1995], in Israel Bartal and Israel Gutman (eds), *The Broken Chain: Polish Jewry Through the Ages* [Kiyum vashever: yehudei polin ledoroteihem], 2 vols (Jerusalem, 2001).

—— 'The History of Jewish Women in Early Modern Poland: An Assessment', *Polin*, 18 (2005), 25–50.

—— 'Innovative Tradition: Jewish Culture in the Polish-Lithuanian Commonwealth', in David Biale (ed.), *Cultures of the Jews: A New History* (New York, 2002).

—— 'Jewish Perceptions of Insecurity and Powerlessness in 16th–18th-Century Poland', *Polin*, 1 (1986), 19–27.

—— *The Lords' Jews: Magnate–Jewish Relations in the Polish–Lithuanian Commonwealth during the Eighteenth Century* (Cambridge, Mass., 1990).

—— 'A Minority Views the Majority: Jewish Attitudes Towards the Polish–Lithuanian Commonwealth and Interaction with Poles', in Antony Polonsky (ed.), *From Shtetl to Socialism: Studies from Polin* (London, 1993).

—— 'On the History of a Historical Source: *Shivḥei habesht* and its Editing' (Heb.), *Zion*, 58 (1993), 175–214.

—— 'Reflections on the State of Polish-Jewish Historical Study', *Jewish History*, 3 (1988), 115–30.

—— 'To Be a Jewish Woman in Early Modern Poland–Lithuania' [Liheyot ishah yehudiyah bepolin-lita bereishit ha'et haḥadashah] in Israel Bartal and Israel

Gutman (eds), *The Broken Chain: Polish Jewry Through the Ages* [Kiyum vashever: yehudei polin ledoroteihem], 2 vols (Jerusalem, 2001).

ROTH, CECIL, *A Bird's-Eye View of Jewish History* (Cincinnati, Ohio, 1935).

—— *The Jewish Contribution to Civilization* (London, 1938).

—— *The Jews in the Renaissance* (Philadelphia, 1959).

ROTH, PHILIP, *The Plot Against America* (Boston, Mass., 2004).

ROUBEY, LESTER W., 'Simeone Luzzatto's "Discorso" (1638): An Early Contribution to Apologetic Literature', *Journal of Reform Judaism*, 28 (1981), 57–63.

RUBINSTEIN, H. L., D. COHN-SHERBOK, A. J. EDELHEIT, and W. D. RUBINSTEIN, *The Jews in the Modern World: A History since 1750* (London, 2002).

RUDERMAN, DAVID, 'Cecil Roth, Historian of Italian Jewry: A Reassessment', in David N. Myers and David B. Ruderman (eds), *The Jewish Past Revisited: Reflections on Modern Jewish Historians* (New Haven, Conn., 1998).

—— 'Israel's *European Jewry in the Age of Mercantilism*', *Jewish Quarterly Review*, 78 (1987), 154–9.

—— 'Jewish Cultural History in Early Modern Europe: An Agenda for Future Study', in Jeremy Cohen and Moshe Rosman (eds), *Re-Thinking European Jewish History* (forthcoming).

—— *Jewish Enlightenment in an English Key: Anglo Jewry's Construction of Modern Jewish Thought* (Princeton, 2000).

RUNES, DAGOBERT D., *The Hebrew Impact on Western Civilization* (New York, 1951).

RYLE, GILBERT, *Collected Studies*, 2 vols (London, 1971).

SARNA, JONATHAN, *American Judaism* (New Haven, Conn., 2004).

SARTRE, JEAN-PAUL, *Anti-Semite and Jew* (New York, 1948).

SATLOW, MICHAEL, 'Beyond Influence: Toward a New Historiographic Paradigm', in Y. Eliav and A. Norich (eds), *Jewish Cultures and Literatures* (Providence, RI, 2007).

—— *Creating Judaism: History, Tradition, Practice* (New York, 2006).

—— 'Defining Judaism: Accounting for "Religions" in the Study of Religion', *Journal of the American Academy of Religion* (forthcoming).

SCHACTER, JACOB J., 'Facing the Truths of History', *Torah U-Madda Journal*, 8 (1998–9), 200–76.

SCHIPER, YITZHAK IGNACY, *History of Yiddish Theatrical Art and Drama* [Geshikhte fun der yiddisher teater-kunst un drame], 3 vols (Warsaw, 1927–8).

SCHIPER, YITZHAK IGNACY, *History of Yiddish Culture in Poland in the Middle Ages* [Di Kultur—geshikhte fun Yidn in Poyln beysn mitlalter] (Warsaw, 1926).

—— ARIEH TARTAKOWER, and ALEKSANDER HAFFTKA (eds), *Żydzi w Polsce odrodzonej*, 2 vols (Warsaw, 1932–1935).

SCHOLEM, GERSHOM, 'Reflections on Modern Jewish Studies', in id., *On the Possibility of Jewish Mysticism in Our Time and Other Essays*, trans. Jonathan Chipman, ed. Avraham Shapiro (Philadelphia, 1997).

—— *Sabbatai Sevi: The Mystical Messiah* (Princeton, 1973).

—— 'What Others Rejected: Kabbalah and Historical Criticism', in id., *On the Possibility of Jewish Mysticism*.

SCHORSCH, ISMAR, 'From Messianism to Realpolitik: Menasseh ben Israel and the Readmission of the Jews to England', *Procceedings of the American Academy for Jewish Research*, 45 (1978), 187–209.

SCHORSCH, ISMAR, 'The Myth of Sephardic Supremacy', *Leo Baeck Institute Year Book*, 34 (1989), 47–66.

—— 'The Place of Jewish Studies in Contemporary Scholarship', in Shaye J. D. Cohen and Edward L. Greenstein (eds), *The State of Jewish Studies* (Detroit, Mich., 1990).

SCHWEID, ELIEZER, 'Changing Jewish Identities in the New Europe and the Consequences for Israel', in Jonathan Webber (ed.), *Jewish Identities in the New Europe* (London, 1994).

SCOTT, JOAN W., *Gender and the Politics of History* (New York, 1988).

SEGAL, AGNES, 'Yiddish Works on Women's Commandments in the Sixteenth Century', in *Studies in Yiddish Literature and Folklore* (Jerusalem, 1986).

SEGRE, DAN V., 'Colonization and Decolonization: The Case of Zionist and African Elites', in Todd M. Endelman (ed.), *Comparing Jewish Societies* (Ann Arbor, Mich., 1997).

SELIKTAR, OFIRA, *Divided We Stand: Jews, Israel and the Peace Process* (Westport, Conn., 2002).

SHAPIRO, HARRY L., *The Jewish People: A Biological History* (Liège, 1960).

SHAROT, STEPHEN, 'Judaism and Jewish Ethnicity: Changing Interrelationships and Differentiations in the Diaspora and Israel', in Ernest Krausz and Gitta Tulea (eds), *Jewish Survival* (New Brunswick, NJ, 1998).

—— 'Religious Syncretism and Religious Distinctiveness: A Comparative Analysis of Pre-Modern Jewish Communities', in Todd M. Endelman (ed.), *Comparing Jewish Societies* (Ann Arbor, Mich., 1997).

SHEFFER, GABRIEL, 'From Israeli Hegemony to Diaspora Full Autonomy: The Current State of Diaspora Ethno-National Diasporism and the

Alternatives Facing World Jewry', in S. Ilan Troen (ed.), *Jewish Centers and Peripheries: Europe between America and Israel Fifty Years after World War II* (New Brunswick, NJ, 1999).

—— 'A Nation and its Diaspora: A Re-Examination of Israeli–Jewish Diaspora Relations', *Diaspora*, 11 (2002), 331–58.

SHENHAV, YEHUDA, *The Arab-Jews: Nationalism, Religion and Ethnicity* [Hayehudim ha'aravim: le'umiyut, dat ve'etniyut] (Tel Aviv, 2003).

SHMERUK, CHONE, *The Esterke Story in Yiddish and Polish Literature* (Jerusalem, 1985).

—— *The Illustrations in Yiddish Books in the 16th–17th Centuries* [Ha'iyurim lesifrei yidish bame'ah ha-16–17] (Jerusalem, 1986).

—— *Yiddish Literature in Poland* [Sifrut yidish bepolin] (Jerusalem, 1981).

SHMUELI, EPHRAIM, *Seven Jewish Cultures*, trans. Gila Shmueli (Cambridge, 1990).

SHOHAT, AZRIEL, 'The Jewish Community of Pinsk, 1881–1939', in Z. Rabinowitsch (ed.), *Pinsk*, vol. i, pt. 2 (Tel Aviv, 1977).

SHOUB, MYRA, 'Jewish Women's History: Development of a Critical Methodology', *Conservative Judaism*, 35 (1982), 33–46.

SHULMAN, NISSON E., *Authority and Community: Polish Jewry in the Sixteenth Century* (New York, 1986).

SHULVASS, MOSES, *Jewish Culture in Eastern Europe: The Classical Period* (New York, 1975).

SHWARTZ, SHULY RUBIN, *The Emergence of Jewish Scholarship in America: The Publication of the Jewish Encyclopedia* (Cincinnati, Ohio, 1991).

SILBERSTEIN, LAURENCE J., 'Benign Transmission versus Conflicted Discourse: Jewish Studies and the Crisis of the Humanities', *Soundings*, 74 (1991), 485–507.

—— *The Postzionism Debates: Knowledge and Power in Israeli Culture* (New York, 1999).

—— (ed.), *Mapping Jewish Identities* (New York, 2000).

—— and ROBERT L. COHN, *The Other in Jewish Thought and History: Constructions of Jewish Culture and Identity* (New York, 1994).

SILVERMAN, MAX, 'Re-figuring "the Jew" in France', in Brian Cheyette and Laura Marcus (eds), *Modernity, Culture, and 'the Jew'* (Oxford, 1998).

SLEZKINE, YURI, *The Jewish Century* (Princeton, 2004).

SLONIK, BENJAMIN, *Seder mitsvot nashim*, ed., trans., introd. E. Fram (forthcoming).

SMITH, ANTHONY D., *The Antiquity of Nations* (Cambridge, 2004).

—— *The Nation in History* (Hanover, NH, 2000).

SMITH, DENNIS, *The Rise of Historical Sociology* (Philadelphia, 1991).

SMITH, JONATHAN Z., *Imagining Religion: From Babylon to Jonestown* (Chicago, Ill., 1982).

SOLOMON, NORMAN, 'Judaism in the New Europe: Discovery or Invention?', in Jonathan Webber (ed.), *Jewish Identities in the New Europe* (London, 1994).

SOLOVEITCHIK, HAYIM, 'Migration, Acculturation and the New Role of Texts in the Haredi World', in Martin Marty and R. Scott Appleby (eds), *Accounting for Fundamentalism* (Chicago, Ill., 1994).

—— 'Piety, Pietism and German Pietism: *Sefer Hasidim I* and the Influence of *Hasidei Ashkenaz*', *Jewish Quarterly Review*, 92 (2002), 455–93.

—— 'Religious Law and Change: The Medieval Ashkenazic Example', *AJS Review*, 12 (1987), 205–21.

—— 'Rupture and Reconstruction: The Transformation of Contemporary Orthodoxy', *Tradition*, 28 (1994), 64–130.

SOMBART, WERNER, *The Jews and Modern Capitalism*, trans. M. Epstein (New Brunswick, 1982) (*Die Juden und das Wirtschaftsleben* (Leipzig, 1911)).

SORKIN, DAVID, *The Transformation of German Jewry, 1780–1840* (New York, 1987).

SPIEGEL, GABRIELLE, 'History, Historicism and the Social Logic of the Text in the Middle Ages', *Speculum*, 65 (1990), 59–86.

STAMPFER, SHAUL, 'The 1764 Census of Polish Jewry', *Bar-Ilan*, 24–5 (1989), 41–147.

STEINBERG, MILTON, *A Partisan Guide to the Jewish Problem* (New York, 1945).

STEINER, GEORGE, 'A Season in Hell', in id., *In Bluebeard's Castle: Some Notes Towards the Redefinition of Culture* (New Haven, Conn., 1971).

STOCKING, GEORGE W., JR., *Functionalism Historicized: Essays on British Social Anthropology* (Madison, Wis., 1984).

STONE, LAWRENCE, 'History and Postmodernism', *Past and Present*, 131 (1991), 217–18.

STONEHILL, CHARLES A. (ed.), *The Jewish Contribution to Civilization* (New Haven, Conn., 1940).

SUTCLIFFE, ADAM, 'Enlightenment and Exclusion: Judaism and Toleration in Spinoza, Locke and Bayle', *Jewish Culture and History*, 2/1 (1999), 26–43.

TCHERNOWITZ, CHAYIM, *History of the Jewish Codes* [Toledot haposekim], 3 vols (New York, 1947).

TELLER, ADAM, 'Hasidism and the Challenge of Geography: The Polish Background to the Spread of the Hasidic Movement', *AJS Review*, 30 (2006), 1–29.

—— *Money, Power and Influence: The Jews on the Radziwill Estates in Eighteenth Century Lithuania* [Kesef, ko'aḥ vehashpa'ah: hayehudim be'aḥuzot beit radzivil belita bame'ah hashemoneh esreh] (Jerusalem, 2006).

TETER, MAGDA, 'The Legend of Ger Żedek of Wilno as Polemic and Reassurance', *AJS Review*, 29 (2005), 237–63.

THOMAS, M. E., M. E. WEALE, A. L. JONES, et al., 'Founding Mothers of Jewish Communities: Geographically Separated Jewish Groups Were Independently Founded by Very Few Female Ancestors', *American Journal of Human Genetics*, 70 (2002), 1411–20.

TOEWS, JOHN E., 'Intellectual History after the Linguistic Turn: The Autonomy of Meaning and the Irreducibility of Experience', *American Historical Review*, 92 (1987), 879–907.

TOPOLSKI, JERZY, 'The Double Image of Postmodernism in Historiography', in Adam Teller (ed.), *Studies in the History of the Jews in Old Poland in Honor of Jacob Goldberg* [=*Scripta Hierosolymitana* 38] (Jerusalem, 1998).

TURNIANSKY, CHAVA, 'On Old Yiddish Biblical Epics', *International Folklore Review*, 8 (1991), 26–33.

TWERSKY, ISADORE, Review of Jacob Katz, *Tradition and Crisis*, *Jewish Social Studies*, 24 (1962), 249–51.

—— 'The Shulḥan 'Arukh: Enduring Code of Jewish Law', in Judah Goldin (ed.), *The Jewish Expression* (New York, 1970).

URUSZCZAK, W., *Próba kodyfikacji prawa polskiego w pierwszej po łowie XVI wieku: korektura praw z 1532 r.* (Warsaw, 1979).

VAKSBURG, ARKADY, *Stalin Against the Jews* (New York, 1994).

VAN CREVELD, MARTIN, *The Transformation of War* (New York, 1991).

VITAL, DAVID, *The Future of the Jews* (Cambridge, Mass., 1990).

—— *A People Apart: The Jews in Europe, 1789–1939* (Oxford, 1999).

VOISÉ, W., *Andrzej Frycz Modrzewski, 1503–1572* (Wrocław, 1975).

Volumina Legum, 2 vols (St Petersburg, 1859).

WADDY, CHARLES, *Shaping a New Europe: The Muslim Factor* (London, 1991).

WALZER, MICHAEL, MENAHEM LORBERBAUM, NOAM J. ZOHAR, et al. (eds), *The Jewish Political Tradition*, vol. ii: *Membership* (New Haven, Conn., 2003).

WASSERFALL, RAHEL R. (ed.), *Women and Water: Menstruation in Jewish Life and Law* (Hanover, NH, 1999).

WASSERSTEIN, BERNARD, *Vanishing Diaspora: The Jews in Europe Since 1945* (London, 1996).

WAXMAN, CHAIM I., *Jewish Baby Boomers: A Communal Perspective* (Albany, NY, 2001).

WEBBER, JONATHAN (ed.), *Jewish Identities in the New Europe* (London, 1994).

WEIN, BEREL, *Echoes of Glory: The Story of the Jews in the Classical Era, 350 BCE–750 CE* (New York, 1995).

—— *Herald of Destiny: The Story of the Jews in the Medieval Era, 750–1650* (New York, 1993).

—— *Triumph of Survival: The Story of the Jews in the Modern Era, 1650–1990* (New York, 1990).

WEINBERG, DAVID, 'Between America and Israel: The Quest for a Distinct European Jewish Identity in the Post-War Era', *Jewish Culture and History*, 5/1 (2002), 91–120.

WEINRYB, BERNARD D., *The Jews of Poland* (Philadelphia, 1973).

—— *Texts and Studies in the Communal History of Polish Jewry* (= *Proceedings of the American Academy for Jewish Research*, 19) (New York, 1950).

WEINRYB, ELAZAR, *Historical Thinking* [Ḥashivah historit], 2 vols (Tel Aviv, 1987).

WEISSLER, CHAVA, 'The Religion of Traditional Ashkenazic Women: Some Methodological Issues', *AJS Review*, 12 (1987), 73–94.

—— *Voices of the Matriarchs* (Boston, Mass., 1998).

WHITE, HAYDEN, *The Content of the Form: Narrative Discourse and Historical Representation* (Baltimore, Md., 1987).

—— 'Historical Emplotment and the Problem of Truth', in Saul Friedlander (ed.), *Probing the Limits of Representation: Nazism and the 'Final Solution'* (Cambridge, Mass., 1992).

—— 'Historical Text as Literary Artifact', in id., *Tropics of Discourse*.

—— *Metahistory: The Historical Imagination in Nineteenth-Century Europe* (Baltimore, Md., 1973).

—— *The Tropics of Discourse: Essays in Cultural Criticism* (Baltimore, Md., 1978).

WHITFIELD, STEPHEN, 'Multiculturalism and American Jews', *Congress Monthly* (Sept./Oct. 1995), 7–10.

WISSE, RUTH (ed.), *A Shtetl and Other Yiddish Novellas* (New York, 1973).

WISTRICH, ROBERT S., 'The Dangers of Antisemitism in the New Europe', in Jonathan Webber (ed.), *Jewish Identities in the New Europe* (London, 1994).

WOLOSKY, SHIRA, 'Moral Finitude and the Ethics of Language: A New World Response to Gianni Vattimo', *Common Knowledge*, 9 (2003), 406–23.

WOOLF, JEFFREY R., 'Medieval Models of Purity and Sanctity: Ashkenazic Women in the Synagogue', in M. J. H. M. Poorthuis and J. Schwartz (eds), *Purity and Holiness: The Heritage of Leviticus* (Leiden, 2000).

YASSIF, ELI, 'Folklore Research and Jewish Studies, B' (Heb.), *Yedi'on ha'igud ha'olami lemada'ei hayahadut*, 28 (1988), 3–13.

—— 'Legends and History: Historians Read Hebrew Legends of the Middle Ages' (Heb.), *Zion*, 64 (1999), 187–220.

—— 'Legend and History—Second Thoughts' (Heb.), *Zion*, 65 (2000), 219–27.

YAWITZ, ZE'EV, *History of Israel* [Toledot yisra'el], 14 vols (Warsaw and Tel Aviv, 1895–1940).

YEHOSHUA, A. B., 'An Attempt to Identify and Understand the Underpinnings of Antisemitism' (Heb.), *Alpayim*, 28 (2005), 11–31.

—— *For Normalcy: Five Essays on the Questions of Zionism* [Bizkhut hanormaliyut: hamesh masot al she'elot hatsiyonut] (Jerusalem, 1980).

—— 'Who Is a Jew?', *Contemplate*, 3 (2005–6), 73–5.

YERUSHALMI, YOSEF H., *From Spanish Court to Italian Ghetto: A Study in Seventeenth-Century Marranism and Jewish Apologetics* (New York, 1971).

—— *Zakhor: Jewish History and Jewish Memory* (Seattle, Wash., 1982).

YINGER, J. MILTON, 'Contraculture and Subculture', *American Sociological Review*, 25 (1960), 625–35.

—— *Countercultures: The Promise and Peril of a World Turned Upside Down* (New York, 1982).

YSANDER, TORSTEN, *Studien zum B'estschen Hasidismus in seiner religions-geschichtlichen Sonderart* (Uppsala, 1933).

YUVAL, ISRAEL J., *Two Nations in your Womb: Perceptions of Jews and Christians* [Shenei goyim bevitenekh: yehudim venotserim, dimuyim hadadiyim] (Tel Aviv, 2000).

—— 'Yitzhak Baer and the Search for Authentic Judaism', in David N. Myers and David B. Ruderman (eds), *The Jewish Past Revisited: Reflections on Modern Jewish Historians* (New Haven, Conn., 1998).

ZAGORIN, PEREZ, 'History, the Referent and Narrative: Reflections on Postmodernism Now', *History and Theory*, 38 (1999), 1–24.

ZFATMAN, SARA, *The Jewish Tale in the Middle Ages: Between Ashkenaz and Sepharad* [Bein ashkenaz lisefarad: letoledot hasipur hayehudi bimei habeinayim] (Jerusalem, 1993).

ZIMMER, ERIC, *Society and its Customs* [Olam keminhago noheg] (Jerusalem, 1996).

ZINBERG, ISRAEL, *A History of Jewish Literature*, vol. vii: *Old Yiddish Literature from its Origins to the Haskalah Period* (Cincinnati, Ohio, and New York, 1975).

ZIPPERSTEIN, STEVEN J., *The Jews of Odessa: A Cultural History, 1794–1881* (Stanford, Calif., 1986).

ZOHAR, TSEVI, *Tradition and Change: Halakhic Responses of Middle Eastern Rabbis to Legal and Technological Change* [Masoret utemurah] (Jerusalem, 1993).

Index